Chinese
Migrants Abroad

Chinese
Migrants Abroad

Cultural, Educational, and
Social Dimensions of the Chinese Diaspora

Editors

Michael W. Charney
University of London

Brenda S. A. Yeoh
National University of Singapore

Tong Chee Kiong
National University of Singapore

SINGAPORE UNIVERSITY PRESS
NATIONAL UNIVERSITY OF SINGAPORE

World Scientific
New Jersey • London • Singapore • Hong Kong

Published by

Singapore University Press
Yusof Ishak House, National University of Singapore
31 Lower Kent Ridge Road, Singapore 119078

and

World Scientific Publishing Co. Pte. Ltd.
5 Toh Tuck Link, Singapore 596224
USA office: Suite 202, 1060 Main Street, River Edge, NJ 07661
UK office: 57 Shelton Street, Covent Garden, London WC2H 9HE

British Library Cataloguing-in-Publication Data
A catalogue record for this book is available from the British Library.

CHINESE MIGRANTS ABROAD
Cultural, Educational, and Social Dimensions of the Chinese Diaspora

ISBN 981-238-041-8

Printed by FuIsland Offset Printing (S) Pte Ltd, Singapore

Contents

List of Figures

List of Tables

List of Contributors

Charney, Michael W. is currently Lecturer of Southeast Asian History in the Department of History at the School of Oriental and African Studies, University of London. In 1999, he completed his Ph.D. in Southeast Asian History at the University of Michigan, on the topic of the emergence of Buddhist religious communalism in western Burma. From 1999 until 2001, he was a postdoctoral fellow with the Centre for Advanced Studies, National University of Singapore, where he undertook research on Burmese migrant communities outside of Burma, the role of transnational religious communities in migrant adaptation to host societies, and the history of Chinese migration into Burma. Dr. Charney has published articles on Southeast Asian history in *Journal of the Economic and Social History of the Orient, Oriens Extremus, Journal of Asian History, Journal of Burma Studies*, and *Journal of the South Seas Society*.

Chin, James is Assistant Professor in the Department of History at the National University of Singapore. Dr. Chin works in the field of Chinese maritime history and the Chinese overseas diaspora and has published dozens of articles on Chinese maritime history, Chinese sojourning communities overseas, and early Sino-Portuguese relations.

Hibbins, Ray is currently a Senior Lecturer in the School of Leisure Studies, Griffith University, Queensland, Australia. His Ph.D. in the Department of Anthropology and Sociology, the University of Queensland was concerned with Migration and Masculinity and explored the experiences of recent Chinese male migrants in Brisbane. He is working on chapters of a book that will be published from this thesis. Over the past ten years, research undertaken by Dr. Hibbins has focused on the links among ethnicity, social class, sexuality, gender, and leisure experiences and behaviour. He has chapters in several books on these issues. Currently, his work centres on the Vietnamese community and indigenous Australians. A comparative study of the effects of migration experiences on constructions of masculinities among men of different ethnic backgrounds is planned for the future. Dr. Hibbins is the author of many articles on migration and gender identity among Chinese males, and is currently working on articles for the *Journal of Sociology, Men and Masculinities*, and *Sexualities*.

Khoo, Siew-Ean is Executive Director of the Australian Centre for Population Research at the Research School of Social Sciences, The Australian National University. She has a BA in Liberal Arts and both a MSc and a DSc in Population Sciences from Harvard University. She was previously Senior Lecturer in the Demography Program at the Australian National University. She had also been on the research staff of the Australian Bureau of Immigration, Population and Multicultural Research and the Department of Immigration and Multicultural Affairs. Dr. Khoo has published extensively on population and immigration issues including immigrant settlement and the demography of immigrants in Australia.

Lee Guan Kin is currently an Assistant Professor in the Centre for Chinese Language and Culture at the Nanyang Technological University. In 1998, she completed her Ph.D. on the topic of Singapore Chinese intellectuals at the University of Hong Kong. In 2001, She spent three months in the Department of East Asian Languages and Cultures at the Columbia University as a Visiting Scholar. Her major research interest is the history of the ethnic Chinese in Singapore and Malaysia with respect to personage, ideology, education, and culture, and has published numerous articles on them. She is now focusing on the project of the history of Nanyang University (or Nantah in abbreviation), the first Chinese University established in Southeast Asia by overseas Chinese. In 2001, she published a book on the response of Singapore Chinese intellectuals to Eastern and Western Cultures, and edited a book, *The Nantah Scholar*.

Li Zong is currently an Associate Professor of Sociology at the University of Saskatchewan and an affiliated researcher of the Prairie Centre of Excellence for Research on Immigration and Integration (PCERII) in Canada. His research projects have been funded by the Social Sciences and Humanities Council of Canada (SSHRC), the Prairie Centre of Excellence for Research on Immigration and Integration (PCERII), and other funding agencies. His recent research project, funded by SSHRC, is entitled "Systemic Racism and Foreign-Trained Chinese Professional Immigrants in Alberta".

He teaches Sociological Theory, Research Methods, Race and Ethnic Relations, Cross-Cultural Perspectives on Poverty, and Social Stratification. His areas of research include race and ethnic relations, immigration and racism, and Chinese society. He has co-authored a sociological book and published articles and reviews in *Canadian Ethnic Studies*, *Journal of Comparative Family Studies*, *American Journal of Sociology*, *Pacific Affairs*, *Journal of Multilingual and Multicultural Development*, and *Journal of International Migration and Integration*. He has also contributed several chapters to published books.

Mackie, Jamie is retired and is Professor Emeritus of the Australian National University and, since 1990, a Visiting Fellow in the Economics Department of the Research School of Asian and Pacific Studies, ANU, attached to its Indonesia Project. He was formerly Foundation Professor in the Department of Political and Social Change in the same School from 1978–89. Previously, he was the first Research Director at the Centre for Southeast Asian Studies at Monash University (1968–78) and founding Head of Department of Indonesian Studies at the University of Melbourne (1968–67), after spending two years in Jakarta, 1956–58, working as an economist with the State Planning Bureau. He works on the borderlines between political science, economics, and economic history, with a particular interest in the economic and political situation of the Indonesian Chinese.

His main publications are *Konfrontasi. The Indonesia-Malaysia Dispute 1963–66* (Kuala Lumpur: OUP, 1974) and (as editor and contributor) *The Chinese in Indonesia* (Melbourne: Nelson, 1975) and (again as co-editor with James Fox and Howard Dick, and a contributor) *Balanced Development: East Java under the New Order* (Singapore: OUP, 1993), as well as various journal articles and chapters in books.

Mak, Anita is currently Senior Lecturer in Applied Psychology at the University of Canberra, Australia. She holds a Ph.D. in Psychology awarded by the Australian National University, and both a Master's of Social Sciences (Clinical Psychology) and a Bachelor's of Social Sciences in Psychology and Statistics (Honours) from Hong Kong University. Dr. Mak has published extensively in the areas of Chinese migrants in Australia, professional immigrants' workplace adaptation, international education, ethnic identification, and social efficacy in cross-cultural encounters. Her latest book, entitled *Relocating careers: Hong Kong professionals and managers in Australia* (2001), has been published by the Centre of Asian Studies Press, Hong Kong University. Dr. Mak is also an intercultural trainer and consultant, and a co-developer of the EXCELL (Excellence in Cultural Experiential Learning and Leadership) Program for the enhancement of sociocultural competencies among migrants, international students, and expatriates.

Ng, Wai-ming Benjamin is currently an Associate Professor in the Department of Japanese Studies at the Chinese University of Hong Kong. He is an intellectual and cultural historian specializing in Sino-Japanese relations. He received his doctorate in East Asian Studies from Princeton University in 1996 and was an Assistant Professor in the Department of Japanese Studies at the National University of Singapore from 1996 to 2001. He is the author of *The I Ching in Tokugawa Thought and Culture* (University of Hawai'i Press, 2000, selected as a Choice Outstanding Academic Book in 2001 by the American Library Association and the Significant University Press Title in 2001 by the Association of American University Presses). His articles have appeared in a number of journals, including *Philosophy East and West, Asian Philosophy, East Asian History, Journal of Asian History, Tsing Hua Journal of Chinese Studies*, and *Korean Studies*.

Pawakapan, Niti is currently Assistant Professor of the Southeast Asian Studies Programme in the Faculty of Arts and Social Sciences, National University of Singapore. He obtained his Ph.D. in Anthropology from the Australian National University. He taught at Chulalongkorn, Kasetsart and Rangsit Universities in Thailand, and was the Henry Hart Rice Fellow at the Center for International and Area Studies, Yale University, between 1998 and 1999. His research interests include migration, ethnicity, and economic anthropology. Dr Pawakapan's work has appeared in the *Journal of Southeast Asian Studies* and *South East Asia Research*, as well as in various Thai-language journals and books.

Tong Chee Kiong is Associate Professor in the Department of Sociology at the National University of Singapore. His research focuses upon the Chinese in Southeast Asia, Chinese business firms and their institutional foundations, and comparative religions.

Wee Tong Bao is a Masters' degree candidate with the Department of History at the National University of Singapore. She is working on Chinese vernacular education in Singapore from the early 20th century until the outbreak of the Second World War. She is a co-contributor of the article — "A Brief Note on Prewar Singapore Sources Relating to Chinese Business History", published in Cornell University East Asia Program's *Chinese Business History Bulletin* 10.2 (Fall 2000).

Wong, Tze-Ken Danny is currently Lecturer of Vietnamese and Southeast Asian History at the Department of History, Faculty of Arts & Social Sciences, University of Malaya. He is in the process of completing his Ph.D. on Vietnamese history at the University of Malaya. He is the author of *The Transformation of an Immigrant Society: A Study of the Chinese of Sabah* (London: Asean Academic Press, 1998) and has published articles in *Journal of Southeast Asian Studies*, *Archipel*, *Journal of the Sabah Society*, and *Journal of the Malaysian Branch of the Royal Asiatic Society*.

Yao Souchou is Senior Lecturer in the Department of Anthropology, University of Sydney, Australia. His research interests are the cultural politics of Southeast Asia and identity formation in the Chinese diaspora. He has done fieldwork in Hong Kong, Singapore and Malaysia. His articles have appeared in *Parallax, Australian Journal of Anthropology*, and *New Formations*. He is the editor of *House of Glass: Culture, Modernity and the State in Southeast Asia* (Singapore: ISEAS, 2001). He is also the author of *Confucian Capitalism: Discourse, Practice and the Myth of Chinese Enterprise* (Richmond: Curzon, 2001).

Yen Ching Hwang formerly Chair Professor of History at the University of Hong Kong, is Reader/Associate Professor in History at the University of Adelaide, Australia.

Yeoh, Brenda S. A. is Associate Professor in the Department of Geography at the National University of Singapore. Dr. Yeoh completed her B.A. (Hons) at Cambridge University and obtained her D.Phil from Oxford University. She specializes in social and historical geography. Her research foci include the politics of space in colonial and post-colonial cities, as well as gender, migration and transnational communities. She has published over forty-five scholarly journal papers and is also the author/editor of *Portraits of Places: History, Community and Identity in Singapore* (Times Editions, 1995, with Lily Kong), *Contesting Space: Power Relations and the Urban Built Environment in Colonial Singapore* (Oxford University Press, 1996), *Singapore: A Developmental City State* (John Wiley, 1997, with Martin Perry and Lily Kong), *Community and Change: The Tanjong Pagar Community Club Story* (Armour, 1997), and *Gender and Migration* (Edward Elgar, 2000, with Katie Willis).

Acknowledgements

This volume is a result of the international conference, "Immigrant Societies and Modern Education", held in Singapore, 31 August–3 September 2000. This conference was jointly organised by the Tan Kah Kee International Society and the Faculty of Arts and Social Sciences of the National University of Singapore. Over the course of 1999–2000, the preparations for the conference involved close collaboration and interaction between the Society and FASS. The success of the conference is thus due in large part to the commitment, organisational skills, and vision of those with whom we served on the organising committees for the ISME conference: Prof. Wang Gungwu (Chairman of the Tan Kah Kee International Society and Professor, East Asian Institute), Mr. Tan Keong Choon, Dr. Tong Ming Chuan, Dr. Phua Kok Khoo, Prof. Hew Choy Sin, Prof. Goh Thong Ngee, Prof. Lim Hock, Prof. Hew Choy Sin, Assoc. Prof. Lee Fook Hong, Dr. Low Hwee Boon, Assoc. Prof. Chen Kang, Assoc. Prof. Hui Weng Tat, Assoc. Prof. Lee Guan Kin, Assoc. Prof. Lee Cheuk Yin, Dr. Low Hwee Boon, Prof. Ong Choon Nam, Prof. Shang Huai Min, Mr. Han Suan Juan, Miss Tan Kuan Swee, Miss Cher Meng Chu, Miss Joelle Cheng, and Miss Kathleen Melissa Ke.

The editors of this volume also wish to thank the individuals whose assistance was necessary, after the dust had settled from the conference, for the compilation of this volume. Miss Ke and Mr. George Wong served as contact persons and organisers of incoming materials. Miss Lynsey Lee Yoke Cum compiled the reference list for this volume. The staff of the former Centre for Advanced Studies also provided various essential services during both the conference and in the year that followed. We are also grateful to Miss Karen Lai and Miss Theresa Wong for assistance with proof-reading and the checking of references. Ultimately, the editors would like to thank the authors of the articles themselves for putting up with the various demands that we, as editors, placed upon them and for sticking with us to the completion of this volume.

Michael W. Charney
Brenda S. A. Yeoh
Tong Chee Kiong

27 August 2001

Introduction: The Chinese Abroad

Michael W. Charney
Brenda S. A. Yeoh
Tong Chee Kiong

As one observer noted a little over a half-decade ago, fast-paced economic growth in Southeast Asia from the late 1960s until the mid-1990s brought increased attention to the Overseas Chinese as an economically successful diaspora and their role in this economic growth (Mackie 1996, p. xii). Events that followed, such as the transfer of Hong Kong and Macao (and with them a susbtantial portion of the Overseas Chinese) to the Peoples Republic of China, the election of a non-KMT government in Taiwan (and the possibility of the abandonment of the "one China" principle by Taiwan), the Asian economic crisis and the plight of Overseas Chinese in Indonesia as a result, and the durability of the Singapore economy during this same crisis, have helped to sustain this attention.

The study of the Overseas Chinese has by now become a global enterprise, raising new theoretical problems and empirical challenges. New case studies of Overseas Chinese, such as those on communities in North America, Cuba, India, and South Africa, continually unveil different perspectives. New kinds of transnational connectivities linking Chinese communities are also being identified. It is now possible to make broader generalisations of a Chinese diaspora on a global basis (McKeown 1999). Further, the intensifying study of the Overseas Chinese has stimulated a renewed intellectual vigor in other areas of research.

The transnational and transregional activities of Overseas Chinese, for example, pose serious challenges to analytical concepts of regional divides such as that between East and Southeast Asia (Liu 2000).

Despite the increased attention, new data, and the changing theoretical paradigms, basic questions concerning the Overseas Chinese remain. To alter slightly the question Leo Suryadinata has asked in terms of the Chinese in Southeast Asia (Suryadinata 1997b, p. 1), should the Overseas Chinese commmunities be considered in their local or national context or as part of a transnational "Chinese" community? Similarly, what do we mean by diaspora and is it appropriate to use this term in reference to the Overseas Chinese? These issues will certainly remain for some time to come.

This authors in this volume take a local approach. The papers in this volume, in other words, seek to understand the Overseas Chinese migrants not just in terms of the overall Chinese diaspora *per se*, but also local Chinese migrants adapting to local societies, in different national contexts.

Part One focuses upon questions of the national, cultural, and gender identities and identifications of Chinese migrants in Southeast Asia and Australia. Jamie Mackie (Chapter 1), for example, warns us against the temptation to overgeneralise and essentialise "Chineseness" among the Overseas Chinese, especially the frequently assumed cultural determinants of Chinese business success. Using five case studies of Chinese empire-builders, Mackie demonstrates that entrepreneurial successes of certain businessmen from the Chinese diaspora cannot be tied to shared "Chinese" characteristics. That is, factors beyond their "Chineseness" must be considered if one is to understand Chinese migrant entrepreneurs and their successes. As Mackie finds, differences more than similarities were critical to the success of the business tycoons he examines.

Ray Hibbins (Chapter 2) turns to the special situation of gender identity among Chinese male migrants in a European-dominated society, that of Australia. Hibbins uses data collected from interviews with Chinese male migrants in Australia and finds that Chinese males in Australia perceive masculinity differently than do their Euro-Australian counterparts. While Euro-Australian men mark maculinity with engagement in physical sports, cars, drinking, and women, Chinese male migrants in Australia see masculinity in terms of hard work, being a strong guardian and the sole provider for the family, educational and occupational achievement, the accumulation of wealth, and sexual conservativeness. As Hibbins explains, consciously or unconciously, the influence of tradition on attitudes toward masculinity remains strong among Chinese male migrants in Australia.

Yao Souchou (Chapter 3) examines the "othering" of the Chinese in Malaysia and how this process is partly reflected in the provisioning of Malay politicians with Chinese women by Chinese businessmen. This process has also involved the creation of an image of the competitive Chinese migrant as a threat to the uncompetitive Malay, an image created for use by Malay politicians and encouraged in Malaysian Prime Minister Mahathir's *The Malay Dilemma*.

Chinese who return from migrant communities in Southeast Asia to live in mainland China, Hong Kong, Macao, or Taiwan face additional challenges to their identity and identification as Chinese. James Chin Kong (Chapter 4) examines the unusual place held by members of return migration of Chinese from Indonesia to mainland China, and then on to Hong Kong. As Chin explains, despite initial self-perceptions as native Chinese among these migrants, these migrants were still viewed as foreign guests or at least as a different kind of Chinese by local mainland Chinese society. At the same time, they were not allowed to return to the Southeast Asian countries they had left, where they were also now seen as outsiders. Not fully accepted in China nor welcome in Southeast Asia, many returned Overseas Chinese moved on to Hong Kong. As Chin demonstrates, the way identities are formed and identifications are constructed has changed in recent years and new forms of organization and community formation have produced additional challenges and new opportunities for assimilation and accommodation by the host society.

Part Two looks at the important cultural role of education in Chinese migrant communities and how these reflect both cultural and economic choices. In either case, they have a decisive impact upon understandings by the Chinese of tradition and modernity. Chinese culture also places special emphasis both on success and respect for education, which helps to increase the importance of education to, and thus the impact on, Chinese migrants.

Using the case study of Kobe's Chûka dôbun gakkô (*Tongwen* Chinese School), the largest Chinese school in Japan, Ng Wai-ming (Chapter 5) examines the role of Chinese schools as sites for the mediation of changing Overseas Chinese identities and of equally dynamic Sino-Japanese relations. Ng first examines the transition from regional identities to a national Chinese identity among Chinese migrants in Japan in the early days of the Chûka dô bun gakkô and then turns to the identity crisis among Chinese migrants in early postwar Japan. As the Chinese communities in Japan have themselves changed, so too has role of Chinese schools, as they continue to change to meet new demands and to serve a new kind of Chinese migrant community. As Ng demonstrates, these schools continue to play a significant role in easing the transition among Chinese migrants from Chinese residents (*kakyo*) to Overseas Chinese (*kajin*) in modern Japan.

Wee Tong Bao (Chapter 6) illustrates the extensive development of Chinese vernacular education in prewar Singapore as a foundation block for the emergence of Singapore's Chinese community. A major problem in trying to assess the place of Chinese vernacular education in the history of Singapore's Chinese community is that while the primary sources have been used extensively, there was either little attempt at a comprehensive historical narrative for Chinese vernacular education in Singapore or the narrative was framed by non-educational factors and interests. In Wee's analysis of the discussion of Chinese vernacular education in Singapore, for example, she found that English accounts tended to look at Chinese vernacular education in the context of colonial administrative and political developments. Chinese-language accounts similarly constructed their narrative of Chinese vernacular education around political events in China. As a result, local social factors critical to the emergence of Chinese vernacular education in Singapore are overlooked.

Wee draws attention to the role of different dialect groups (the Hokkien, Cantonese, Teochiu and other Chinese dialect groups) within the "Overseas Chinese" label in the establishment of Chinese vernacular schools in colonial Singapore. As Wee explains, a variety of social factors identified in the sources, but generally ignored in the secondary accounts, were at work in the emergence of these schools. One of the most important of these was the role of dialect bangs in coming together to found and support schools for the children of their communities. Dependence upon policy- or politically-oriented historical narratives for education in Singapore, however, hides such factors.

Yen Ching Hwang (Chapter 7) gives an overview of the emergence of modern education among the Chinese in Malaya. He ties this development first with educational reforms in the late Qing period in China, and follows through with the continuing influence of educational and other developments in Republican China that had a serious impact upon Chinese education among Chinese in South China and Southeast Asia. Yen is mainly concerned with the experiences of one particular dialect group, though, the Hokkiens. As the first of the dialect groups to migrate to and settle in Southeast Asia, and as the most economically successful of the dialect groups among Chinese migrants to Southeast Asia, the Hokkiens were able to sponsor modern Chinese schools earlier and more intensively than other dialect groups within the Chinese diaspora. While many Chinese, especially businessmen, were involved in promoting Chinese education in Malay, Yen's case study, one visionary, Tan Kah Kee, merits special attention due to his commitment and sponsorship of educational enterprises in both South China and in Malaya.

Danny Wong (Chapter 8) examines a different Chinese dialect group, the Hakkas, in Sabah, where they form the overwhelming majority of the Chinese population. Wong's Hakka Christians sought English education and English schools, by contrast with Yen's Hokkiens and their pursuit of Chinese education. According to Wong, the Hakkas developed connections with Christian missionaries in the middle of the 19th century in China, and these connections were developed further when Hakkas migrated to Sabah later in the Qing period. As a result, many Hakkas were Christian and sought out English education in mission schools, giving them an advantage in competing for white-collar jobs in the employment of the British Chartered Company, which governed Sabah. As Wong explains, changes from the 1970s, such as the shifts in Malaysian government policy in the independence period and the replacement of English with Malay as the language of government, has brought an end to the advantage of an English education and thus to the Hakka domination over white collar and government jobs.

Part Three turns to other factors involved in the Chinese migrant relationship with host societies, including economic, occupational, and national integration. Li Zong's (Chapter 9) case study focuses upon Chinese-Canadian and Polish-Canadian professional immigrants in Toronto, Canada. As Li explains, foreign-trained immigrants face special challenges in gaining work in their professions. These challenges go beyond poor command of English on arrival, poor networking, and lack of prior Canadian work experience.

A more significant barrier is that it is difficult to get employers in Canada, or the professional gatekeeper associations in Canada to recognize their education and credentials gained outside of Canada. This problem is more acute, Li finds, among Chinese migrants than among Polish migrants who are otherwise very comparable as immigrant professionals. This has led to very different occupational choices, especially by Chinese migrants, often in stark contrast to their personal qualifications. Furthermore, more Chinese believe that their situation is a result of being visible minorities (due to skin colour). Li clearly illustrates the social impact of this aspect of immigrant integration into one host society.

Siew-Ean Khoo and Anita Mak (Chapter 10) provide an analysis of the factors that encourage permanent settlement of Asian migrants, mostly Chinese, in Australia. As Khoo and Mak explain, the degree of retention of Asian immigrants as permanent settlers in Australia varies depending upon the country of origin, migrants being broken up into China, Hong Kong, Korea and Taiwan, Malaysia and Singapore, and India and Sri Lanka countries of origin. As Khoo and Mak indicate, factors that encourage permanent settlement include whether or not the immigrant has found employment and the level of satisfaction with that employment, their level of English proficiency, whether or not the immigrant already had relatives in Australia, the degree to which having the goal of a better future for their family was a reason for migration in the first place, and whether or not the immigrant had school-aged children. Differences, such as those between Chinese migrants from the PRC and Hong Kong also depended upon whether or not returning to the place of origin was a realistic option. Ultimately, traditional Chinese values including providing educational opportunities for one's children has clearly remained strong among migrants of the Chinese diaspora.

Niti Pawakapan (Chapter 11) provides new perspectives and data on the Chinese migrant community in Dunedin (New Zealand). Chinese migrants to New Zealand came in two waves. The first, in the late 19th century, consisted of temporary, male migrants who only sought to find their fortune in mining gold and who intended to return to China as wealthy men. The second wave, from the 1920s, consisted of Chinese, many of them refugees and eventually women as well as men, who came to New Zealand to settle permanently. Pawakapan provides valuable insights into their occupational choices, which were determined in large part by their attempt to fit into niches available in the New Zealand economy. These choices were largely characterized by self-employment and included market gardening, vegetable and fruit vending, shopkeeping, and work as launderers.

These occupational choices had a serious impact upon the integration of Chinese migrants into the host society of New Zealand. Pawakapan suggests that different approaches to employment and the challenges of settlement in a new land fostered social distance between White and Chinese that has been confused with racism. Pawakapan thus challenges previous work on the Chinese in New Zealand that has previous oriented studies on this migrant group around issues of White racism

Lee Guan Kin (Chapter 12) examines the role of language in nation-building in independent Singapore. As Lee explains, the Chinese community in Singapore is facing a cultural crisis. As the Malay minority clings to its Malay heritage, the cultural identity of the Chinese in Singapore is in decline. This is in large part due to the role of language as a cultural transmitter to the young. While Malays use their native language in the most important cultural spheres of their lives, Singaporean Chinese are becoming decreasingly acquainted with the Chinese language. As Lee explains, this development is ironic, as Chinese language was promoted and played a significant role in the cultural life of Singaporean Chinese, especially seen in the growth of Chinese-language schools, under British colonial rule, but has suffered instead at the hands of the independent and Chinese-dominated Singaporean state. Lee suggests that a major reason for this decline has been the government insistence on the use of Mandarin, both in the schools and in the home, at the expense of sub-Chinese dialects.

PART ONE

Chineseness and "Overseas" Chinese Identifications and Identities of a Migrant Community

CHAPTER 1

Five Southeast Asian Chinese Empire-Builders: Commonalities and Differences

Jamie Mackie

It is appropriate that a conference co-sponsored with the Tan Kah Kee Society should include a panel with the words 'entrepreneurship', 'business empires', and 'education' in its title, for they all have direct relevance to Tan Kah Kee and his remarkable career. But while the first two words could also be applied to many other Southeast Asian Chinese businessmen of the last century or more, the last could not. None have made such generous, sustained contributions to the creation of schools for their fellow-citizens, or attached such great significance to education, both modern and traditional, as he did. And this despite having had little more than rudimentary schooling in the Chinese classics in Xiamen, before he was set to work in his father's business in Singapore at the age of sixteen.[1] Like many other self-made men who became captains of industry or commerce in other parts of the world (Carnegie, Ford, and Nuffield are striking examples) he was well aware of the advantages of a good education and the opportunities for advancement and wider freedoms missed by those who have not had access to it.

A good education of the right sort can prove highly beneficial for a modern entrepreneur (especially in today's world of IT and fast-changing technologies) but it has clearly not been a necessary or sufficient condition for business success previously. Many of the foremost Southeast Asian Chinese tycoons of the 20th century, probably most, have had very little education, and almost none of them very much. A study of the Chinese in the Central Javanese city of Semarang in the 1950s found, in fact, that those who had been able to get some education were inclined to prefer professional or salaried jobs with security and higher status rather than an exhausting, sweaty life as a self-employed businessman in the marketplace, with all its risks and difficulties (Willmott 1960). The more entrepreneurial types tended to come from the poorly-educated, hard-driving, Chinese-speaking new arrivals, not the older-established *peranakan* families. But that too may now be changing as times and circumstances change. Of the five outstanding Chinese empire-builders to be discussed here, only Robert Kuok owed much to his good schooling (although the maverick Lucio Tan could claim higher formal qualifications), while Liem Sioe Liong, once the wealthiest tycoon by far in all Southeast Asia, and a very smart businessman, probably had the least schooling of them all.

These five men, each of whom could be regarded as among the foremost entrepreneurs in his country, intrigue me because their differences seem so much more striking than any commonalities we might discern. They differ in their personal characteristics, their career paths, and in the ways they have adapted to the very diverse socio-economic and political conditions each has encountered in the several countries of Southeast Asia. It is hard to find any one common factor or combination of factors that can be held to account for their extraordinary success, apart from their obvious entrepreneurial talents (of strikingly different types), their risk-tasking propensities and their ability to adapt to rapidly changing circumstances (Mackie 1992, 1998).

That quality of adaptability strikes me as one of the most interesting qualities of the Overseas Chinese, not just here but also in many other parts of the world (in Australia particularly). It is a characteristic of the poor as well as the rich, and one that deserves closer scrutiny than it has yet been given. It may owe something to the personal qualities and values deriving from their ancient Chinese cultural heritage, although that explanation needs to be investigated far more rigorously than it has been so far. But the adaptability of the Overseas Chinese has enabled them to fit amazingly well into a wide range of other countries, societies and cultures all over the world, not just the Thai, Malay, Indonesian, and

Filipino but also Canadian, American, or Australian, as shown in the splendid set of country studies edited by Lynn Pan (1999). It is a feature they share with my ancestors, the Scots, one of the world's other great diasporic peoples, but a much more stubborn, inflexible and ornery lot.

The differences among these five men must be stressed — and of the circumstances in which they achieved their success — rather than any common features, in order to guard against any temptation to slide towards the essentialist fallacy of assuming that all Overseas Chinese businessmen possess essentially the same characteristics (if only we could identify them properly) among which we might be able to find the key to their entrepreneurial drives and talents. The latter are often said to be derived from their Chinese cultural heritage or values. But without meaning to be disrespectful of that great heritage I would argue that it is only one element among many that go into the complex alchemy that produces strong entrepreneurial drives and talents in so many Overseas Chinese. We still have a very poor understanding of that alchemy.[2] Most of us can easily recognize a successful entrepreneur when we see one, but no one has succeeded in explaining why some succeed while so many others fail. Even if we can account for their strong propensity towards risk-taking, very common among people famous for their love of gambling, strongly inclined towards geomancy and often desperate to rise out of poverty, that alone does not give us the key to what makes so many of them highly entrepreneurial in character. In fact, according to Schumpeter's famous definition, risk-taking is not the quality that distinguishes entrepreneurs, for in his view all capitalists are risk-takers to some degree, but very few are entrepreneurs. He regarded the true entrepreneur as something more, one who creates those 'new combinations' of factors of production (not just innovators, but far more than that) which entirely transform the business scene, generating the waves of 'creative destruction' of older enterprises which open up the way towards whole new industries (Casson 1990, pp. 114–34). On that definition, however, very few Overseas Chinese would qualify. We do not have to accept Schumpeter's theory as the canonical last word on the subject, of course — or Max Weber's, for that matter — influential and fruitful though they have been by stimulating new thinking about the well-springs of entrepreneurship.

The success of Southeast Asian Chinese entrepreneurs is often attributed to one or more of the three well-known structural features of their business life — their family firms, both small-scale and large, which are still the most common form of business enterprise among them; their reliance on inter-personal trust (*guanxi* and *xinyong*) as the basis on which so many business transactions are conducted; and their legendary networks of personal connections which are an extension of *guanxi*, sometimes a pillar on which big business empires have been created. It is not enough just to point out how widespread these features have been, as if that alone will lead us towards the secrets of entrepreneurial success. In a perceptive introduction to the book he has edited on *Chinese Business Networks*, Chan Kwok Bun (2000, p. 5) has warned of the deceptiveness of 'monolithic cultural labels' and reminded us it is "fallacious to lump varied and varying Chinese experiences into a singular history and destiny". We are likely to come closer to the truth by exploring the differences hidden behind such notions than we will by trying to discover common elements as the key to Chinese commercial success, which exponents of the essentialist fallacy often seem to be seeking. The strikingly diverse careers of these five great empire-builders show this very clearly.

Tan Kah Kee

Tan Kah Kee (1874–1961, b. Xiamen) became known as 'the rubber king' of Singapore-Malaya in the 1920s, and a multimillionaire, although his businesses collapsed in the Depression years. He was not a classic example of the rag-to-riches entrepreneur, for he came from a moderately wealthy family; yet he lived a very frugal, almost spartan life. It was his ability to adapt shrewdly and decisively to changing business conditions that was a key factor in his success.

His business career started in 1890 when he was summoned by his father from his home village in Xiamen to work in the family's rice trading company in Singapore. He was soon appointed its manager, and the business flourished as Tan proved himself to be a "sound, dedicated and competent manager" (Yong 1987, p. 42). But for reasons beyond his control the company collapsed in 1905. Meanwhile he had launched his own pineapple-canning and rice importing enterprise, which soon profited greatly from rising European demand for canned pineapple. In 1906 he branched out into two new ventures, a rice mill producing cooked rice for the Indian market, which proved very profitable, and a small rubber plantation.

The timing of his move into rubber was lucky, for Malayan rubber was just starting to make a big impact in Britain and his trees began to come into production a few years later just as the crazy 1910 rubber boom in London led to sky-rocketing prices for both rubber and Malayan plantations. Tan sold his Singapore estate at a big profit and reinvested in two others in Johore that he put under rubber, interplanted with pineapples. In fact, pineapple canning remained his main source of income over the next few years and by 1914 he was already close to being a millionaire.

The outbreak of World War I brought an abrupt change in his fortunes, as shipping shortages made it impossible to export canned pineapples to Europe and difficult to send his cooked rice to India. So he began to lease ships to transport the rice and thus became briefly but heavily involved in the shipping business. Through several further strokes of luck he made huge windfall profits there with which he converted one of his pineapple factories into a rubber remilling plant that soon became a lucrative money-spinner during the post-war rubber boom.[3] He then branched out in yet another new direction into a rubber manufacturing operation in Singapore, producing rubber-soled shoes, tyres for bicycles and horse carts (not yet for motor cars) and much else.[4] This daring venture also proved very profitable for a few years, although it later proved to be a disastrous millstone around his neck

His businesses were doing so well by then that Tan returned to Xiamen for three years to attend to the schools and university he had established there, leaving his brother in charge in Singapore. Another phase of rapid expansion and big profits followed in the mid-1920s, when he established nine more rubber mills across Malaya and also founded the famous newspaper, *Nanyang Siang Pau*. But while those years were the pinnacle of his success, he made one fatal error of judgement. He had borrowed three million Singapore dollars from Singapore banks to finance both his rubber interests and his schools in Xiamen, which he could easily have repaid out of his cash reserves at that time, but chose not to do so. When rubber prices began to decline in 1926, however, he had to sell assets on a declining market and cut back on his ambitious plans.

By 1929, "his financial foundation had been shaken and he was left with serious liquidity problems", with debts to local banks of nearly ten million Singapore dollars (Yong 1987, p. 64). His plight worsened disastrously as the worldwide depression struck the entire Malayan rubber industry a devastating blow. He then made another strategic error by pouring more money into rubber manufacturing operations in the belief that the firm's future could develop on that base, a bad misjudgment in the colonial economic context at a time of collapsing prices, shrinking world markets and rising tariff barriers. The financial position of his businesses deteriorated inexorably in the early 1930s despite efforts to restructure it as a limited liability company. Finally in 1933–34 his creditors took over and eventually wound up the enterprise.[5] That was virtually the end of his career as an entrepreneur and business empire builder.

In the years following, Tan Kah Kee, who was still "by no means a pauper" (Yong 1987, p. 70), went on to achieve a new form of greatness as a community leader of the Singapore Chinese and as the Southeast Asia-wide leader of the anti-Japanese resistance movement after 1937. That is another story, however, too complex to go into here. Instead, I will offer three brief comments on his entrepreneurial characteristics.

First, he was undoubtedly extremely enterprising, a daring risk-taker, with a sharp eye for new business opportunities. He built up an unusually large and diverse business enterprise through his adaptability and capacity to maintain tight control over a large and varied group of companies. Second, his success during the expansion phase of his empire was due largely to his shrewd assessments of market trends, although he miscalculated badly when the rubber market started to contract after 1926, especially by clinging to his ambitious vision of a future based on rubber manufacturing, instead of consolidating on his strongest assets, rubber remilling and cultivation. Finally, he differed most from other successful towkays of his time (and later) in that his primary aim was not simply to make money but to contribute to the modernisation and emancipation of China (and, by extension, the Chinese community of Singapore) through education and the creation of new industries. In this he was indeed a remarkable visionary, quite unique in the recent history of Southeast Asia.

Robert Kuok

Robert Kuok Hock Nien (b. Oct. 1923, Johore), the most accomplished and cosmopolitan of all the 20th-century tycoons of Southeast Asia, is an utterly different kind of entrepreneur from Tan Kah Kee.[6] He came from a wealthy family in Johore who owned a well-established commodities trading business that he took over on his father's death in 1949 and rapidly transformed into a major sugar-trading empire. He had the benefit of a good education at Raffles College, where he established personal connections with Malaya's later political leaders, and later built up a wide range of business associates and political contacts throughout the East Asian region while creating a vast, diversified business empire. He suffered no major setbacks except those resulting from the 1997 economic crisis which afflicted nearly all of the large enterprises in East Asia, but from which he has survived with fewer losses than most. He has never been as buccaneering or adventurous as Tan or the other entrepreneurs mentioned here, and may never have been the wealthiest of them. Yet of the five, he is the one best worth studying for clues to the secrets of success in the modern world of big business in Southeast Asia.

Consider the following remarks that have been made about him. He has "a solid reputation for reliability, honesty and skill" (Verchere 1977, p. 12) and is "the consummate deal-maker" (Hiscock 1997, pp. 207–209). He is "loyal to his business associates and employees, supportive of friends and discreet to the point of near invisibility ... [he has] a reputation for fairness ... and will always leave the other guy some meat on the bone" (Friedland 1991, pp. 46, 47). He has "superlative cross-cultural networking skills ... [being] equally at home in the hermetic world of Chinese *sinkehs* ... as he is in the cosmopolitan boardrooms of New York, London or Paris" (Heng 1997, p. 33).

Kuok has always been a trader and investor rather than an industrialist, although he was involved early on in shipbuilding and steel processing as well as sugar refining and flour milling in Malaya. He laid the foundations of his fortune in sugar trading (and flour) in the late 1950s, making a reputation as the "sugar king of Asia" before he was forty, reaping big profits from the steady rise in world sugar prices over the next twenty years. His career divides into two distinct phases: the first, until 1976, based mainly in Malaysia in sugar and related enterprises, the second based mainly in Hong Kong and China, with hotels (the Shangri-La chain) and property (Kerry Properties) at its core.

Kuok took over his family's commodities trading business in 1949 and soon began to focus on sugar trading, but moved to London briefly when the firm came under suspicion from the colonial security services because his brother had joined the Malayan Communist Party. In 1954, he was back in Malaya and acquired a small British agency house with a shipping arm that he built into Pacific Carriers Ltd., later to be the largest dry-goods bulk shipping company in Southeast Asia. His first large-scale enterprise, Malayan Sugar Manufacturing, was established in 1959 as a joint venture with Japanese companies, importing raw sugar from Thailand and processing it for export as well as for local consumption. Over the next decade or so he built up a complex network of business contacts in Thailand, where a new, dynamic sugar industry was developing, and in Indonesia, in partnership with Liem Sioe Liong, buying and selling sugar, flour, veneer, plywood and other commodities throughout the region.[7]

By the early 1970s, Kuok was being described as "the sugar king" of Southeast Asia, said to control about ten percent of the world's sugar trade. He had also started Malaysia's first major sugar cultivation project, Perlis Plantations, in association with a government agency, still a very profitable and efficient part of his vast business empire, although now only a tiny part of it (Malaysia is one of the world's most insignificant sugar producers, but had a lucrative protected domestic market that he dominated.) During that Malaysian phase of his career he also set up the Malaysian International Shipping Corporation and also Malaysia's first shipbuilding operation, which later branched out into a wide range of other heavy engineering projects there. He thereby built up close personal connections with two Prime Ministers, Tun Razak and Hussein Onn, whom he had earlier known at Raffles College, as well as a wide range of senior government officials. They came to trust him and rely heavily on his financial and technical knowledge. He was also diversifying his own investments into real estate and hotels in Malaysia and Singapore, with the first Shangri-La hotel opening in Singapore in 1971. But he moved to Hong Kong in 1976, henceforth developing his main business interests there and in China, reportedly because he was growing uneasy about the increasing constraints on Chinese business enterprises in Malaysia.

In the Hong Kong–China phase of his career, Kwok's business interests have diversified much further, mainly into hotels (the Shangri-La chain, with a dozen hotels in China) and Kerry Properties, although his older investments in sugar and flour trading are still important. He also has property investments in the Philippines and many other parts of the Pacific. Some of his ventures in China have entailed delays and cost overruns which have reduced their profitability, but not to a disastrous extent. He has cultivated good personal relations with China's leaders through his part in constructing the (initially far from profitable) World Trade Centre in the 1980s, building the Shangri-La hotels, becoming a shareholder in CITIC Pacific and purchasing the *South China Morning Post* from Rupert Murdoch (to ensure it would be in friendly hands prior to Hong Kong's transfer to China in 1997). While the 1997–98 crisis in East Asia caused setbacks for some of his companies, their very diversity enabled him to survive it relatively unscathed.

Friedland (1991) gives a good explanation in terms of three main factors for Kuok's success as an entrepreneur and empire-builder, and of "his ability to overcome adversity". The first was his use of a competent and loyal cadre of professional executives, alongside his two sons and two nephews who are the core directors of a close-knit family group. Second was his prudent financial management, exemplified in his practice of making each unit of his diverse business empire a separate profit centre so that there was minimal cross-subsidisation. Third was his unrivalled network of *guanxi* connections with leading businessmen and the political authorities in the Asian countries (and others) where he has business interests. There were no doubt other elements behind his success, but these seem the most important.

Liem Sioe Liong

Liem Sioe Liong (b.1917, Fujian) is a self-made man with perhaps the most remarkable rags-to-riches story of all the penniless Chinese migrants who came to Southeast Asia over the last 150 years.[8] He came to Java to join his brother at the age of 20, and worked initially in very menial jobs as a kind of travelling hawker providing credit on instalment terms (*cinamindring*) to very poor villagers (Twang 1998). During World War II and in the turbulent years of Indonesian-Dutch conflict that followed, Liem lived dangerously and prospered sufficiently from his daring to set up in business on his own. He was able to live comfortably through the next twenty years, during which he became *inter alia* a supplier to the Army's Central Java division and thereby acquainted with the then Colonel Soeharto, its commander at one period. He did not achieve exceptional wealth during those years, but almost no businessmen did at a time when the Indonesian economy was stagnant and grossly over-regulated. But soon after Soeharto came to power in 1966–67 and restored the economy to healthy growth, Liem rocketed to the fore.

As one of the many Sino-Indonesian *cukong* on whom Soeharto initially depended for supplementary funds, Liem soon became very wealthy through the business favours he received in return.[9] He first obtained monopoly rights over flour milling and cloves imports for the fast-growing *kretek* cigarette industry, which provided him a substantial cash flow for many years; later he also got preferential access to all sorts of contracts, licenses, cheap credits and much more, as he built up a vast range of new industries which became an important basis for the industrial transformation Indonesia experienced through the 1970s. Liem set out to achieve market domination in all these fields and succeeded in most of them, as Yuri Sato (1993) has commented in the best survey available of Liem's business empire and strategies, relying on 'conglomerate power' as much as on 'politically affiliated power'.

From then until the 1997–98 financial crisis his business interests just kept on expanding, with only a few setbacks. He moved first into crumb rubber milling (then a new technology) and logging, then textiles and various forms of food production (most notably noodles) cashing in on the growth of middle-class and urban demand as the economy recovered from the disasters of the Sukarno era. Meanwhile, he broadened into cement manufacture and real estate development as the construction industry started to boom in response to the growing demand for housing. Later, he moved into banking, insurance and financial services, auto and motor-cycle production (a field in which he was a late starter and never as dominant as the rival Astra group), the Krakatau cold-rolled steel mill — at Soeharto's behest — oil-palm plantations and cooking oil, and petrochemicals.

The collapse of his empire (within Indonesia, but not the large offshore portion), after the 1997–98 financial crisis and the overthrow of Soeharto was a tangled process. Liem's enterprises were the most obvious targets for popular hostility to the excessive cronyism and corruption of the Soeharto regime (especially the many ostentatious branches of his Bank Central Asia chain), and the backlash against Chinese businessmen generally. His house was wrecked during the anti-Chinese riots of May 1998. He has since found it prudent to remain abroad, leaving the task of recovering what remains of his assets there to his son Anthony.

On the question of Liem's entrepreneurial capacities three points stand out. First, he certainly benefitted from his crony status and the rent-taking opportunities that yielded him far more extensively than any of the other four tycoons discussed here have done, and it was crucial to his success. Second, he was able to amass huge profits within a highly protected domestic market system, with monopoly rights in some areas and preferential advantages in many others. Indonesia's markets have never represented a 'level playing field', being riddled with distortions of all sorts which ensured big profit margins to early-bird operators or any who could gain market dominance, as he constantly did. That was how many of the top twenty or so big conglomerates of the Soeharto era became so wealthy, but none on his scale. Finally, the question recurs endlessly: "Was he a 'real entrepreneur' as well as a crony and rent-seeker?" In his youth he was certainly highly enterprising, and successful in very adverse circumstances. Later, he successfully made the difficult transition from small-scale peddling to the vastly different demands of the new modern world of large-scale multinational conglomerate enterprises. The fact that a man of so little education could do that, even with the advantages of political patronage he enjoyed (which many others had also), is alone remarkable.

He managed a huge industrial empire more effectively than any of his rivals in Indonesia. And Soeharto put great trust in him. He must have achieved an uncanny knowledge of the workings of the New Order political and economic system within which he had to operate. So, while he certainly owed a huge amount to the rent-taking opportunities he was allowed, his detractors get it badly wrong when they attribute his success solely to that.

Dhanin Chearavanand

During Thailand's extraordinary boom decade prior to the 1997–98 financial crisis, Dhanin Chearavanand (b.1939, Bangkok) presided over a phase of headlong expansion by his family's Charoen Pokphand (CP) group, which led it to be ranked close to the Bangkok Bank group (or ahead of it in some estimates) as the country's largest conglomerate.[10] This culminated in a wildly ambitious investment spree in China, which made it for a time the biggest foreign investor there, with outlays estimated at close to one billion US dollars. Dhanin came to be regarded as an empire-builder of extraordinary capacities, although always with some doubts about his more enigmatic qualities. Yet his story tells us not so much about the benefits of entrepreneurial daring as about the dangers of building castles on sand.

In the early 1980s, Dhanin embarked upon a new business strategy that was a radical deviation from CP's previous path. Ever since being founded by his father in 1924 as a modest seed and farm feedmill business, CP had grown steadily but gradually for over 50 years around that line of business, mainly on the basis of its "superior technology and efficient trading".[11] By the 1970s, it had become one of Thailand's top twenty business groups and the largest in the agro-industry sector. It had developed high-yielding strains of chickens for egg-laying, built up an integrated set of feedmill, fertiliser and poultry enterprises and created an effective system of contract farming of chickens and later prawns. It opened an offshore company in Indonesia and later half a dozen other countries, becoming one of the first regional multi-national companies in all Southeast Asia.

Under Dhanin's leadership, after his father's death, CP maintained and further developed its activities in agro-industry, but also began to diversify vigorously into other activities across a wide range, not only in Thailand where it became a major player in the fast-developing telecommunications sector and retailing, but also in China after its opening up by Deng Xiao-peng in the 1980s. By the mid-1990s, CP was involved in a wide array of agro-industry projects in many of China's provinces as well as motor-cycle manufacturing in Shanghai, in a joint venture with China's largest auto company, and a shaky telecoms operation. In Thailand it moved into retail food outlets, Seven-Eleven convenience stores, supermarkets, property development, telecommunications, petrochemicals and petroleum refining, and much else. All this occurred at a time when capital for expansion was easily available from the banks and demand was growing fast in Bangkok and other Thai cities. It seemed as if the sky was the limit for CP.

Dhanin's aim was to make CP into a large-scale industrial conglomerate similar to the South Korean *chaebol*, with strong backing from the state as the champion of national industrial growth, more tightly integrated than Thailand's other rather haphazard financial or commercial groups, able to gain sufficient market share in various fields to become a price-setter over a wide range of products (Handley 1996). But because he felt that Thailand's market was too small to sustain such an organisation, he was determined to establish a strong presence in China by making CP's technology indispensible to the local and national authorities there.

Yet weaknesses in this strategy were becoming apparent even by the mid-1990s, well before the crisis of 1997. Handley (1996) has noted that "its conservative management style and heavily *guanxi*-reliant approach ... had in many ways become a drag on progress", blaming this on the fact that "diversification has been based too much on entrepreneurial opportunism and obtaining concessions through connections, and too little on existing group skills and attentive, capable management". CP's core agribusiness activities continued to be successful and its investments in property were very lucrative; but in other areas the results were 'mixed at best'. Many of the group's larger projects were performing badly and the attempt to move into China as a major international conglomerate was not doing as well as had been hoped.

When the 1997 crisis broke, CP was caught like most other big Thai companies with large unhedged loans from the banks that suddenly turned into huge unpayable debts. It had no choice but to retrench sharply, sell off non-performing assets wherever possible, even at bargain-basement prices, and concentrate its resources again on its core strengths, agribusiness and telecommunications (*Nation Multimedia* 31 Dec. 1998). It has survived the disaster so far, but Dhanin's ambitions to create Thailand's first great *chaebol* and establish a strong presence in China are things of the past. Business empires need to be built on solid foundations.

Lucio Tan

I will end with the maverick Lucio Tan (b. 1934, Xiamen), who is not only a daring empire-builder and risk-taker in the Tan Kah Kee mould but also a highly controversial figure among Manila's 'Six Taipans' who have emerged as dazzling new Philippines-Chinese stars on the business scene there since the fall of Marcos in 1986.[12] They are a remarkable group of men who have built up large business empires at a time when the country's economy was relatively stagnant. Yet Tan is not at all like them. He is an outsider, a loner, a rough diamond, a rags-to-riches entrepreneur, a bit of a hustler, not highly regarded by either the Philippines indigenous elite or by wealthy Philippines-Chinese. He became notorious as one of the hated 'Marcos cronies' in the 1970s, as a result of which he fell badly out of favour with the two presidents who followed him, Corazon Aquino and Fidel Ramos. Yet he has since shown remarkable resilience as a survivor and an empire-builder of unusual talents.

By the mid-1990s, he controlled Fortune Tobacco, Asia Brewing, Allied Banking Corporation and Philippine Airlines (PAL), all of them among the largest enterprises in their fields, plus an array of lesser enterprises within the Philippines and others off-shore. Just how he did so is not easy to pin down, except that his connections with Marcos were obviously crucial in his early years. But he is certainly an entrepreneur of unusual ability, although something of an enigma to those who have tried to analyse him (Tiglao 1986).

Tan came to the Philippines in his youth as an impoverished immigrant. After various low-level jobs in cigarette factories, he set up one of his own in Ilocos in the 1960s. His first big break came when he luckily obtained an American agency for down-market cigarettes which he built into the 'Fortune' tobacco company, soon to become one of the country's largest (Yoshihara 1988, pp. 188–89). By establishing a close crony relationship with President Marcos he received government help in taking over a struggling bank in 1977 which soon grew into one of the country's largest banks as the Allied Banking Corporation. Later he established Asia Brewery that effectively challenged the near-monopoly of the mighty San Miguel corporation by producing a cheaper but very popular beer for the mass market rather than just the middle class (Tiglao 1996).

After the fall of Marcos, when the Aquino regime sequestered much of the 'ill-gotten wealth' of the cronies, Tan found himself in the political wilderness for some years. Yet by the early 1990s he was being mentioned as one of the country's 'Six Taipans'. Then in 1993, after fighting off serious charges of tax evasion, he achieved his most spectacular coup by obtaining control of PAL in the face of fierce opposition from both the government and the old-established Spanish-descent elite families, the Ayalas, Sorianos, and even the influential Cojuangco family, with whom he had earlier been in partnership.

What sort of man is he? He is described as reclusive, highly secretive about his business activities, but also as a "rather austere, somewhat ascetic character, more interested in intellectual activities than in the hedonistic pleasures of the wealthy". He neither drinks nor smokes. He is the only one of the five empire-builders discussed here who actually has a university degree, in chemical engineering.

Why has he been so successful? Several reasons are obvious. First, his political connections with Marcos were crucial in the years when he was getting started — although that became a disadvantage later when Cory Aquino and Ramos hounded him. But he was later very close to President Estrada, and is said to exert considerable influence with various Congressmen by contributing to their campaign funds. His political networks seem much wider and better developed than those of the other big taipans. Second, he has utilized the well-tried Chinese business strategy of accepting low profit margins on goods in mass markets and large volume of production for the sake of rapid turnover and large economies of scale (Tiglao 1996, p. 62). Third, he is said to have had a loyal and competent staff consisting mainly of family members, but also some strategically chosen ex-generals whose military contacts have been useful in various ways. Fourth, he has clearly possessed a high degree of resilience as well as an eye for emerging business opportunities of any sort — plus the means to pursue them.

What significance, then, does Lucio Tan's story have for us here? He has been far more of a risk-taker than our other entrepreneurs, or any of the other Philippines taipans. Living dangerously seems not to perturb him. But he seems to be a shrewd gambler (and is reportedly quite ruthless in getting his way). His business empire is relatively diversified if compared with those of his rivals, with four major segments, whereas they have nearly all built up around one main base. His Chinese origins are far more apparent than is the case with any other of the 'Six Taipans', some of whom barely speak any Chinese, whereas Tan speaks little English. He is said to have a wide knowledge of the Chinese classics. Not an easy man to pigeon-hole neatly at all.

Conclusion

Are we now any closer to an answer to my question about the commonalities and differences between these men? The differences between them are indeed very striking — as could be said also of the group of Southeast Asian Chinese entrepreneurs described by Chan and Chiang (1994) or the many more listed by Yoshihara (1988). But the differences are not sharp black-and-white contrasts so much as shades of grey, or a matter of where they might be located between the two poles of various spectra — e.g. between, say, 'traditional' and 'modern' in their world-views, or 'diversified' or 'concentrated' in their business strategies.

It is clear, however, that these five have all been risk-takers to an exceptional degree, far more so than the average Chinese small trader or artisan, with Tan Kah Kee and Lucio Tan the most notably so and Robert Kuok probably the least. They could all be located towards the 'modern' end of the spectrum rather than the 'traditional' in respect of their business practices and general outlook — with Kuok the closest to the modern end and Dhanin (and perhaps Lucio Tan) towards the traditionally 'Chinese' end, while Liem and Tan Kah Kee hover somewhere in the middle, not easy to place with any precision — although all five of them retain some strong Chinese socio-cultural characteristics in varying degrees. How far have they relied on Chinese-style commercial networks and *guanxi* links to build up their enterprises? All of them to some extent, but Lucio Tan perhaps the least and Tan Kah Kee not very much (beyond his family circle), and Dhanin the most heavily. How diversified or concentrated have their business empires been? All rather diversified, it seems, Liem's and Lucio Tan's especially, for none of them has concentrated on only one or two main spheres of activity (as a few of the second-rank enterprises observable in all these countries have been), except insofar as Tan Kah Kee and Kuok have at various times put most of their efforts into one or two sectors. In the nature of things, the building of a large business empire in a developing economy is almost bound to create strong pressures towards diversification (as a strategy for hedging one's bets), even if the core of the empire is in sugar, as in Kuok's early years, or hotels as it became later.

It would be absurd to imply that any firm conclusions can be drawn about the mainsprings of Overseas Chinese entrepreneurial drives or talents on the basis of such a small sample as this. Yet I doubt if we would get much further ahead by working with a sample many times larger, if it were feasible. Nor is it likely that any significant commonalities would emerge if we were to look instead towards particular personality traits or motivations that differentiate these men from their lesser rivals or from the average medium-sized towkays to be found throughout Southeast Asia (hard working? frugal? ambitious? determined? persistent? focused in their efforts? smart? flexible? adaptible? Are any of these likely to lead to an adequate explanation?). But it could perhaps be said that they must be driven by some urge to excel or dominate, or to create an ever-growing business empire rather than just rest on their laurels once they have made enough money to last them and their families for a life-time (or several).

It is hardly rational to keep on driving oneself relentlessly to the end of a life just to make more and more money. Tan Kah Kee was in this respect the most rational of them all both in his initial reasons for wanting to do so (to build schools) and in his socially valuable utilisation of his other talents after the collapse of his business empire in 1935.

Why do the more entrepreneurial types in any country keep on making more and more money? Not for the reasons Schumpeter put forward, I am sure, or Weber's. And I doubt they have much to do with Confucian values either, apart from the desire to excel. But that is too wide (and contentious) a topic to open up here. It is more enlightening just to keep on finding out as much as we can about the lives of these men and how they handled the twists and turns of fortune they encountered, and what that tells us about their many and varied entrepreneurial talents.

Notes

[1]For a good account of the life of Tan Kah Kee, on which I have relied heavily here, see Yong (1987).

[2]I have attempted a preliminary analysis of this alchemy in "Overseas Chinese Entrepreneurship" (Mackie 1992), which also gives a literature survey on the subject, as well as a further assessment of the factors most commonly said to explain Southeast Asian Chinese commercial success in Mackie (1998).

[3]A rubber remilling plant involved a fairly rudimentary manufacturing operation to produce higher-grade sheet rubber from low-grade 'blanket' and 'slab' rubber after extracting stones and extraneous matter from it through a simple milling process.

[4]In 1928, Tan's factory was described by Ormsby-Gore, the British parliamentary Under-Secretary for Colonies in his report on a study tour of rubber-producing countries, as "one of the most remarkable enterprises in Asia ... a vast and varied factory that he has entirely built up and extended himself with Chinese management" (Yong 1987, p. 66).

[5]For a fuller account of the events leading to the final collapse of the company and some of the reasons he sees for it, see Yong 1987, pp. 66–68. In any assessment of Tan's achievements, it should be noted that two men who got their start as his employees, Lee Kong-chian (who became his son-in-law) and Tan Lark-say, went on to build up the two greatest rubber-dealing enterprises in Southeast Asia over the next thirty years — and many others in lesser measure.

The Lee Rubber corporation is still a dominant force in Southeast Asia's rubber industry, at the end of the 20th century, an indirect legacy from Tan Kah Kee.

[6]For information on Kuok I have drawn upon the works of Verchere (1978), Friedland (1991), Heng (1997), Gomez (1999), and Searle (1999).

[7]In the process, Kuok built up good personal ties with some of the most prominent Sino-Thai tycoons whose stars were then rising, notably Chin Sophonpanich, the Bangkok Bank head, whom he later called "his financial godfather", the Techaphaibun family, and the Thai Rung Ruang sugar group. He was also building valuable connections with political and business leaders in Kuala Lumpur and the emerging Indonesian tycoon, Liem Sioe Liong, whose sugar and flour operations complemented his.

[8]For the best brief account of Liem's career, see Schwartz (1994, pp. 109–115). Members of the Hok-chia *pang* to which Liem belonged were among the last to come to Java in large numbers and found themselves confined to the least desirable jobs, such as his. Yet an amazingly high proportion of them have since achieved outstanding commercial success in Indonesia and still form a close-knit, mutually-supportive group (Twang 1999).

[9]The word *cukong* was used by Soeharto's bag-men, who provided him with funds in return for commercial privileges.

[10]I was of two minds whether to use Dhanin as Thailand's representative for inclusion here or the founder of the Bangkok Bank, Chin Sophonpanich, who in an earlier time was not only one of the region's most remarkable entrepreneurs but also the real founder of Thailand's largest and most durable conglomerate. I decided against him because it is not easy to pin down the reasons why he proved so much more successful than his rivals. Some say he got his start through his financial backing for Army-related drug trafficking in the 1950s, others that he was a financial wizard at handling complex foreign exchange transactions at a time of tortuous, fluctuating exchange rates in the turbulent postwar years — and yet others that his skill at manipulating political connections was the key, at least in his early years. He was very much a product of his times and circumstances during a turbulent postwar phase of Thai history which is too complex to deal with adequately here. Dhanin's story of both success and failures is more readily explicable.

[11]For information about Dhanin, I have relied mainly on Handley (1996) and Biers and Vatikiotis (1999).

[12]On Tan's business career, see Palanca (1995) and Rivera and Koike (1995). He was at one time regarded as the wealthiest of the 'Six Taipans', although George Ty of fast-growing Metrobank may have outranked him in the late 1990s (Hiscock 1997, pp. 202–203). Estimates of his wealth vary greatly (up to $8 billion by one unlikely guess; Hiscock's figure is US$1.6 billion). Because he is very secretive and none of his companies are listed publicly, all such figures are highly speculative.

CHAPTER 2

Providers, Protectors, Guardians:
Migration And Reconstruction of Masculinities

Ray Hibbins

Since the gold rushes of the 1850s, Chinese people from Southern China have been migrating to Australia and North America. During that time and over the period of the world wars Chinese people experienced racism, prejudice, and discrimination at the hands of the Anglo-Celtic majority. The predominantly all-male Chinese groups were infantalised and emasculated by the big-spending European groups (Murphy 1993) who violated them and found them guilty of strange and exotic sexual customs and being a threat to the jobs of locals, particularly women. Chinese males were marginalised and subordinated by the hegemonically masculine European groups. While the socio-economic characteristics of Chinese migrants have changed since those earlier times the question arises if Chinese males experience forms of marginalisation and subordination in terms of gender identity in Australian culture. Therefore, this paper raises the issue of the construction, deconstruction, and reconstruction of male gender identity among Chinese male migrants, and concurs with the view that within migration research there is a need for a much greater explicit recognition of men's migration experiences and the social construction of masculinities (Willis & Yeoh, eds. 2000).

In keeping with a grounded theory approach the voices of the males interviewed in-depth in this study, will be introduced at the outset.

Moreover, selected literature will be introduced later in the discussion section so that theoretical propositions can be inductively developed in a grounded way from the data. The forty males migrated to Australia over the past fifty years from various countries of origin. Their duration of settlement varies from two years to approximately fifty years. Some have prior migration experiences, some of the respondents are gay and others are married with children. Some have experienced relationships with non-Chinese males or females. They tend to be employed in IT, engineering, importing-exporting, and hospitality or be academics. Several themes that emerged from open, axial and selective coding (Strauss & Corbin 1998) will be used to integrate some of the emerging ideas. These themes will then be linked into relationships (theoretical propositions) which were inductively developed from the coded data. The qualitative software package Atlas/ti was used to manage the data and code, filter, develop memos, code families and networks that facilitated the emergence of the theoretical propositions.

Socio-cultural Context and Dominant Masculinities

Together with the thumbnail historical context provided in the introduction, this section provides some idea of the socio-cultural context into which the Chinese males migrated. Australia is a country that has experienced migrant waves consistently throughout its history since the first group of Anglo-Celtic migrants confronted the indigenous inhabitants in the latter part of the 18th century. The gold rushes in the 1850s saw the first influx of non-Anglo-Celtic groups and since then there have been waves of Italian, Greek, middle Eastern and Asian migrants. The Asian groups have been predominantly Vietnamese and Chinese. The Chinese group has been rather consistent migrants and has come predominantly from Hong Kong, Taiwan, Malaysia and Singapore and more recently, PRC. The Chinese diaspora is well established in Australia and recent immigration policies that have concentrated on skilled migrants have resulted in Chinese migrants of higher socio-economic status. On average Chinese migrants have higher levels of education, professional and business skills than the Anglo-Celtic majority.

While Australia is multicultural its dominant institutions are based on Anglo-Celtic traditions and values. Historically, sport, the beach and surfing and the pub have been central to the Australian way of life. These have been locales frequented by males (Edgar 1997) and have been testing grounds for masculinity. Connell (1995) has argued that participation and success in sport, ability to consume copious amounts of alcohol and have sexual achievement with women are important rites of passage for Australian males. Hegemonic masculinity in Australia is characterised by homophobia, car fetish, heterosexuality, DIY interests, sporting and sexual achievement (either actually or in fantasy), physical violence and mateship. Some would argue that these are stereotypes of Australian males while others would point to the diversity of masculinities in Australian culture. Recent post structuralist and postmodernist writing (Woodward 1997; Gilroy 1997; Segal 1997; Rutherford 1990; Butler 1989) in the area of identity refer to the multiple and fluid nature of gender identity, to hybridity and the influence of social milieu on the fractured nature of identity.

Some Selected Themes

In this section of the paper, the voices of the Chinese male migrants will be used to facilitate discussion of the following themes: the importance of hard work and male as sole provider; the centrality of family and education; the secondary nature of sport and recreation; sexual "conservativeness". These themes are linked to and situated among a larger number of themes that emerged from this study, and are displayed in Figure 2.1. Many of these themes contained common codes, the properties and dimensions of which, facilitated linkages and allowed for depth and variation.

The Importance of Hard Work and Male as Sole Provider

While these male migrants indicated that they were not attempting to project a particular image or wanted to be perceived in a particular way, most of them pointed to the importance of hard work and to their role as sole provider and head of the family.

Figure 2.1: Major Themes and Their Relationships

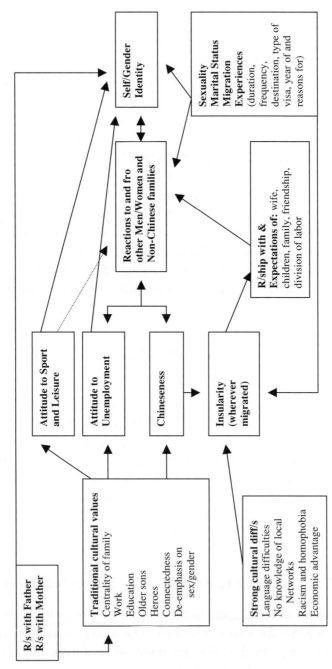

"Chinese men um just can't afford to … to lose their, their credibility as the as the head of the family. Simply because I do not have work, they couldn't find a job and er er that has a lot of problem with … their being the head of the family and their problem on the er in the eye of their children have changed since their migration from somewhere. That's the reason why it affects so much the relation between the er er within the family" (C 96).

This respondent is also referring to the problems of unemployment for Chinese men particularly in their relationships in the immediate family, the extended family and broader social networks. Later this respondent had this to say:

" … they need to have a role in order to demonstrate to their children that they are useful person who can really protect and make a living for the family. I think that's very important" (C 96).

"This is still typical um father that most children will look up to, you know, they want to have er a very well successful of course, in terms of their career. In terms of um their position in the … in society, not just in the family" (C 97).

" … I don't think they (women, the mother) can replace the um the husband or the father in, in leading the family … in terms of their leadership in the family … most children, particularly Chinese children … they look up to the father as the role model rather than the mother" (C 97).

Most of these males suggested that models for most young Chinese males were wealthy Chinese businessmen. Sportsmen like Michael Jordan and martial artists like Jackie Chan were models and sometimes heroes because of their wealth rather than their athletic abilities. There was also a strong indication of hierarchy within Chinese families and an emphasis on patriarchy.

It was of interest that irrespective of age or sexuality, these Chinese male migrants emphasized their role as sole provider and protector.

"My father is more, more powerful in family" (PW).

"I think they're (Chinese males) still quite dominant, some of them particularly the older ones ..." (S).

" ... the Chinese father is usually ah the authority figure in the family. So, yes there was some distance" (L95).

" ... I am the one who make more money then her, I don't want her to make money for me I want to make money ... as the head of the family I am the one to make money for her" (M).

" ... ah normally the man, the man is expected to support their family. If you don't do that you'll become, you lose everything. Your ... reputation" (A).

" ... in my *opinion* I work and it is my own responsibility to support the whole family. My wife, she can have her choice whether she work outside ... or prefer to stay at home, up to her" (W).

This choice for women was referred to by some of the male informants but, in general, there was some ambivalence about women going outside the home to work. Some referred to changes brought by feminism particularly in the West, others referred to powerful Chinese women. Most of the married males indicated that it was the woman's responsibility to look after children even where they worked outside the home.

"Yeah, I expect (she might have a career) but you know she has got a lot of responsibility, responsibility to look after you know house work, house work, house work you know ... basically wife also take some responsibility for home and for children" (BJ).

Migration and duration of settlement seemed to have had little influence on these traditional processes. Where changes in the division of labour had occurred they made sufficient difference for male respondents to comment on how their spouse had noticed and commented on the changes in the amount of assistance they provided in the home. There were some indications that changing economic circumstance since leaving the home territory had influenced attitudes to wives working. Such decisions were pragmatic and instrumental.

> "Yeah I would (expect my wife to work) because ah if I just my work, if I work then the money would be not enough to support the family because everything is getting expensive. I expect my wife to go out to work" (A).

Wider social structural factors like the presence of children, the absence of domestic assistance more typical in the home territory and increases in the cost of living appear to be influencing changes in the role of the male as the sole provider. Nevertheless unemployment was perceived to be the antithesis of being a 'good' Chinese male and most males experienced ambivalence about women working.

The Centrality of Family and Education

Education was viewed as the solution to attaining a career and eventually accumulating status, power and wealth.

> " ... once you've got knowledge in your head it's there forever until your life is ended. It is knowledge. It is really part of, I guess, um the enthusiasm that Confucian knowledge ... is power. Those people who can become important are people who ah have knowledge" (BT).

Issues of control and discipline as well as status were associated with knowledge and acquiring a high level of education. Many of these males had placed on " hold" other aspects of life like relationships with women while they achieved educational qualifications.

> "I do not want to know all of the girls. I must concentrate on studying. So I stop going to the um to the co-educational school. Only boys school" (W).

> "OK, but he would be expected like you for expected to continue your education, do well, get a job, get married" (PW).

Many respondents referred to the competitive pressures in secondary school, and to the support and sometimes pressure from parents to achieve well. Sometimes respondents who failed exams were physically punished.

"… parents expected you to work hard all the time … They want you to succeed well" (BJ).

"Because we couldn't you know let our parents down, because I mean you know we had to compete, we had to be good you know on top of everyone else" (DI).

These males referred to their success being reflected collectively on their families and for some, this meant increased family status.

"… they were aware of the value of education and the importance of education and they started to put pressure on in Years 11 and 12 … University is much more competitive" (K).

Even where parents were not well educated there was pressure from them on respondents to achieve well educationally.

"… we are from a family you know although our parents might not have a very good education but they very keen on our kids, you know their kids to have good education … you know in a way … good education up to the tertiary level" (E).

There were cases where males (sons) were encouraged to proceed to higher education while daughters were sent out to work. In other cases a male who achieved well in secondary school or was the oldest son was encouraged to proceed to tertiary education while other children went to work to support them. Most of the Chinese male migrants believed there was greater equality in Chinese families today and that females were encouraged to have careers. While some of these male respondents physically punished their children for lack of educational success, most encouraged their children sensitively, to achieve well.

Respect for older parents and for family order and harmony were all central for these male respondents. Many of the males referred to a close relationship with their mothers but a more distant one with fathers.

"... I grew up, I just did not like him, his way of treating us. I mean treating me and my brother ... like babies ... become distant ... sometimes I ignored him" (RIC).

Some of the males referred to their relationship with their fathers as like a "teacher-student" relationship. The relationship was often distant.

Gay men in particular often had conflictual relationships with fathers when they were younger. With maturity, many of these relationships had mellowed and most of the respondents with children desired a much closer relationship with their children than they had experienced.

"Yes to be obedient to your parents but if you still do, you do that and you look after your parents, you respect them. I think your children will learn from it, they will see what you did, then" (PC).

"Well I think it's still honouring your parents and respecting ... and what do you call respect for authority" (FY).

"Sharing ... sharing things together and uh, helping one another out ... he still the head of the family. It's good to have someone the head of the family, like the male" (S).

"... my father is always there ... the main caretaker of the family ... he has the income ... more or less the head of the house" (FC).

"... should respect them, sometimes it's very difficult, because I disagree with their decision but because they are my parents I obey them" (NE).

Respect for authority, obedience and emphasis on the extended family and the collectivity were emphasized by these male migrant respondents. There was an emphasis on patriarchy however and the importance of the male as the provider for the family.

The Secondary Nature of Sport and Recreation

Unlike many non-Chinese males in Australia, ability to converse at length about sport, knowledge of sporting heroes, participation in

competitive and often physically aggressive body-contact sport and
spectating at various sporting events are not markers of masculinity for
Chinese male migrants.

Some of the Chinese male migrants referred with some amazement
to the importance placed on sport in secondary schools, at the expense
of education.

> "Here I understand there are kids, that compete against each other
> in sports but ah academically it seems that they don't care that
> much. No it's very different from Asian society" (PIN).

Another male referred to the adulation, in Australia, of male sporting
heroes at school by other males and teachers. This particular male was
also concerned that few awards were given for academic achievement.

> "Sport … I don't like it very much. Sport was very important and
> the school captain has to be a sports person … sportsman of the
> week get an award … prizes … certainly weighted heavily toward
> all sports people … sports heroes. I'm still not aware of them …
> I never follow sport in terms of sporting heroes" (CL).

This respondent joined other 'nerd' males who were frequently not of
Anglo-Celtic background, and enjoyed academic achievement and the
challenge of intellectual pursuits. The sporting 'jocks' frequently challenged
this group verbally and physically.

Other Chinese migrant respondents referred to the way in which sports
and physical education teachers pressured male students into sport
participation.

> " … during my all boys school days I'm not very keen on sport. I
> think I pick up sport in the later stagesü… it's forced by school,
> you have to do all the physical training in school (in Australia)"
> (IS).

A small minority of these Chinese males who had migrated to North
America to attend secondary school and university discovered that sport
participation was an important ingredient to receiving the adulation of
females, and being popular among other males.

"Ah, I would have to say very important. Um, if ah, the way I've been brought up is um you know it seems like if you, you can play sport, and you are very good at it you can be very popular, and make your life a lot easier. No, I hadn't known sports before America" (X).

These males participated in sport and one of them engaged in sexual activity with non-Chinese females. Because of pressure from family and increasing demands of educational performance these males reduced participation in sport and commenced dating Chinese girls. They referred to the problems of adapting to the expectation of Chinese girls for them to be providers and guardians, after modifying their behaviour to accommodate to the desires for independence and individuality of non-Chinese females.

Many of the migrants referred to an increasing reduction in sport participation as pressure to achieve well educationally took hold in late secondary school and in university.

" ... in primary school ... actively to about form 3 or form 4 ... not as actively in form 5 and form 6 when the external examination pressure began to mount. After form 6, I've never found myself on a soccer field any more" (L95).

" ... in the school um or in the family they expect the student, the children to study harder in academic rather than sports ... gradual reduction in the amount of time given to sport ... " (PC).

"Well ah I mean they expect me to pay more time in study ... they think if I don't study, I don't study hard I can't find job, I've got a problem later. But at that time I'm, I'm quite ah interested in sport and think about developing a career in sports. But that's not accepted, I mean according to traditional Chinese point of view. They think sport is no good, they think just hobby or leisure but not a job" (C-W).

Where the informants adulated professional sportspersons it was because of their ability to accumulate wealth or their actual wealth rather than their sporting prowess. Heroes included Michael Jordan, Jackie

Chan, and Michael Chang. Wealth was a central feature of 'manhood', not ability to use one's body as a weapon on the sports field. One respondent (C97) in particular suggested that "blood is spilt on the stock market floor and in corporate offices rather than on the sporting fields" among Asian men, as they test out their masculinity.

Those informants who participated in sport like volleyball or basketball did so for social reasons or for diversion from the stresses of work. These social groups were usually Chinese or other Asian friends and they provided opportunities for the males to talk about business opportunities, to catch up on issues in the Chinese community or merely, to have fun.

Two exceptions to this pattern placed a slightly different spin on sport participation. One younger respondent referred to the changing attitudes to sport among the younger generation.

> "They (older generation) just know ah about hard work, work hard and earn enough money to support my family. But now this, for my generation, my generation all next generation the concept of ah life is different. It's changed. But the leisure is more important, now more and more it's getting important in our lives" (A).

The other exception was a male who had lived in New Zealand prior to coming to Australia. He had migrated when young and had been educated away from his home country. This respondent had strong homophobic attitudes and believed that women did not make suitable managers because of their emotional approach to the job. Like the stereotypical hegemonically masculine male in Australia, this male believed he knew more about Australian Football than most of his neighbours and he celebrated grand final time by inviting them to his home. Both of these exceptions indicate some interesting potential changes in gender identity among Chinese males in Australia in the future. For the majority of these Chinese male migrants however, educational achievement, career and status, being the sole provider, ability to accumulate wealth and maintain a competitive advantage were more important markers of masculinity than sport participation, and thus displayed little change of attitude since migrating.

Sexual "Conservativeness"

This theme is consistent with the others discussed in this paper in the sense that educational achievement, fostering a career and the accumulation of wealth or prospects of this were given priority by these Chinese male respondents, over early relationships with women and sexual involvement. These men referred to the greater sexual openness and freedom, the independence and greater physicality of relationships among non-Chinese males and females in Australia. While there was some suggestion by the informants that sexual attitudes and practices were becoming more liberal in home territories among younger generations of Chinese, this was rarely obvious among these men. The exceptions were the gay males in the sample. In this regard they were more like hegemonically masculine non-Chinese males.

For most of these males, their first sexual experience was with their spouse after marriage. This was attributed to traditional Chinese mores concerning sexuality and sexual relations, to conservativeness compared with Western people, and to the suppression of conversation about sexual matters in some home territories. Reference was made to the influence of religion, particularly Islam and the State on these issues.

Those respondents who had experienced sexual relationships prior to marriage were generally those who had migrated overseas to study, or were gay, or indicated they were exceptions in their society.

> "I had sexual relations in USA. Ah I think if I was in Taiwan it would be much different. Ah, but at that time when I was in US, I had been very Americanised" (X).

> "Fairly early. At that stage I think I'm ahead. Ah it (sexual relations) is not seen as very common I think. I think I'm a bit too early" (TON).

Most of the males in this sample who attended secondary school in Australia referred to the importance for masculinity of sexual relations among non-Chinese males. Some of them experienced pressure from non-Chinese males to become involved.

" ... none of us really want to have sexual relations with any girlfriend in high school ... everyone like pressure each other you know even though no one want to do it themselves". (CT)

"This is high school. You are supposed to enlarge the number (of sexual conquests) by ten digits or something. That happened for everyone just a little bit to have popularity ... if you talk like that in Taiwan ... people think think you are dickhead ... They don't care. So people don't show it that way" (CT).

Reported discussions among non-Chinese males included banter about the frequency of sexual relations and the number of sexual conquests. It appeared to be a central rite of passage for the Western males, but not for the Chinese respondents. The Chinese male migrants were warned by their parents about the sexual openness in Australia, and they encouraged their sons to concentrate on educational achievement and hard work. The latter were central markers of Chinese masculinity.

Some of the respondents referred to the privacy of sexual relations in Chinese society, to not talking about sexual matters in public and to the resistance of governments to talk more about the need for sex education.

" ... don't talk about sex in the public ... no big deal" (DI).

"In the Chinese way. No you never you never you know, you never tell anyone if that happens" (CT).

"Sexuality is a very suppressed subject in the Chinese community" (TON).

It was the gay males among the respondents who experienced sexual relations much earlier in life and often across ethnic boundaries. These males made reference to the importance of fitness and a 'good' body and suggested that 'good looks' were important in a prospective partner. Unlike the heterosexual males in this sample, some of the gay males referred to the need to be protected by another male. On the other hand, the gay males indicated that they were popular among females because of their interests in shopping and fashions and because they were not perceived to be a threat. The gay males also emphasized their role as protector of their female friends. They suggested that Chinese women were sexually naïve. Most of these gay Chinese migrants believed they needed to be circumspect in their general behaviour in Australia. They had dual concerns about racism and homophobia and therefore, found it necessary not to communicate their sexuality to strangers and to restrict their spatial sphere of influence. Most of them felt more comfortable with their sexuality in Australia than in PRC, Hong Kong or Taiwan. Among the Chinese male migrants however only the gay males perceived themselves to be rather marginalised on ethnic grounds and subordinate on grounds of sexuality, and therefore needed to protect themselves from the homophobia and racism of hegemonic masculinity. There were also suggestions of homophobic attitudes among some of the heterosexual Chinese male migrants. The majority of the heterosexual males were opposed to homosexuality on religious, medical or political grounds.

Discussion and Conclusions

Among these Chinese male migrants there appeared in general terms, to be no perceived need to model their behaviour on local variants of masculinity. They retained many of the traditional markers of masculinity viz., the centrality of hard work; educational achievement; career advancement and status; acquisition of wealth; maintaining a competitive edge; being the sole provider for and protector/guardian of the family. Because of the higher socio-economic status and the importance of cultural traditions concerning the collectivity and interdependence in the wider socio-cultural group these males saw no need to change their gender behaviour. Most had almost exclusively mono-ethnic friendship groups with whom they recreated. It was rare for these male migrants to express a need for more "blokey" friends with whom they could consume alcohol and talk sport. Only one respondent expressed a desire to mix in non-Chinese friendship groups. While the workplace in Australia was for some, less hierarchic, more friendly and a place where cross-gender social interaction occurred they tended not to mix in "happy" hours or participate in extra curricula activities. This resonates with the Confucian variant of masculinity (Connell 2000, p. 54) which has a stronger commitment to hierarchy and social consensus compared with a secularized Christian variant based in North America which shows more hedonism and individualism. Their tests of manhood were measured against their abilities to be protector, provider and guardian for the immediate and extended family. The patriarchy seemed to be alive and well for these men. Their gender identity was reinforced in the private sphere.

The minor exceptions to this pattern were males who were married with children and gay males. It was apparent that the former group were experiencing changed expectations about fatherhood. Their children who were experiencing the influences of acculturation were inclined to expect their fathers to demonstrate interest in their sporting and recreational activities. While in nearly all cases fathers emphasized the importance of education for their children, these informants with children were less severe on and less distant from their children than their fathers had been. Most of these males with children however, retained a belief about a gendered division of labour where wives were expected to care for children and fulfil domestic duties. These expectations persisted even where women worked outside the home. These informants were similar in attitudes to division of labour to those held by recently arrived Asian migrants to the United States in a study by Chua and Fujino (1999). There were indications among these males, even the younger ones, of ambivalence about wives working. These married males retained a strong desire to be sole provider for the family. This was central to their masculinity.

Among gay males in this study, there were indications of a heightened awareness of the importance of sexual behaviour, a desirable body and good looks to them as gay men. In most other respects these males were similar to the heterosexual males in the study. For them hard work, educational achievement, having a competitive edge, the accumulation of wealth and status were central to how they perceived themselves as Chinese men. They also wanted to be providers, protectors and guardians of women. It was among these gay males and the married Chinese male migrants with children however that changes in expectations of male gender identity were being flagged.

The Chinese male migrants in this study displayed little change in their gender identity since migrating to Australia. Unlike the Mexican male migrants investigated by Hondagneu-Sotelo and Messner (1994) who were of lower socio-economic status, who experienced unemployment and were highly dependent on the political-economic system in North America, the Chinese males were of much higher socio-economic status and often were skilled professionals who had not experienced unemployment or dependence on the broader social structure. Their main reasons for migrating centred on economic work, where the Mexican immigrants experienced challenges to their masculinity from dominant variants, these Chinese migrants, who placed little importance on the centrality of their gender identity and overt dominance, rarely felt that their manhood was being challenged by hegemonic variants. The exceptions were gay Chinese males. In general, the masculinities of these Chinese male migrants were reinforced by their friendships, family structures, their workplaces and recreational milieu. The Chinese males in this study were different from the Iranian male migrants studied by Shahidian (1999) and the Mexican male migrants investigated by Hondagneu-Sotelo (1992). In these latter two cases there was evidence of extensive negotiation over division of labour between spouses. This seemed to be influenced by past history and traditions, by changing power relations where women and children were left behind in the home country or by challenges to the masculinity of new arrivals by dominant local variants.

Duration of settlement and age differentiate these male migrants on some issues of gender identity but the differences within the sample are not significant. The influence of prior migration particularly to North America certainly sensitised those males to the importance of sport and sexual behaviour for masculinity but even these males eventually adopted more traditional markers of masculinity. Sexuality and the presence of children for married migrants appear to be more sensitive variables. There is a need however to broaden the social class dimension in future studies of reconstruction of gender identities among male migrants.

Several important issues are raised by this research. The use of Western (Connell 1989) and Asian-American variants (Chua & Fujino 1999) as benchmarks for measuring the gender identities of Chinese male migrants as is typical of most studies, seems extremely hazardous. Asian American males in the work by Chua and Fujino (1999) appear to be much more sensitive to issues of gender identity than relatively recently arrived

Chinese male migrants to Australia. Actually the attitudes to household division of labour of the recently arrived Chinese migrants in Chua and Fujino's study were remarkably similar to those of the Chinese male migrants in the research reported here. More generally the relevance of the Western concept of masculinity for investigating the gender identities of non-Western males is called into question. There appears to be a need for the development of a comparative methodology for investigating gender identities across cultures. It is apparent that markers of masculinity used by Chinese male migrants are different from those more typical of dominant variants used by non-Chinese males in Australia. While they may not be conscious of it the significance of tradition for the masculinities of these Chinese male migrants to Australia remain central to "reconstructions" of male gender identities. For social scientists there is a rich yet untapped vein of research data on male migrants and their gender identities especially when a more nuanced analysis includes diversity of class, sexuality, and ethnicity.

CHAPTER 3

Tasting the Night: Food, Ethnic Transaction, and the Pleasure of Chineseness in Malaysia*

Yao Souchou

Jalan Alor, a narrow street running next to the busy Jalan Bukit Bintang, has always enjoyed a certain reputation among residents of the Malaysian capital Kuala Lumpur. By day it is a parking space for shoppers; but by night it transforms itself into a site of pleasure. For Jalan Alor is one of the city's red light districts; and here, not surprisingly, are also found some of its best food stalls. At eight p.m. each night, as if by clockwork, they magically spring to life on the shop verandahs and parking spaces in the street. There, in the cool of the evening air, families, courting couples, drug addicts, and sex workers and their 'guests' rub shoulders with each other, consuming fresh seafood, soups of turtle, python, fruit bat, and other wild meat stewed in Chinese herbs, and the speciality of the area: Hokkien fried noodles in dark soya sauce garnished with pork crackling and raw garlic. For many, it is Jalan Alor's delicious and diverse foods that have taken them there; but as they eat, they cannot help but be reminded of the other offerings of the place. Above their tables, as they look up, are a myriad of neon signs advertising services of massage parlours, *karaoke* lounges, beauty clinics (offering face whitening and "breast enhancement

---

*A different version of the paper appears as "*Xiao Ye*: Food, Alterity and the Pleasure of Chineseness in Malaysia", *New Formations* 40, Spring 2000, pp. 64–79.

without surgery"), and Chinese physicians promising delivery from 'weaknesses of the kidney' and relief from 'exhaustion of the *yang qi*' (masculine rigour).

To this place of secret carnality and culinary pleasure arrive Diana, a 19-year-old Chinese hostess from the Sakura Karaoke Lounge, and her lover Ah Keong. They are in deep conversation and she is in tears. They sit down and, with his arm around her shoulder, Ah Keong tries to comfort her. The anthropologist who accompanies them for supper already knows the story. Diana has just returned from an assignment with a client at the Federal Hotel just down the road. Having been in the trade for barely two months, it is the first night out with a client that Ah Keong has arranged for her. What rubs salt into the wound is that, as she only finds out at the hotel room, the client is an old Malay man, a politician and businessman from Sarawak, and he has demanded — with insistence, as she tells Ah Keong — 'kou jiao' (fellatio). Apparently Ah Keong has arranged Diana's visit on instructions from two Chinese merchants, who pay handsomely for his services. The Malay man is a backbencher in the Sarawak state parliament who has promised the merchants an introduction to the 'right people' in Kuching who can deliver a lucrative timber concession. Diana has been a part of the 'gift' to the Malay man, who has specifically requested the company of a Chinese girl during his stay in Kuala Lumpur.

The anthropologist silently recalls the 'ethnographic background' as he shares the meal with the lovers, as a quiet drama slowly unfolds before him at three o'clock in the morning. Interrupting his whispers of comfort and endearment to Diana, Ah Keong signals to the waiter that he is ready to order.

We are having *bak ku teh*, the only item on the stall's menu. Literally meaning meat-bone-tea in Hokkien dialect, the dish is a thick stew of pork knuckles and ribs, simmered for hours in a stock flavoured with Chinese herbs, garlic cloves and soya sauce. With its full-bodied flavour, dense with medicinal goodness and nutritional value, there is perhaps no food more appropriate for restoring the tired and defiled bodies of those in the sex trade. As the waiter takes the order, Ah Keong retrieves two small packets from his breast pocket, and asks him to put some of the contents in the dish. These are ginseng and deer horn powder — the most expensive Chinese tonics available — that Ah Keong has brought with him. As he hurries the waiter to be quick with the dish, he smiles and kisses Diana on her cheeks, and says, in Cantonese, "See, how much I care for you."

History, Memory, Enjoyment

To partake of the pork dish, spiced with medicinal goodness and flavoured with personal solicitude, is to nestle in a private sanctuary away from the glaring light of public judgement and conventional culinary taboo. This is perhaps the lesson of the 'deep play' I have just described. As in the anthropology of Clifford Geertz, what takes place on this evening in the foodstall at once connects the personal with the public, linking immediate social concerns with wider structural realities (Geertz 1973). Located in this dialectics, the ethnographic episode is portent of the foundational elements of national life in Malaysia. All the real and imaginary peculiarities are there: the pain and social estrangement of ethnic relations, Malay hegemony and Chinese complicity, the pecuniary rewards of political office, the arrogation of private pleasure as a 'sanctified' place of personal meaning, and of course, the gender disparity in these transactions. These features give *bak ku teh* a certain allegorical quality at the heart of Chinese self-recognition in Malaysia. Not only the dish, but the site of culinary enjoyment too, is imbued with significance, "imprinted with our tenacious, inescapable obsession", to borrow a phrase from Simon Schama's masterly *Landscape and Memory* (Schama 1995, p. 18). In this site, what we have to reckon with is precisely the immediacy of our own 'topofilia' that couples sentiment with place, cultural memory with locality, where "imagination augments the values of reality" (Bachelard 1964, p. 2).

For Chinese diners in Jalan Alor, the culinary enjoyment of *bak ku teh* is never purely that; it is also about something else, incited by something beyond the senses. That pleasure can be located in history and in the political is, of course, the tradition of the Frankurt School. In the conceptions of Adorno, Hormheimer and Marcuse, the enjoyment of cultural products in capitalism is a sign of the degradation of European culture, and a major force in the mystification of the individual mind (*vide* Adorno 1991). In spite of its elitist — and humanist — assumptions, it is nonetheless the crucial insight of the Frankfurt School in highlighting the secret and insidious presence of the political/ideological in pleasure. In this sense, pleasure may be said to have a material base. And the task of discursive intervention, as Jameson suggests, must involve writing history back to pleasure:

> "[A]s far as 'pleasure' is concerned, it may readily be admitted that it is materialist; whether or not 'unconsciousness' (the psychological subject is always and in all moments of history and modes of production constitutionally and irrecuperably idealistic, the generalization is probably safe for us.... Pleasure is finally the consent of life in the body, the reconciliation — momentary as it may be — with the necessity of physical existence in a physical world" (Jameson 1985, p. 10).

If the senses indeed have a history, then we can fruitfully use the phrase 'social formation of pleasure'. We may speak of its origin which charts its social arrival as embodiment of the 'consent of life'. All things visceral are located in a sensual geography of individual sensation and collective historical experience. In this dialectical realm, pleasure mystifies by its endless return to the preserve of private experience, and by offering a powerful affirmation of selfhood through the senses. And the task of deconstructing the social formation of pleasure may well begin here: by retracing the history of its social judgment and cultural consensus in the first place.

Eating Bitterness (*Chi Ku*) for the Body

Among Chinese in Southeast Asia, *Bak Ku Teh* is normally eaten as a stew, either by itself, with a bowl of rice or with pieces of fried rice dough bread called *you zha gui* (literally 'oil fried devil'). In a culture that believes that food must not only give nutrition but also provide therapeutic values, this pork dish has a distinct 'culinary identity'. Rich in protein, heavily spiced with garlic and Chinese herbs, the stew sits in that hybrid category between a *tang* or soup and a *bu* or tonic. Without a restrictive culinary tradition, *Bak Ku Teh* has proved to be a highly versatile dish subject to creative innovations in restaurants and domestic kitchens. At home, it is a common practice to add fried tofu (bean curd) and Chinese white radish (*Raphanus sativus*) cut into cubes, as a way of improving the 'texture' of the dish, and to absorb and 'disguise' the medicinal taste of the herbs. But herbs and spices are major ingredients of the recipe. For the discriminating cook, the herbs and spices — always hand-packed in a muslin satchel by a Chinese medicine shop rather than from the supermarket shelf — are chosen according to the taste and medicinal effects one wishes to achieve. In the foodstall we visit in Jalan Alor, what goes into the pot includes, besides pork rib pieces, dark soya sauce, garlic cloves, peppercorns and seasonings, the following herbs: *tang kuei* (*angelica sinesis*), *yu zhu* (*polygonatum odoratun*), *yu gui* (*Fructus lycii*), *ji zi* (*Radix codomopsitis*), *dang shen* (*Rhizoma linguistici*). These herbs give the stew a slightly tangy, bitter taste, a sign of its medicinal goodness and its status of being more than simply a flavourful food. Partly because it would, according to Chinese medical beliefs, undo the effects of expensive herbs like ginseng, Chinese radish or any other root vegetables are not added to the pot. Indeed at the foodstall, the medicinal flavour of the dish, rather than as something to be disguised, becomes a significant 'trademark' for a tasty *bu* stew which 'patches up' the weak body and restores the spirit (*vide* Ahern 1975, pp. 91–114).

For Diana, whose five years in a Chinese primary school have given her a rich repertoire of useful proverbs, the sharp medicinal taste of the dish must seem like a culinary reflection of her favourite expression *chi ku* or 'eating bitterness', which she often uses to describe the common fate of her and her 'sisters' in the trade. In this instance, partaking of the dish becomes the literal enactment of a linguistic metaphor. Eating and speaking, the bitterness of food and the bitterness of life's experiences: their connections may not be too far fetched after all. If nothing else, as Derrida in his critique of Western logocentrism has pointed out, speech and eating are bodily functions that deploy the same organ — the tongue (Derrida 1986, p. 161). Derrida might as well have turned to the Chinese proverb, for *chi ku* shames the logocentric privilege of speech by the crucial reminder that words too — their concepts and associations — have 'taste'. If *chi ku* bridges the literal and the metaphoric, then what Diana 'spits out' as she consumes the dish with a quiet melancholy are not only grit and bone, but text itself (Derrida 1986, p. 161). *Chi ku*, the 'swallowing' of the excruciating 'bitterness' of one's life and work, signifies an experience

of endurance and suffering. However, just as partaking of a dish like
Bak Kuh Teh has a 'surplus of operations' (Ulmer 1985, p. 55) flooding
into the realm of medical therapy, *chi ku* too promises redemption by
validating the virtue of silent endurance and fortitude. Diana and
Ah Keong may well remember the ancient tale of Qui Yuan who, having
lost the kingdom of his emperor, tastes each night the bitterness of gall
bladder hung above his bed to remind himself of his humiliation and the
urgent task of revenge and the restoration of the kingdom. If the pork
dish needs a point, it perhaps lies in the subtle echoing of its 'bitter taste'
with the social deprivation of the world of Sakura Karaoke Lounge. It is
a 'bitter taste' — in food as in life — that endorses the wisdom of patient
forbearance as a strategy of recovery, just as it nurtures the longing for
life's redemptive possibilities.

What the stall in Jalan Alor cooks up is indeed a food of the place. As a
metaphor of moral hope, a tonic stew of humoral balance will not do. It
must carry 'excess' ingredients in order to do battle with all that conspires
to wear down the body and spirit. Indeed, the dish — for the heavy
protein stock and the addition of *dang gui* (*Angelica sinensis*) — is geared
towards producing an appropriate 'heatiness' in order to compensate
for, in their different ways, the loss of *yang* among the sex workers and
the male clients. For the former, late nights and the menstrual irregularity
that seems to plague women in the trade, and for the latter, loss of
semen and sexual over-exertion, tend to produce in the body an
insufficiency of *yang* — the positive *qi* of rigour and strength in
the Chinese humoral system. Mildly 'warming' rather than aggressively
'heating', the dish improves the pallor, cures anaemia, and rebuilds the
body drained of vitality by cigarettes, alcohol and late nights. As though
united by a common destiny of loss, men and women devour the herbal
stew, not with grimaces on their faces, but with relish and the knowledge
that suffering its bitter 'taste' is precursory to the reaping of therapeutic
benefits.

If it is moral hope as much as medicinal goodness that makes *bak ku
teh* so tasty a dish, then Ah Keong's charming solicitude that night at the
foodstall is charged with a similar significance. What Ah Keong offers is
indeed a culinary epitome of himself. The tonic dish gives bodily strength
and social comfort, just as he as a lover would, to a young woman crushed

by the circumstances of her trade and frailty of her body. The addition of expensive ginseng root and deer horn powder to the dish may be a self-conscious gesture of male bravado, but it is no less genuine as an expression of care and affection still possible in a world of flagrant transactions of the flesh. And such a gesture is surely as sustaining of body and spirit as the tasty and nutritious dish.

Here, however, lies a catch. For if eating the bitterness of the pork stew promises bodily cure and social redemption, its final purpose is inescapably a preparation for re-entering a world without atonement. For all its culinary enjoyment and social comfort, the pleasure of the tonic dish merely blunts the brutish reality of world of the karaoke lounge. Somewhat inevitably, it is a pleasure that mystifies as it paves the way for further transactions of sin and hopelessness. This is surely the gloomy understanding of the lovers that evening at the foodstall. It may be suggested that the private realm they have so anxiously carved out for themselves is futile and impossible from the beginning. For a province of personal emotions cannot prevent the intrusion of the wider social forces, any more than the lovers can long nestle in its comfort blind to the world in which the trading of Diana's body is a stark reality. This understanding must have cut deeply in Diana's feelings of hurt and disappointment, and these feelings take us at once to that world, and further still, to the terrain of state power and the violent politics of ethnic relations.

Xiao Ye and Bodily Trade

For Diana and Ah Keong, social regrets, the misfortunes of gender and state power therefore cannot but intrude upon and reshape their very enjoyment. Instead of pleasure being a haven from the woes of the world, it reproduces and intensifies them; in place of the paradise of private comfort, the oral enjoyment and companionable warmth sadly prepare the ground for further trading of Diana's body. At the foodstall in the early hours after midnight, the enjoyment of *Bak Ku Teh* seems remarkably close to that fetishistic, dreamy quality of the 'calamitous state' before breakfast which Benjamin describes:

> "A popular tradition warns against recounting dreams on an empty stomach. In this state, though awake, one remains under

the sway of the dream. For washing bring only the surface of the body and the visible motor function into the light, while the deeper strata, even during the morning ablution, the grey penumbra of dream persist, and, indeed, in the solitude of the first waking hour, consolidates itself. He who shuns contact with the day, whether fear of his fellow men or for the sake of inner composure, is unwilling to eat and disdain his breakfast. He thus avoids a rupture between the nocturnal and the daytime world. ..." (Benjamin 1979, pp. 45–46).

Against the soporific pull of sleep, to break out from the "protection of dreaming naivete" (Benjamin 1979, p. 46), one has to muster all the strength and clear-headedness that a nutritious breakfast brings:

"The narration of dreams brings calamity, because a person still in league with the dream world would betrays it in his world and must incur its revenge. Expressed in modern terms, he betrays himself.... For only from the far bank, from broad daylight, may dream be recalled with impunity. This further side of dream is only attainable through a cleansing analogous to washing yet totally different. By way of the stomach" (Benjamin 1979, p. 46).

It is not too much to read Benjamin here, as Terry Eagleton does, in terms of his virulent injunction against the fetishistic power of ideology as he outlines a tactics of its subversion. History and its narrative, too, like dreams, reside in a terrain beclouded by the seduction of memory, by the siren song of ideology and mystified unconscious. To recall such a history, Eagleton suggests, both the past and the unconscious must be subject to the violent rupture of rude awakening:

"Dream may fructify history, but only it is first subjected to a certain violence — ruptured, distanced, purged, and only thus refracted into the vigilance of conscious life.... It is only through the radical discontinuity of past and present, through the space hollowed by their mutual eccentricity, that former may be brought to bear explosively upon the latter" (Eagleton 1990, pp. 43–44).

From breakfast to memory and history and its subversion; the 'taste' of a dish like *Bak Ku Teh* is thus never innocent. With this in mind, it is not surprising to find another 'use' of *bak ku teh* and its enjoyment. For all its health fostering qualities, it is simply the favourite dish for karaoke lounge hostesses when they go for *xiao ye* or 'late night supper' after work. *Xiao ye* is the late meal of the day. In tropical Malaysia, to sit in the foodstall near midnight and order a bowl of noodles, sticks of satay or spicy soup of mutton (*sup gambing*) is as much about meeting the body's call for food, as for trying to stretch out a few more hours of the cool of the evening before bedtime. In the world of karaoke lounges, this pleasant ritual — of 'eating the air' (*makan enging*, in common Malaysian parlance, — is given a subtle semantic twist.

Xiao ye is in fact a jargon of trade; it refers to the practice of a hostess spending a night out with a male client. For the six hostesses in the Sakura Karaoke Lounge — a number occasionally supplemented by young women from Thailand and China on tourist visas — to be invited out for late night supper is both a privilege and a burden. In the first place, such an invitation is a clear sign of their desirability and professional attainment. For it is only the more popular — and thus physically more attractive and financially more viable — hostesses who can entice men to 'buy ticket' (*mai piao*) from the manager in order to take them out for supper after closing time. For the 'star' of the place, this popularity complements her flirtatious charm and social skills, most evident as she strains her voice, while applauding the similar effort of the clients, in following the lyrics on the television monitor of songs by Neil Diamond, Air Supply, Andy Lau, and Anita Mui. All the time, she urges the men to order drinks from the bar to soothe the throat, coyly asking for herself the in-house specialty — 'brandy' (Chinese tea) in a large cognac balloon glass.

But having 'late night supper' is not always a matter of choice, nor only with a client one likes. At times, a hostess is sent out by the manager to partake of *xiao ye* with a man because he has bought tickets and specifically asked for her company. For her at least, the outing seems like an expedition of doom. The dishes arrive, and she barely touches them with the fidgety play of chopsticks; though she might order for herself a single bowl of soup to keep him company and because it is all she has appetite for.

Duplicity and the Pleasure of Chineseness

For the women in the karaoke lounge, *xiao ye* is indeed all these things: the partaking of delicious food, a pleasant respite from the tropical heat, a sign of their desirability among men, a euphemism for commodified sex, and above all, a comforting and an ironic ritual which smooths the path for the trading of (their) bodies. If *xiao ye*, not only the herbal soup of pork, embodies a grammar of pleasure which redeems the 'damaged' body, then Diana's anguish clearly signifies an extra burden to all that is associated with Sakura. Even as *xiao ye* is not a matter of choice, Diana's evening out with an old Malay man elicits universal sympathy among her 'sisters'. And we have to ask a cold analytical question: in a world where trading of the body is the norm, why does the ethnic origin of the client matter so much, and cause so much grief? The answer to the question at once takes us back to the social formation of Diana's own bitter feeling and unhappy fate, and the futility of private bliss immune from the intrusion of state power and political relations.

In Malaysia, the idea of the procuring of a young Chinese female body for a Malay politician all too eager to exploit the opportunities of his office, has all the flavour of a 'social myth'. Indeed, tales abound in Sakura among Chinese men about their busy wheeling and dealing in bidding for government tenders by working with a Malay *bumiputra* (literally, 'son of the soil') partner, and in following the devious routes of contacts and middlemen in fixing a final purchase order from a government department. Part real and no doubt part masculine boasting to impress the ladies, these tales are frequently garnished with one spicy detail. This is regarding the supplying of a young Chinese woman as a part of the 'deal'. And in more substantial transactions involving a senior politician, as some stories go, a 'gift' of no less than a film starlet from Hong Kong or Taiwan is specified.

The demand for Chinese flesh by Malay politicians, to summarize an informant's convoluted explanation, is a privilege of office which allows them to indulge in their 'special attraction to the white skin'. In the absence of *Mat Salleh* (European) women, Chinese women with their fairer skin, are objects of carnal interest among Malay men. There is no need to take too seriously this scandalous and self-serving narrative but for the kind of normal, common sense quality it seems to enjoy among those in the sex trade. Blind to their own complicity and almost proud of their moral misadventures, Chinese informants spin out enticing tales which draw from and fuel the myth of the erotic fantasy of whiteness among Malay men. In the El Dorado of new economic riches of East Malaysia, the timber trade offers another elaboration of the myth. To Kuala Lumpur now come 'State Assemblymen', some genuine, some carpetbaggers, out to make a quick *ringgit* from equally duplicitous Chinese *towkays* (merchants), promising government contacts and useful connections for acquiring highly lucrative logging concessions. Perhaps aware of the frailty of their pledges, these men do not demand exotic imports, but are content with the more modest choice of a local Chinese girl during their stay in the capital.

In Sakura, as though to give these tales of new riches and transactions a more solid and believable foundation, Chinese men come to talk about their own enjoyment with the language of timber trade. When timber merchants gather, they would down glasses of Remy Martin or Black Label Johnny Walker and shout, in appreciative approval, "Ah, that is worth a log or two." And, since there is no higher evaluation of things than the price of a log of stripped timber extracted by hardy men from deep in the Sarawak jungle, they would, in what they think as a flirtatious compliment, call out to a young hostess: "Now you are worth two logs, but don't forget your old love like me." The crudity of such jokes, like other 'compliments' about bust size, for instance, marks the very routine in the way a hostess has to 'look after' her clients. For some women, these jokes are at once embarrassing and a reminder of the reality of their world. It is only the more seasoned hostesses who can deflect the phallic reference with a reply suggestive of a comparable insult: "Well, we have to see how much your log is worth (for me to love you again)."

What all these add up to in fact is a set of collective cliches that one comes to identify with political life in Malaysia. Here, to the idea of the corrupt Malay politician is added another dimension, that of the duplicity of rich Chinese who manage to make money even when government policies are stack on them. Returning to our ethnography, for Diana, what the medicinal goodness of *bak ku teh* has to work against, we might say, is as much the health draining lifestyle of a karaoke hostess as the wider state processes which impose their impeccable, violent logic on her body. The pleasure of the body is at once traceable to the desires and social impulses constitutive of the order of political life. Moving beyond their physiological self-obsession (Jameson 1983, p. 1), the 'realms of the senses' in the pork dish, as in Diana's body, are opened up to their public lives and social significance. The taking of Diana's body is at the same time the sad fate of her gender and profession, an exercise of epistemic violence, and the logical destiny of a state discourse anxiously affirming the need to possess and manage the enjoyment of the Other: to this complex field of power and desire we shall now turn.

State Hegemony, Ethnicity and Alterity

To contemplate the nature of state power, and ethnic identity in Malaysia — what it means to us and the way it gives significance to others, is to place the conventional narrative of the state under a new critical light. All narratives, Hayden White reminds us, carry "an illusionary coherence", and the process of their telling invariably "charges them with the kinds of meanings more characteristic of oneiric than of waking thought" (White 1987, p. 124). There is nothing more illustrative of this than the measured normalcy of the 'story' of modern Malaysia. Bathed in the radiance of national progress and the wise political leadership which has helped to achieve it, the story tells of Malaysia's struggle for nationhood from British colonialism, the success of the anti-communist campaign during the Emergency of 1948–60, the installation of Malay political, cultural, and economic hegemony as a necessary condition of ethnic peace and, of course, the rapid industrial modernization under the Prime Minister Dr Mahathir bin Mohamad, whose tough political skills and pragmatic economic management will steer the country out of the current financial crisis.

Like all state narratives, this one too is imbued with a seductive magic (see, for example, Coronil 1997). It is a magic that is derived from the narrative's endless retelling, as it recounts one heroic enterprise after another undertaken by the various regimes of wise and capable political leadership. However, as one would expect, the narrative cannot achieve its astonishing power without a quick sleight-of-hand and a rapid shuffling

Natural abundance, in other words, has ironically become an evolutionary trap by protecting Malays from the strenuous logic of natural selection. Here, in the richness of the tropics, even the weakest and feeble minded survive and propagate themselves. However in a multiethnic society, the 'survival of the weak' would not have been as serious if the 'immigrant communities' were not already toughened by the hardy environment in their home countries. All the while as Dr Mahathir outlines the woes of Malays — from genetic fault-lines and poor social discipline to inward-looking Islamic world view — the subtext is clear. Malay frailty has to be seen against the strength of Chinese who came from a tough environment which truly tested the fit and stout-hearted, weeding out the weak and turning them into 'hardened and resourceful' people (Mahathir 1970, p. 25). The intellectual genius of *The Malay Dilemma* lies in its construction of the tragic vision of Malay communal fate — the Faustian dilemma of nature's reward when it undoes at the same stroke, the good work of Darwinian evolution. In this vision, not only Malays, but the figure of the Chinese Other too carries a tragic mendacity because it is primarily an invention, an object of desire's fantasy. The hardworking, cross-breeding, biologically tough and socially outward-looking 'Chinese' has been constructed to fulfill a singular purpose — to mirror the 'relative disadvantage' of Malays, and excavate the analytical depth of the 'Malay dilemma'.

Not surprisingly, both the notions of Chinese endowment and Malays' lack have the ghostly quality of a dream, immortal in their endless rebirth in the state discourse, socially gripping for their haunting realism. For it is at the ambivalent geography of desire in which we can evaluate Dr Mahathir's project. Speaking of the preferential allocation of government scholarships to Malay students, he writes:

> "To answer (the criticism of racial favouritism), one has to go back to the basic reason for the preferential treatment of the Malays. The motive behind preferential treatment is not to put Malays in a superior position, but to *bring them up to the level of non-Malays....* The scholarships are not a manifestation of racial inequality. They are a means of breaking down the superior position of the non-Malays in the field of education.... The

Malays are not proud of the 'privilege' of being protected by law like cripples. They would like to get rid of these privileges if they can, but they have to let pride take second place to the *facts of life*" (Mahathir 1970, p. 75, emphasis added).

Here the destinies of the Malay subject and its (Chinese) Other are fatefully intertwined. Not only is the Other's endowment a gauge of one's lack, but the Malay subject's socio-economic ambitions and the question of their attainability are also ultimately measured by the level of achievement of the Other. This process of Othering, based on the twin convent of promotion of Malay cultural and economic interest and suppressing the enjoyment of the Other, has all the ruling principle of the psychic economy described by Zizek:

> "Nationalism … presents a privileged domain of the eruption of enjoyment into the social field. The national Cause is ultimately nothing but the way subjects of a given ethnic community organize their enjoyment through national myth. What is therefore at stake in ethnic tension is always the possession of the national thing. We always impute to the 'other' an excessive enjoyment: he wants to steal our enjoyment (by ruining our way of life) and/or he has access to some secret, perverse enjoyment … The basic paradox is that our Thing is conceived as something inaccessible to the other and at the same time threatened by him" (Zizek 1993, pp. 202–203).

Returning to Dr Mahathir's text, what explains the "ground of incompatibility between different ethnic subject positions" (Zizek 1993, p. 203) is precisely the mathematics of national enjoyment as a limited good, the principle of "the more of it for the Other can only lead to less for me". But why is the Other so remarkably capable of enjoyment, of always extracting something from his relationship with the National Thing, in a way which fatally threatens my effort to do so? In a way, the genetic biologism in *The Malay Dilemma* has already provided the answer; but not quite. For if Malay subject positionality is, as I have said, constructed out of desire's longing, then neither the 'Malay Problem' nor the project of 'bringing Malays up to the level of the Other communities' can ever find a satisfactory ending and resolution. Like chasing the whistling presence of a phantom, the 'level of achievement of the Other' cannot ever be caught up with simply because the desire which produces the Real in the Malay subject position cannot be pinned down. The Chinese Other in Dr Mahathir's (Orientalist) discourse — genetically endowed, hardened by the good work of evolution — is a screen upon which authorial desire can be displaced or deferred.

This is the most ironic moment in the tortuous discourse. If he is the thief of my pleasure, the Other also offers the final measurement of my achievement. In the context of this contradiction, the Chinese Other becomes at the same time, a target of Malay resentment and an object of cultural adoration. After all, the cultural and biological endowments of the Other are identified as those very qualities which the Malay subject desperately needs in order to bring itself to the same or at least, comparable level of achievement. Moving to the contemporary period, the continuance of the NEP (New Economic Policy) thus has a more significant cause than the greed of Malay elite conspiring to prolong its rich harvest — in collaboration with local Chinese and Indian capital. In spite of the dramatic redefinition of Malay identity by wealth redistribution, and particularly through a modernising secular Islam, the ethnicisation of state policy has meant the enduring need to construct and vitalize the discourse of the tragic and 'natural' disadvantages of Malays (relative to the Other). Seen under this light, the 'Malay dilemma' so evocatively laid out by Dr Mahathir may indeed point to another problematic: how to manage and re-possess the enjoyment by the other, enjoyment that rightly belongs to us.

The Deferred Pleasure of the Chinese Body

There is something in Dr Mahathir's narrative of the 'knotting' quality that Barbara Johnson refers to as charting any representation of the Real in the transference and counter-transference of desire. For all the biological and social determinism in Dr Mahathir's text, the discriminatory differences in the relative cultural and economic endowments of the Malay subject and the Chinese Other cannot be projected 'out there' into the Social Real. Denied of its realist authority, the Malay subject has to

discover its completion in the Chinese Other, which is itself a
construction of desire. Returning to our ethnography, is it this double
fantasy that incites the Malay politician's urgent call for Diana's young
body? The taking of Diana's body is a classic move of desire in the
displacement of its longing for the Chinese Other. What the enjoyment
rehearses is the 'education of desire', to use a potent phrase of Ann Laura
Stoler (Stoler 1995), which circulates in an endless relay between the
narrative of the state and the Malay subject's fantasy. It is a fantasy which
draws succour from the powerful *Bumiputra* discourse of the state, just as
it fuels the subject's imaginary mastery of selfhood through the triumphant
taking of pleasure in/from the Other. The process is one of double
inscription. At the level of official discourse, the need for — and the
erasure of — the Chinese Other is traceable to the social, environmental
conditions and genetic consequences that Dr Mahathir has painstakingly
described. Yet the Real in all these articulations is always already infected
with fantasy's work precisely because it has been "formally composed to
establish itself as 'truly' real, as an element of discourse, the discourse of
truth" (Clough 1992, p. 547). For the Malay subject, the pleasure of the
Chinese body is thus never 'sufficient' nor 'complete' in itself. If such
pleasure is one of sensual enjoyment, then there is pleasure too, ironically,
in its delay and when it falls short of total fulfilment. For the ecstasy
offered by the Chinese body is always deferred to 'something else', as it
draws its constructed significations in 'some other place', located in the
mobile terrain between the sites of fact and fantasy, truth and fiction,
narrative and discourse.

In the world of Sakura Karaoke Lounge, if the nutritious *bak ku teh*
repairs the body and restores the spirit, for Diana it is also from the painful
experience of the night excursion with the Malay man which such
rehabilitation is sought. The sighing acceptance of woman's fate, the
deprecating solicitude of a lover who sells her body, and the harvesting
of redemption from 'eating bitterness' — what lies in the midst of all these
is the deep humiliation of having *xiao ye* with a Malay man. Even in a
world in which the transaction of the female body is a normal affair,
Diana's insistence on the 'ethnic import' of her pain is highly suggestive.
However, if such a transaction is a part of the everyday in Sakura, then
it is precisely in the routine banality of the women's leisure and work that

we find "the hidden present, or the discoverable future" (Blanchot 1987, p. 13) of their lives. It is not only that Diana's humiliation signifies the burden of 'ethnic differences' in repressive state politics and discourse; rather the everyday of her world is always merged with the fragmentary processes of social life, constituting "the very moment of society" (Blanchot 1987, p. 14). And the crucial issue of gender and power is surely this: Diana's suffering signals her (personal) embodiment of the meanings and consequences of the tortuous discourse of ethnicity as they imperceptibly become a part of her life and understanding,[1] as they distribute through her body, as Foucault would say.

The quality of 'unserious seriousness' — the term is again Blanchot's (Blanchot 1987, p. 16) — of the everyday is also crucial when we turn to look at yet another modality of the enjoyment of *xiao ye* and a dish like *bak ku teh*. For the 'privatization' we have witnessed in the subterranean world of Jalan Alor way past midnight is not only discernible in the cosy intimacy and gentle whispers of lovers. More potently, it is also authorised, literally, in the street. For the social comfort of the foodstall's offering, as I have said, lies in their carving a sanctuary out of the tedium and discomfort of daily life. But ironically, this social comfort is only feasible because the banal, quotidian quality of the street renders open what is obscure, what is hidden by forces which conspire to achieve its concealment. In Blanchot's rendering of Lefebvre's political reading of the street, "The street tears from obscurity what is hidden, publishes what happens elsewhere, in secret; it deforms it, but inserts it in the social text" (Blanchot 1987, p. 17). The culinary pleasure offered by the foodstalls in Jalan Alor takes on a similar quality, of linking the enjoyment of the moment to the grim silences and discriminations of the state.

Here the busy and violent interference of the state seems so far away, in some place only discernible in the light of day. In the dead of night no police constables are in sight. Shrouded by the secret transparency of night, what is partaken of at the foodstall suddenly appears to assume a special significance. Is not *bak ku teh* with pork knuckles and ribs a *haram* (polluting) food under the strict Islamic food taboo? Have not we all heard that in the PAS (Party Islam Malaysia)-dominated state of Kelantan such a dish can only be consumed in the inner section of a Chinese restaurant, away from the street? And, by the same token, have not the Chinese businessmen who come to Sakura complained of the increasing difficulty of obtaining restaurant licence from the state authorities when the proposed establishment is to include pork dishes on the menu? In the face of these realities, the pleasure of *bak ku teh* seems to take on an insidious quality perhaps because, as one ponders to suggest, such a culinary choice is forbidden by the state and its official religion; it is only consumed by non-Muslims. For Diana at least, it is as if the enjoyment of the *haram* dish helps to regain a sense of herself, if she would put it so, lost in a transaction in which her body has been a key commodity. 'The everyday escapes' as it slips through the net of significance constructed by the anthropologist, just as it seems to break through the pervasive gaze of the state. There is undoubtedly pleasure too in these ventures of 'disappearance' as one sinks one's teeth into the thick pork chunks, dripping with dark sauce and medicinal goodness.

Conclusion

Looking back at that late evening at the foodstall with Diana and Ah Keong, it seems too easy to recall, with a tinge of the tongue, the bitter-sweetness of the dish and to give shape its taste from memory. However, there is always a danger in narration from memory, as Benjamin has warned. When taste comes to be remembered as an experience of incorrigible innocence affirmed by the senses, then the magic of the fetishistic begins to assert itself. Taste always 'disappears' into itself. If I have evoked Benjamin to drive home the point about the potent, dreamy quality of the fetishistic, my analysis is even more primarily orchestrated by the insight of Marx about the relationship between history and the senses: "Man is affirmed in the objective world not only in the act of thinking but with all his senses. The formation of the senses is a labour of the entire history of the world down to the present" (Marx 1972, pp. 140–141). Just as aesthetics, even that witnessed in the display of food in restaurants and supermarkets, tends to escape into the ideological realm (Eagleton 1990), we can only 'taste' through history. We cannot enjoy a meal without the intrusion of social memory, any more than we can create for the poor in these times of post-Thatcherite economic rationalism, the vulgar optimism of social hope by the display of the temporary abundance of a soup kitchen.

My attempt to retrace the enjoyment of the dish *bak ku teh*, has been to tell another history, other genealogies of pleasure, in the political landscape of Malaysia. In this enterprise, I return to the fundamental feature of Malaysian political life: state power based on Malay hegemony, and its effect in the formation of Malay subjective position. To be foundational in this sense is not, I submit, to commit the theoretical mistake of foundationalism. In a condition where complex and uneven forces work to create collective silence if not social amnesia, the unsettling of the hardrock of state formation is intended as a conscious political gesture. These forces of silence range from state enforcement, complicity of Malays and non-Malays middle class and capitalists alike, to the (vulgar) Marxist fantasy of the progressive circle for whom 'ethnic issues' are but false consciousness to be put right by the unifying project of class struggle. Against these forces, what I have been at pain to bring to light is the very endurance of the ethnic divide in Malaysian life. To witness such divide and its more subtle articulations, one has to turn away from places where the instrumentalities of the state are immediately visible, but to the sites of the everyday and ordinary pleasures.

Instead of communal peace, a 'fact' invariably brought up by the state to justify its racist policies, intense passion and anguish are witnessed in these sites. And this is precisely the remarkable insight of Benjamin and Blanchot which underpins my analysis: in Malaysia, it is not that ethnic violence has somehow disappeared from daily life, with the dying traces hidden in places of the quotidian; rather it has always been self-evidently and pervasively 'there' in the shadow. For those who have eyes to see, and those who live and work there, these banal and marginal places are never what they are commonly perceived but charged with profound significance. As in taste, what nestles in these places is another history, another narrative of life's ambitions and disappointments. And like taste, history too has to be perceived, not as a factual 'thing' — like a supermarket shelving into which we slot all our understandings and passions, as Michael Taussig has sardonically described (Taussig 1987, pp. 151–69) — but as a narrative subject to the vagrancy of its telling. It says much about the ideological tenor of the *Reformasi* movement organized around the former Deputy Prime Minister and Finance Minister Anwar Ibrahim following his arrest that ethnic-based policies are to be upheld as a part of its political platform, because they are "in the constitution and put there by the forefathers (of the nation)" (Email interview with spokesperson of Parti Keadilan Nasional, 12 July 1999). For all its anti-Mahathir radicalism and appeal to democratic reform, *Parti Keadilan Nasional* (National Justice Party) under the leadership of Anwar's wife Dr Wan Azizah Wan Ismail fails to attract wide support across the ethnic groups. The ambivalence many Malaysians feel about the *reformasi* movement may well lie in this ideological blindspot, in its inability to resolve a historical burden at the centre of political life. If the past indeed repeats itself, then the *reformasi* project too, like the taste of *bak ku teh*, is spell bound by the intimate merging of state narrative and collective amnesia, cultural enjoyment and ethnic aspirations.

CHAPTER 4

Multiple Identities among the Returned Overseas Chinese in Hong Kong

James Chin Kong

The Chinese in Hong Kong have never been a homogeneous ethnic community. Hong Kong is both a migrant society and a former British colony (prior to 1997) and as a result, there are several major ethnic communities in Hong Kong. These ethnic communities consist mainly of Chinese migrants from mainland China and Indian migrants from some former British colonies in Asia. Further, numerous mainland Chinese emigrated to Hong Kong in different periods. The large number of returned overseas Chinese who moved into Hong Kong after the 1970s are of particular interest to the students of Chinese diasporas, since they provide a special perspective from which to examine Chinese overseas communities.[1] Despite this, in the literature on the overseas Chinese, little attention has been given to those returned overseas Chinese currently living in Hong Kong.[2] This study is a preliminary exploration of this special Chinese community of Hong Kong based on the author's observations of, and participation in, their activities over a six-year period. This paper will focus on the associations established by these returned overseas Chinese, tracing the development and change of this overseas Chinese community, and examining its multiple identities.

The Historical Setting

After the end of World War II, various countries in Southeast Asia successively rid themselves of colonial rule and attained independence. With independence and the nation building that followed, however, Southeast Asian Chinese faced difficult challenges such as those involved in choosing new identities within the new nation-states. In addition, discriminatory economic policies towards overseas Chinese were quietly put into practice by the new indigenous authorities in the early years of independence. Indonesian Chinese, including the local-born *peranakan*, suddenly realised that they had been deliberately expelled from rural areas and their economic activities were confined to intermediary trade.[3] In the meantime, a new wave of Chinese nationalism gradually reached its height among Southeast Asian Chinese with the establishment of People's Republic of China (PRC) in late 1949.

A large number of local-born young Chinese students who felt discriminated against in their host countries decided to go to mainland China. They were encouraged and persuaded by principals and teachers of Chinese schools, many of whom were later found to be underground Chinese Communist Party (CCP) members. These young Chinese students left their families in Southeast Asia for the PRC to continue their Chinese language education or to serve the new government.

The majority of these young Chinese were Indonesian Chinese. Based on interviews and other sources, it appears that there were five major migratory waves of overseas Chinese to mainland China in the 1950s and early 1960s. These occurred in 1950, 1953, 1957, and 1960, with the last one being generated by the anti-Chinese storm of "30 September 1965" in Indonesia. Estimates vary as to the number of Southeast Asian Chinese who went to China during this period. It is widely held that about 600 thousand Southeast Asian Chinese travelled to China between the early 1950s and 1969, with more than half of them coming from Indonesia (Frolic 1980, p. 100).

While these young Southeast Asian students tried very hard to integrate into the PRC's socialist system, they confronted various problems, both political and economic. Frequently they were distrusted and criticised because of their previous foreign connections (*haiwai guanxi*), which in turn led to them being further abused during the numerous political movements launched by the CCP in the 1950s and 1960s, the Anti-Rightist Movement of 1957, and the decade-long Cultural Revolution in particular, in which they were labelled as "foreign spies" or "capitalists' dogs".[4] Disappointed with and discouraged by what they had experienced in the PRC, hundreds of thousands of returned overseas Chinese quietly left mainland China on various excuses, joining in a mass exodus crossing the Lo Wu Bridge, the bridge marking the border between the PRC and the British colony of Hong Kong, in the hope of eventually returning to their homes in Southeast Asia. Unfortunately, only after they crossed the Lo Wu Bridge and landed in Hong Kong, did they realise that they would not actually be able to reunite with their family members in the Nanyang as they had come from the PRC. Consequently, almost all the Southeast Asian nation-states shut their doors to them. In other words, for political reasons, a large number of overseas Chinese were unable to return to their homes in Southeast Asia in the years following the Cultural Revolution, after they had finally given up their naïve commitment to make contributions to the PRC and had been forced to leave mainland China. Apart from a small number who were successfully smuggled back to Southeast Asian countries, most of these people had no option but to remain in Hong Kong, and there they pioneered new enterprises.

More than one thousand returned overseas Chinese had reached Hong Kong by 1964, under the pretext of reunion with family members from Southeast Asia, visiting friends, medical treatment, or marrying someone from overseas. The largest wave of migration from mainland China, however, did not come until 1972, when Beijing's Overseas Chinese Affairs Commission finally agreed to let the returned overseas Chinese leave China for Hong Kong and Macau in batches. As a result, a huge number of returned overseas Chinese rushed into Hong Kong from various parts of China within a few months, which brought great pressure to bear on Hong Kong society. Possibly due to complaints from the Hong Kong government, the Beijing authorities suspended the issuing of exit permits to those who still remained in mainland China for a short period in late 1973. Nevertheless, once the stream of migration began, it continued to flow. According to contemporary reports by Hong Kong's media, not more than 100 thousand returned overseas Chinese were said to remain in mainland China by the end of 1976. At the same time, more than 300 thousand of them had left for Hong Kong and Macau. Of these, more than 250 thousand entered the British colony while another 25 thousand migrated to Portuguese Macau (*Mingpao Monthly* 12.10, Oct. 1977, p. 8; Liu 1979). From then onwards, small numbers of returned Overseas Chinese kept moving into Hong Kong. By the middle of the 1980s, excluding those who were determined to settle down in mainland China, the majority of the returned Overseas Chinese had crossed the Lo Wu Bridge and migrated into Hong Kong.

Unlike the Overseas Chinese community in Macau that consists predominantly of ethnic Chinese from Myanmar, the Overseas Chinese community in Hong Kong mainly consists of the Indonesian Chinese. According to the local overseas Chinese leaders' estimates, 90 percent of the Overseas Chinese in Hong Kong are from Indonesia while Chinese migrants from other Southeast Asian countries, such as Myanmar, Thailand, Malaysia, Vietnam, the Philippines, Singapore, and Cambodia constitute the remaining ten percent. It is estimated that among 6,680,000 Hong Kong permanent residents, about 350 thousand are returned Southeast Asian Chinese and their family members.

For most of these returned Overseas Chinese, after landing in Hong Kong, life was initially extremely bitter. The British colonial government did not recognise their professional qualifications or working experience, though they had been experienced engineers, physicians, teachers, writers, and artists for many years in mainland China. To survive, they had to engage in physically demanding jobs for long hours with low wages, such as working in garment factories or carrying cargo as dock porters.

They worked hard, however, to improve their circumstances. Many of them attended night schools to improve their English, while doing their best to make money to maintain their families. After several years' effort, some of them passed the colonial qualifying examinations and started anew their professional careers as private physicians or accountants. While those who were able to grasp daily English were admitted into private trading companies or shipping companies with the recommendation of relatives and friends, those who had been teachers or media workers in mainland China gradually managed to obtain positions in local Chinese media, with some becoming employees of PRC-owned enterprises in Hong Kong. Others, with the help of their relatives in Southeast Asia, established their own trading companies, conducting import and export business between China and the countries of Southeast Asia. Typical Indonesian-style grocery stores run by some of the returned Indonesian Chinese quietly came into being in the areas where the ordinary Indonesian Chinese lived. Almost all local products produced in Indonesia, such as clove cigarettes, dried shrimp slices, paintings, clothes, flavourings, popular movies, and music cassettes could be found in these groceries.

A few wealthy returned overseas Chinese soon emerged as business representatives of their families or clans in Hong Kong. They were actively involved in investments in mainland China on behalf of the family business, with offices based in Central, Hong Kong's financial district. It would be misleading, however, to consider the returned overseas Chinese of Hong Kong as a group of well-to-do businessmen. On the contrary, most of them have remained in the working class and, even until the late 1980s, many lived in the poor wooden housing area in Diamond Hill, a poorer suburb.

Voluntary Associations and Organising Principles

Strictly speaking, the returned overseas Chinese did not form a cohesive and independent community in Hong Kong prior to the early 1980s, even though more than 250 thousand of them had settled down in Hong Kong by that time. The first voluntary association of Southeast Asian Chinese of Hong Kong — *Xianggang qiaoyoushe* (Association of Overseas Chinese in Hong Kong, hereafter QYS) did not come into being until 1982.

Why did it take almost two decades for people to establish such associations? During interviews with senior overseas Chinese leaders from various associations, I was given several reasons that can be summarised as follows. First, several hundred years' of sojourning in Southeast Asian countries by their forefathers had made them aware that politics can be very dangerous and it brings serious trouble for sojourning Chinese if they carelessly get involved in it. Moreover, overseas Chinese were never allowed by the colonial authorities or indigenous governments to have a hand in local political affairs. As a result, most overseas Chinese in Southeast Asia used to concentrate on their businesses and were afraid to concern themselves with the politics of their host countries or to establish their own organisations.

Secondly, they had not yet moved on from the scar left by the successive political mass movements they experienced in mainland China from the early 1950s to the mid-1970s. Although they had migrated to British Hong Kong, bitter experiences and a fear of politics still prevented them from establishing any associations.

Thirdly, almost all of them had to struggle for survival in the early years and were frequently exhausted from earning a living through two different jobs. As a result, they actually had no time or energy to consider how to unite their fellow Southeast Asian Chinese through establishing organisations.

Fourthly, most of them had a strong nostalgia towards their Southeast Asian homes. They always believed that someday in the near future they could return to their tropical homelands. With this sojourning psychology in mind, the majority of the returned overseas Chinese were not willing to join any voluntary associations, fearing that they would be forbidden to return to their homes in Southeast Asia once their activities were observed and recorded by officials of the Southeast Asian consulates in Hong Kong.

Finally, since many returned Southeast Asian Chinese had close business relations with Taiwan, they feared that they might be drawn into political disputes between mainland China and Taiwan by events beyond their control, which in turn would affect their business. Consequently, not many returned overseas Chinese of Hong Kong were interested in establishing their own associations or even joining one up until the 1980s.

In any case, as noted above, October 1982 saw the first returned overseas Chinese association headed by an Indonesian Chinese emerge in Hong Kong. And once someone had taken the initiative, this organization was quickly followed by others. Six months later, a group of Chinese from Medan in Sumatra set up another similar association in the colony. From then on, returned Southeast Asian Chinese established various types of voluntary associations. There are now 46 overseas Chinese associations formally registered with the Hong Kong government and most of these were formed from the mid-1980s to the early 1990s. Of these, 25 are comprised entirely of Indonesian Chinese. One organization comprises Thai Chinese, one was established by Chinese from Malaysia and Singapore, one consists of Burmese Chinese, 13 are alumni associations based on mainland Chinese schools and universities, and the other five are cross-national. While the associations created by Indonesian Chinese thus appear to only constitute approximately half of such voluntary organizations in Hong Kong, a closer observation reveals that Indonesian Chinese have actually been the most active members and have been preponderant in most of these associations.

In so far as their organising principles are concerned, voluntary associations established by the overseas Chinese of Hong Kong exhibit a number of different characteristics when compared with their counterparts in Southeast Asia. Historically, Chinese associations outside of mainland China were usually constructed through three traditional principles: lineage, dialect, and locality. These three major traditional organising principles, however, have transformed or have disappeared from Hong Kong's overseas Chinese associations. Almost all of the Southeast Asian Chinese were young students when they returned to China in the 1950s and 1960s. They were not Chinese families or lineages moving back from overseas. Instead of being sent directly to their ancestral home villages, most of these young Southeast Asian Chinese were sent to study in overseas Chinese preparatory schools before being admitted into universities to continue their education or to be assigned to overseas-Chinese farms scattered throughout the southern provinces, notably on Hainan Island and in Guangxi, Yunnan, Fujian, and Guangdong. Thus, the traditional Chinese lineage ties that once played a key role in organising Chinese communities overseas vanished from among these returned overseas Chinese.

Dialect ties, another important organising principle, also underwent fundamental change. Although some of the overseas Chinese were able to speak southern Chinese dialects when they migrated back to China (those from the Medan area, for example, would habitually use Hokkien to communicate with one another), the majority of them preferred to speak *Bahasa Indonesia* among themselves. In addition, two decades of education and working in the mainland enabled them to speak fluent Mandarin (*putonghua*). Consequently, when they moved to Hong Kong, though the prevalent dialect ties were still there, the components had basically changed. Traditional southern Chinese dialects such as Hokkien, Teochiu, and Hakka are no longer widely spoken among these people in Hong Kong. Cantonese, one of the major southern Chinese dialects, remains the most frequently used language in the Chinese society of Hong Kong, but it does not necessarily mean that it also became the working language of the Overseas Chinese community of Hong Kong. Instead, *Bahasa Indonesia* and Mandarin have become their special *lingua franca* in daily life and a new organising principle in the formation of voluntary associations.

A similar situation can be observed in terms of locality ties. Although most of the Southeast Asian Chinese in Hong Kong clearly know where their home villages are in the mainland, their personal experiences have never provided them with direct or close links with these ancestral native places. On the contrary, they really miss their tropical homelands in Southeast Asia where they were born and spent their pleasant teenage years. The towns and cities of Southeast Asia where sizable ethnic Chinese communities could be found thus unconsciously replaced their ancestral homes and emerged as another new organising principle by which to bring returned overseas Chinese from the same place in the Nanyang together. The locality ties or native place connections are still widely recognised among them but have been redefined. To them, the *Qiaoxiang* (homeland of overseas Chinese) ties obviously mean hometowns in Southeast Asia rather than the ancestral home villages of south China. As a result, a group of Indonesian Chinese from Samarinda, the capital of East Kalimantan Province, formed an association in 1983 with the interesting name *San-ma-lin-da lugang tongxianghui* (Association for Samarinda Chinese Sojourning in Hong Kong), while another group of Chinese from Bangka Island registered their association with the Hong Kong government in October 1995 under the name of *Xianggang bangjia qiaoyouhui* (Hong Kong Association for Overseas Chinese from Bangka Island). Indeed, among 46 overseas Chinese associations in Hong Kong, none of them is linked with any traditional Southeast Asian Chinese homeland in China.

With the disappearance of lineage ties, a more influential and stronger link — alumni associations — emerged among the returned overseas Chinese, particularly among those from the Indonesian Archipelago. As mentioned, almost all of the returned overseas Chinese were young students in the 1950s and 1960s, and they had either just finished their junior education in various Chinese schools in Southeast Asia before travelling to China or intended to pursue their tertiary education in China after finishing language training courses in preparatory schools. Common educational background and study experience thus became key factors in uniting these Southeast Asian Chinese in Hong Kong and various alumni associations gradually developed into some of the most active and popular voluntary organisations.

Two types of returned overseas Chinese alumni associations can be identified. The first one includes those organized on the basis of the so-called "red schools" or the Chinese secondary schools in Southeast Asia. Those from the prominent *Bacheng zhongxue* (The Secondary School of Batavia) or *Ba Zhong*, for instance, established their alumni association with the name *Yinni bazhong xianggang xiaoyouhui* (Hong Kong Alumni Association of the Secondary School of Batavia, Indonesia). Such a phenomenon is not confined to Indonesian Chinese and alumni from the Nanyang Secondary School of Thailand have also organised an alumni association in Hong Kong. If the number of alumni was not high enough to form an independent alumni association, these Southeast Asian Chinese would, as a rule, unite with other schools from the same region to organise a regional alumni association. Quite a number of alumni associations were formed in this way, including *Jugang xianggang xiaoyouhui* (Hong Kong Alumni Association of Palembang), *Yinni sishui lugang tongxuehui* (The Alumni Association HK of Surabaya, Indonesia), *Yinni xijiang tongxuehui* (Association for Alumni from Makassar), and *Subei yaqi lugang tongxuehui* (Association for Sojourning Alumni from Aceh of North Sumatra).

The second type refers to those established on the basis of mainland Chinese schools and universities. Thirteen alumni associations have been organised on this basis, including the *Xianggang jimei qiaoxiao tongxuehui* (Hong Kong Alumni Association of Jimei Overseas Chinese Preparatory School), the *Lugang huaqiao daxue xiaoyouhui* (Hong Kong Association for Sojourning Alumni from Overseas Chinese University), and *Xianggang shantou qiaoxiao xiaoyouhui* (Hong Kong Alumni Association for Swatow Overseas Chinese School).

While the three new organising principles remain very important in terms of the establishment of voluntary associations among overseas Chinese in Hong Kong, not all of the associations under discussion fall within this grouping. Some associations have deliberately eschewed the limits set by the above principles and organised returned overseas Chinese of Hong Kong under the principle of cross-nationality. The *Xianggang qiaoyoushe* (Association of Overseas Chinese in Hong Kong), or QYS, and the *Xianggang huaqiao huaren zonghui* (The Hong Kong Overseas Chinese General Association), or HKOCGA, are two such cases.

Another striking example to be noted is the *Xianggang yinni yanjiu xueshe* or Hong Kong Society for Indonesian Studies (HKSIS). The HKSIS was established in early 1999 by a group of Indonesian Chinese who are very concerned about the current situation of Indonesia and the prospects of ethnic Chinese in Indonesia. They regularly hold seminars and workshops to discuss and analyse what is happening in Indonesia. Apart from local scholars, officials and researchers from the Indonesian government and military have also regularly been invited to give speeches or reports at their meetings. What is more interesting is their journal, entitled *Yinni Jiaodian or Indonesia Focus*, a tri-lingual (Chinese, English and *Bahasa Indonesia*) journal, that provides an up-to-date summary and in-depth analysis of Indonesia's current affairs. Although edited and circulated internally as a private journal, it soon received the attention of local academia and the Indonesian Consulate General in Hong Kong and consequently appeared on the desks of government authorities, both in Jakarta and Beijing, as valuable reference materials.

Thus, four groupings of voluntary associations can be recognised according to the links introduced above. The first group consists of those voluntary associations based upon places of origin in Southeast Asia. The second group consists of cross-national associations. The third group includes alumni associations organised in accordance with schools in Southeast Asia. The fourth group includes those alumni associations based on mainland Chinese schools and universities. There is, however, some overlap in terms of membership.

Multiple Identities among Returned Overseas Chinese

The large number of returned overseas Chinese currently residing in Hong Kong were all born and spent their childhood and youth in Southeast Asia before returning to mainland China in the 1950s and 1960s. While in the PRC, they not only received systematic Chinese education and participated in economic construction, but also experienced various extreme political movements to which many of them fell victim. They were almost middle-aged when they finally decided to leave the PRC and emigrate to Hong Kong. As depicted above, they had tried very hard in Hong Kong for almost three decades before eventually re-establishing themselves in an environment that is culturally less familiar but more fair in terms of individual development and commercial competition. Such a unique experience obtained during three different periods has undoubtedly left deep marks on their multiple identities.

(A) Political Identity

Mainly due to the bitter memory about the political movements they experienced in mainland China, most of the returned overseas Chinese view politics with horror and, on the whole, they hate to be involved in any kind of political activities. It is often the case that these Southeast Asian Chinese maintain a very cautious attitude when asked for their personal opinions on political events. In their articles of association, the majority of voluntary associations clearly express the purpose for which their associations were established. Their sole concern was for their own business and welfare, showing little interest in local politics by limiting their activities to the returned overseas Chinese community. This situation, however, started to change gradually in the 1990s with the approach of 1997 when the sovereignty of Hong Kong was due to be returned to the PRC. More and more association leaders agreed to be appointed by the Xinhua News Agency, a ministerial level of the Chinese government office based in Hong Kong, as Hong Kong affairs advisors, members of the Chinese People's Political Consultative Council (CPPCC), or members of the National People's Congress (NPC).

Three tiers of identity can be observed among the returned overseas Chinese in so far as politics is concerned. The first tier refers to the relations between the PRC and foreign countries, excluding those in Southeast Asia. Whenever there is a conflict between the PRC and foreign countries, the overseas Chinese community of Hong Kong would definitely take sides with the PRC. The majority of the associations admitted in the 1990s, for instance, that they were pro-PRC in the struggle against the British with respect to political negotiations over the hand-over of political sovereignty. What is more interesting is that while some of the influential associations admitted that they contended for what the PRC government advocated, they never confessed that they were "tools" manoeuvred by the Beijing authorities for the purpose of *Tongzhan* (the united front strategy). Political identity, however, changed without being noticed due to the shift of parameters. Thus, the second tier, which concerns the relationship in the Taiwan Strait, saw these returned overseas Chinese carefully maintain a balance between Beijing and Taipei in the 1980s and 1990s and few associations would openly admit their political inclination on the sensitive issue of Taiwan. On 12 October 1987, for example, QYS held a workshop to introduce the investment environment in South Africa to its members and a newly retired Taiwan government diplomat was invited to give a report. Activities such as this were usually kept very low profile. Another interesting case is that their associations not only sent delegates to offer their condolences to the Taiwan government when the former ROC president, Chiang Ching-kuo, passed away in January 1988, but also organised members to attend memorial ceremonies offered to the former PRC leaders such as Ye Jianying and Deng Xiaoping in Hong Kong.

This kind of ambiguity exhibited in their political identity, nevertheless, is slightly modified when countries of Southeast Asia, Indonesia in particular, become the focal point of the community's life. Given that the majority of the returned overseas Chinese are Indonesian Chinese and almost all of them have family members or relatives in Indonesia, anything that happens in the Indonesian Archipelago quickly attracts their attention. Regularly, they would have internal meetings with officials from the Indonesian Consul-General in Hong Kong to discuss the political and economic situation in Indonesia or to express their concerns toward it. Sometimes, senior officials from Jakarta or even government leaders and military generals, such as President Abdurrahman Wahid, Vice-President Megawati Sukarnoputri, People's Consultative Congress Speaker Amien Rais, and General Agum Gumelar of Lemhannas, were invited to give a keynote speech or have a closed-door meeting with these Indonesian Chinese when they visited Hong Kong. Indeed, they are much concerned about Indonesia and their fellow Indonesian Chinese who currently live in the country as compared with the PRC and the mainland Chinese, though they are well aware that they are not Indonesian citizens anymore. In the months following the riots of May 1998, for example, the overseas Chinese community of Hong Kong organised thousands of Indonesian Chinese and local Hong Kong people to march to the Indonesian Consul-General of Hong Kong and protest against the violence against the ethnic Chinese of Indonesia. The third tier, which is relevant to Southeast Asian countries, dominates the political identity of the returned overseas Chinese community. In other words, the Southeast Asian Chinese of Hong Kong have a clear order of importance when choosing their political identity and this kind of identity keeps changing in accordance with the shift of political parameters.

(B) Homeland Identity

Similar to political identity, homeland identity is also multi-faceted. To most of the people in Hong Kong, "Where is your homeland?" should be a very easy question. But for the returned overseas Chinese of Hong Kong, such a seemingly uncomplicated question would be difficult. Most Southeast Asian Chinese feel that both mainland China and their countries of origin in Southeast Asia are their homelands. It thus seems that their homeland identity has undergone a change in the past 50 years. While they were in Indonesia, their Chinese teachers repeatedly told them that their cultural roots are Chinese and China is their real homeland. Indeed, ethnic Chinese were widely perceived as aliens by indigenous people at that time. However, after they returned to China and worked many years in different occupations, as teachers, performing arts actresses, physicians, writers, journalists, technicians, and state farm workers, they suddenly realized that they still belonged to a special category of Chinese in China in local mainland Chinese eyes. No matter how much effort they put into their daily lives and work in the hope of becoming real Chinese, most of them failed to change the image they left in local society as *Huaqiao* (overseas Chinese) or *Nanyang Ke* (guests from Southeast Asia) though they had been learning and working in mainland China for a long period.

This local perception of their difference stranded the overseas Chinese in mainland China in an identity limbo. They were not seen as *pribumi* or indigenous people when they were in Indonesia even though their families had been in the Archipelago for many generations; they again could not be fully accepted by the mainland Chinese as real Chinese when they returned to China. They then started to doubt what their Chinese teachers taught in the classrooms when they were young and decided to leave mainland China, trying to re-identify with their birthplaces or homelands in Southeast Asia. Nevertheless, they were not allowed to return to their homes in Southeast Asia when they reached Hong Kong. They were forced to establish themselves in Hong Kong and to cultivate a new identity.

The returned overseas Chinese of Hong Kong classify their homelands according to their intimacy with an area. Given the fact that all the returned overseas Chinese currently are permanent residents of the Hong Kong Special Administrative Region of the PRC, and taking into account the factor of nationality, most of them would tell you that their first homelands are somewhere in south China from where their ancestors emigrated to Southeast Asia. Their second homelands are in Java, Sumatra, Kalimantan, southern Vietnam, or somewhere else in Southeast Asia where their parents, brothers, sisters, and classmates can be found. Hong Kong is their third homeland where they have settled down. In reality, however, they feel nostalgia for their homelands in Southeast Asia rather than those in south China. An Indonesian Chinese from Surabaya impressively depicted his feeling towards Indonesia in a short article entitled "Revisiting homeland with endless nostalgia" as follows:

"In the early 1950s, I left my wet nurse (Indonesia) and returned to my real mother (China). After being apart for 23 years, I eventually revisited my wet nurse with joy beyond expression. As soon as I alighted from the plane and landed on the soil of Indonesia, I knelt down to touch the ground with tears full of my eyes. I was so excited and emotional that some airport staff thought that I was sick and fainted on the ground, so they rushed to support me with their hands. If there were soil on the ground, I would definitely grab it and kiss it. It is on this land I was born and brought up, and it is this land that gave life to me" (You 1995, p. 116).

Some Indonesian Chinese based in Hong Kong openly admit that Indonesia is their first homeland. Zhou Rongfeng, an Indonesian Chinese from Surabaya, is a case in point. In a poem entitled "Gu Xiang" or homeland, Zhou disclosed his real feelings towards Indonesia:

"Indonesia Surabaya, my beautiful first homeland. It was there I spent my naïve childhood and romantic youth with sweet dreams and hopes. Oh, Indonesia, the most vast Archipelago in the world with more than thirteen thousand islands, how much I have been missing you! I was so familiar with everything in Surabaya, but now all of them are far away from me. Because of the misunderstanding occurred in early 1950s and the tease by the destiny, I left you, left my homeland and left my parents, heading for the north, returned to my second homeland, even without the last glimpse at you" (Zhou 1991, p. 91).

Therefore, it is usually difficult for these Indonesian Chinese to decide which homeland is more intimate to their lives.

Multiple identities are not only demonstrated in the overseas Chinese community as a whole but can frequently be seen in individual families. During my interviews, I asked the question, "Do you believe that you are a Chinese?" To my surprise, family members representing different age groups would give different answers. The elder overseas Chinese said, "To be honest, I am half an Indonesian and half a Chinese, at least in terms of culture." Middle-aged parents gave me another answer, "Of course we are Chinese. There is no doubt about it. We love China, but we also love Indonesia." Their young children who were born in Hong Kong in the late 1970s or 1980s, however, chose their own option and answered me without any hesitation, "No, we are neither Indonesians nor mainland Chinese, we are Hong Kong-nese." Indeed, different life experiences and backgrounds left different cultural marks on members of different age groups, which in turn prompted them to choose different identities.

What needs to be noted here is the interesting sojourning mentality possessed by the returned overseas Chinese. Similar to elder generations who set sail for Southeast Asia and sojourned in local societies while doing business there, these Southeast Asian Chinese have a very strong sojourning mental state. Of 46 voluntary associations established by them, 12 have the Chinese characters "lu-gang" or "sojourning in Hong Kong" in their formal registered association names. Even though they have been living in Hong Kong for almost three decades and have established their businesses and families in this financial centre, they still insist or at least have the dream that someday they can return to their homelands in Southeast Asia. Sometimes they themselves admitted that such a dream is not practical and cannot be realised since the living standard in most of the Southeast Asian countries is much lower than that of Hong Kong, and the prospect for the development of ethnic Chinese, especially in Indonesia, remains pessimistic.

(C) Cultural Identity

Three major categories of cultural identities can be identified, namely language, food, and the performing arts. In order to make a living and to develop business in Hong Kong, most of the Southeast Asian Chinese based in Hong Kong are able to speak Cantonese fluently, although with a discernible accent. Nevertheless, among themselves they prefer to use Southeast Asian languages, *Bahasa Indonesia* in particular. It is often the case among overseas Chinese families in Hong Kong that the parents use *Bahasa Indonesia* to discuss family business while Mandarin or Cantonese are occasionally utilized to communicate with the members of the younger generation. Unlike ordinary Hong Kong people who mainly employ Filipino maids to help with the housework, the returned overseas Chinese habitually employ Indonesian maids, not only because Indonesian maids are cheaper in terms of wages as compared with those from the

Philippines, but with an aim to create an appropriate language environment for their children to learn *Bahasa Indonesia* at home. Normally the working language for these Indonesian Chinese is Mandarin when they attend association activities or discuss something seriously among themselves. However, once someone starts to use *Bahasa Indonesia* to voice out his or her opinion, immediately others would follow and the language channel would suddenly change. The whole meeting would then be conducted in *Bahasa Indonesia* rather than in Mandarin.

The widespread use of *Bahasa Indonesia* among these Indonesian Chinese makes it substantially easier for their dialogue and exchange with friends from Indonesia. On frequent occasions, when the author attended Hong Kong dinner gatherings with Indonesian government officials, scholars, and businessmen, the only language spoken would be *Bahasa Indonesia*, just like a normal meeting to be held anywhere in Indonesia. In their daily lives, the Southeast Asian Chinese would observe the customs of Hong Kong and speak Cantonese with their local business partners or clients. When they meet with friends from mainland China, Taiwan, or Singapore, however, Mandarin replaces Cantonese and becomes the unique working language. They speak these three major languages depending upon the specific circumstances and most of them are able to use these languages with facility. Again, the employment of language among these returned overseas Chinese shows their multiplicity in identifying themselves with something. Moreover, as noted above, Southeast Asian languages as a new organising principle have not only facilitated the formation of various associations but have also enhanced their solidarity and intimacy to a large extent.

The second category concerns food or dietary habits. It is well known in Hong Kong that Southeast Asian Chinese are crazy about tropical dishes. Whenever there is a party or gathering organised by their associations, large quantities and varieties of homemade Indonesian food and desserts would appear on the tables as a rule. Some Indonesian Chinese even opened Indonesian restaurants in Hong Kong to cater to the needs of their fellow overseas Chinese. As this addition to Hong Kong's food culture attracted lots of foreign tourists as well, the returned overseas Chinese community made a great contribution towards Hong Kong's tourism and restaurant business. On the other hand, almost 20 years of living experience in mainland China has altered their dietary habits. Those inhabiting northern China for a long period of time, have come to like cooked wheaten food such as *jiaozi* or Chinese dumplings, *baozi* or steamed stuffed buns, and noodles, and those coming from southern China largely prefer the Chaozhou (Teochiu) dishes, which are the most popular dishes. Different experiences thus embedded different characteristics into their dietary habits.

The third category pertains to performing arts. Among Hong Kong's voluntary associations, those established by Southeast Asian Chinese are famous for their talents in performing arts. Influenced by Indonesian culture and tradition, Indonesian Chinese are skilled at playing music, singing, and dancing. They organised various dance groups, choruses and orchestras. Regular musical competitions or performing parties organised by associations can be seen in this community. And from time to time, they would send their performing groups to mainland China on a performance tour. It is interesting to note that, as is the case with food and language, the performances given by them also show a mixture of Indonesian culture and Chinese culture. On the one hand, they are deeply engrossed in performing Bali-style dance or Madura folk dance and sing the song "The Solo River"; on the other hand, they love to sing popular Chinese songs of the 1960s and 1970s. But they never allow local popular Cantonese songs at their parties. When asked why that was the case, only a simple answer was given: "We do not like it." Such resistance to local Hong Kong culture could probably be cited as a footnote to their sojourning mentality mentioned above.

Conclusion

It is obvious from the above discussion that the returned overseas Chinese community of Hong Kong is a very special Chinese community. Because of their unique experiences, they have developed their own culture differently from that of other ethnic groups in Hong Kong. Although they are part of the Chinese ethnic group, these people who were born overseas still had to learn how to adapt to local society when they moved back to mainland China in the 1950s and 1960s or to the former British colony after the 1970s. Subjected by their own experiences and a variety of influences imposed upon them by local society and culture, they gradually developed new multiple identities in the process of acculturation and accommodation.

At the same time, they have built up their own voluntary associations and networks extending to mainland China and Southeast Asia. In contrast to the traditional Overseas Chinese societies, ties of lineage, dialect, and ancestral homeland are no longer playing an active role in their community. Newly-created ties such as Nanyang homeland ties, Southeast Asian school ties, and Southeast Asian language ties (here mainly referring to *Bahasa Indonesia*) have replaced traditional ones and have become new organising principles for them.

As part of the Overseas Chinese community of Southeast Asia, these returned Overseas Chinese have actually sought their cultural roots more in their tropical homelands than in mainland China. Their bitter experiences in China further strengthened their longing for their Southeast Asian homelands. Partly because of this, multiple identities are frequently seen in this community. At the same time, they identify themselves with China, with Southeast Asian homelands such as Indonesia, and, to a lesser extent, with Hong Kong where their families are now based. It is very difficult for them to decide on any single identity.

Notes

[1]For an overall survey of migration from the mainland China to Hong Kong after World War II, see Li (1997, pp. 24–29).

[2]Thus far, only two Australian historians have studied the returned overseas Chinese. They conducted several short periods of fieldwork in Hong Kong from 1984 to 1986 and interviewed a number of Indonesian Chinese. Based on these interviews, they published two joint articles. Their research interest and emphasis, however, was confined to the tragic experiences of these returned overseas Chinese in mainland China from the 1950s to the 1970s, leaving the history of this community in Hong Kong untouched (Godley 1989, pp. 330–52; Godley & Coppel 1990, pp. 179–98). Apart from these, a fieldwork report focusing on the Hong Kong Alumni Association of Palembang was published in a Chinese journal in late 1999 (Wang 1999, pp. 55–66).

[3]Chiu (1995) provides a detailed account of the discriminatory policies imposed upon Indonesian Chinese in the early nation-building period.

[4]Detailed accounts of the experiences of these returned overseas Chinese in mainland China from the 1950s to 1970s are available (Frolic 1980, pp. 100–121; Godley 1989; Godley & Coppel 1990).

PART TWO

Chinese or Western Education?
Cultural Choices and Education

CHAPTER 5

Chinese Education and Changing National and Cultural Identities among the Overseas Chinese in Modern Japan: A Study of Chûka Dôbun Gakkô [*Tongwen* Chinese School] in Kobe

Benjamin Ng Wai-ming

The situation of the overseas Chinese in modern Japan is an important but neglected area in overseas Chinese studies. Although there are a considerable number of Japanese writings written by popular authors and journalists on interesting topics such as gourmet culture and business practices among Chinese merchants for general readers, scholarly works are few (Ng 1998, pp. 61–67). In recent years, however, there have been some stimulating discussions about the identity of overseas Chinese in modern Japan (Guo 1999 & Zhu 1993). Based on large-scale surveys and interviews regarding the political, social, and cultural life of Chinese residents in the Chinatowns of Kobe and Yokohama, these studies discuss the identity of overseas Chinese in contemporary Japan from a sociological perspective. This paper, however, looks into the issue of changing identities among overseas Chinese in modern Japan from a historical perspective, focusing upon the historical development of the Chûka dôbun gakkô (*Tongwen* Chinese School) in Kobe, the largest Chinese school in Japan. It aims to deepen our understanding of the relationship between Chinese education and the formation and transformation of national identity among overseas Chinese in modern Japan and of the impact of

changes in Sino-Japanese relations on overseas Chinese in Japan. Since
English and Chinese sources are very limited, this paper uses mainly
Japanese sources, both primary and secondary. Some data has been
acquired through interviews.

This paper consists of three major parts. Part one traces the
transformation of the national identity of Chinese residents in prewar
Japan from regional to national through an overview of the early history
of the Chûka dôbun gakkô. Part two discusses the national identity crisis
among Chinese residents in early postwar Japan, using the issue of building
a new campus for the Chûka dôbun gakkô as the main point of reference.
Part three investigates the localisation of overseas Chinese in
contemporary Japan, highlighting the dramatic changes at the Chûka
dôbun gakkô designed to cater to the needs of a different Chinese
community.

From Regional to National Identity in Prewar Japan

Regional identity used to be very strong among Chinese in Japan. In the
late Qing and early Republican periods, the first identity of most Chinese
was their home province rather than the nation. Many considered
themselves as Cantonese, Fujianese, or members of some other sub-ethnic/
dialect group more than they did as Chinese. Likewise, Chinese residents
in prewar Japan had a strong sense of regional identity, supporting schools
and joining organisations associated with their home provinces.

More than ten Chinese schools existed in prewar Japan (Ichikawa
1988, 1.155–62; Ichikawa 1987, p. 168). Founded by southern Chinese,
either revolutionaries or reformists, early Chinese schools in Japan used
Cantonese as the teaching language. During this time, standard Chinese
was not yet established and people spoke their own dialects, such as
Cantonese, Mandarin, Shanghainese or Hokkien. In the Meiji period
(1868–1912), Cantonese was the most widely spoken dialect among
Chinese residents in Japan. Of the six Chinese schools founded in the
Meiji period, four used Cantonese as the teaching language and the
remaining two used Mandarin and Shanghainese respectively.

Before World War II, the Cantonese were the largest Chinese dialect
group in Kobe, and the Cantonese dialect was the main language used in

Chinatown and in Chinese schools in Kobe. The Chûka dôbun gakkô started as a Cantonese school to teach mostly southern Chinese. In response to an appeal by Liang Qichao (1873–1929), a famous political reformer from southern China, to provide new education to Chinese in Japan, the Chûka dôbun gakkô was founded in 1899 as the first Chinese school in Kobe and the Kansai area.[1]

The prewar Chinese community in Kobe was divided into two camps: Cantonese and non-Cantonese. Both camps had very strong regional identites and seldom communicated with each other and, at times, were even at odds. The Chûka dôbun gakkô was established and run by the Cantonese in Kobe. The majority of its teachers and students came from southern China. The school was closely associated with the Kantô kôsho (The Guangdong Association). In 1914, another Cantonese school, Kôbe kakyô gakkô (Kobe *Huaqiang* School) was established in Kobe. While the Southerners had the luxury of choosing schools, the non-Cantonese found it difficult to send their children to these Cantonese schools due to language and clan barriers. In 1919, the first Mandarin school, Chûka kôgaku (Chinese Public School), was founded by Chinese from the central provinces (Jiangsu, Zhejiang and Jiangxi, commonly referred to as Sanjiang) and Fujian. The school was located inside the Sankô kôsho (The Sanjiang Association) in Kobe. Teachers were recruited from northern China.

These Cantonese schools and the Mandarin school in Kobe were geographically close, but they had no formal or regular contacts. For instance, the Chûka dôbun gakkô was only a hundred meters away from the Chûka kôgaku, but their teachers and students only gathered once in a while for ceremonial functions. Students of these two schools created trouble like street fighting every now and then. Li Wanzhi, the principal of the Chûka dôbun gakkô for 40 years, from 1943 to 1982, recalled what he saw in the late 1930s when he was a teacher of the Chûka kôgaku:

> "The existence of these two schools [Chûka dôbun gakkô and Chûka kôgaku] showed how serious the problem of sectarianism among Chinese residents was. The two schools were only two or three minutes walking distance apart, but there was no communication between their teachers or students. Although we were all

Chinese, we saw each other as strangers when we met on the street. Every now and then, small altercations occurred between our students. We only had contacts occasionally to celebrate festivals or to greet visitors from China. During that time, the regional identity was very strong among Chinese residents. The old-generation Chinese residents disapproved of intermarriage with Chinese from other provinces" (Li 1997, p. 47).

The identity of Chinese in Japan began to change in the 1930s and 1940s. Sino-Japanese military confrontation prompted nationalism among Chinese residents in Japan, pushing Chinese residents from different backgrounds together. Chinese education was a good example to show the unity of Chinese residents in this difficult time. In the 1930s, there were only two Chinese schools in Kobe: the Cantonese-speaking Chûka dôbun gakkô and the Mandarin-speaking Shinhan chûka kôgaku (Kobe-Osaka Chinese Public School).[2] At first they had no communications but they gradually started working together when the Japanese government put them under surveillance after the Manchurian Incident in 1931. The Chûka dôbun gakkô and Shinhan chûka kôgaku closed temporarily after the Manchurian Incident, because nearly half of the Chinese population in Kobe (about three thousand) returned to China. When they were reopened, the atmosphere became very unfriendly towards the Chinese in Japan. For example, anti-Japanese textbooks published in China were confiscated by Japanese customs and Chinese schools were forced to use textbooks recommended by the Japanese government (Kôyama Toshio 1979, p. 70).

After the Marco Polo Bridge Incident in 1937, many Chinese residents returned to China. Anti-Chinese feelings grew and Chinese residents in Japan were regarded as citizens of the enemy. Administrators and teachers of Chinese schools were subject to frequent questioning by the police. Textbooks, lectures, and even students' school bags were checked to make sure that Chinese schools in Kobe advocated neither Communism nor anti-Japanese ideas. In the face of scrutiny and suppression from the Japanese government, Chinese sub-ethnic or dialect groups worked together to protect their mutual interests. In 1939, under Japanese government pressure, the Guangdong, Sanjiang, and Fujian associations were merged into the Kôbe chûka sôshôkai (The Kobe Chinese Chamber of Commerce) and the two Chinese schools in Kobe were combined into the Kôbe chûka dôbun gakkô (Kobe *Tongwen* Chinese School). The aim of these mergers was to put the Chinese community and Chinese education under Japanese government supervision, but unintentionally they further strengthened the rising national identity and unity among Chinese residents in Japan.

The Second Sino-Japanese War stimulated national sentiments and cultural pride among Chinese residents in Japan. More and more Chinese in Japan identified themselves primarily as Chinese rather than as Cantonese, Sanjiangese, or Fujianese. Although over 60 percent of students were Cantonese, Mandarin, the official language of China, was adopted as the teaching language at the Kôbe chûka dôbun gakkô. All Chinese, regardless of their place of origin, studied under the same roof. The school suffered from deficits and its survival depended upon the collaborative financial efforts by the Guangdong, Fujian, and Sanjiang groups in Kobe. The heads of these three groups gathered together frequently to discuss educational and business matters.

As the War progressed, the enrolment of the Kôbe chûka dôbun gakkô dropped, because a large number of Chinese residents in Japan returned to China. Why did so many Chinese residents return to China? It was because Chinese residents in prewar Japan regarded themselves as *kakyô* or temporary Chinese residents. They would go back to China one day, alive or dead.[3] They were neither naturalised nor received the status of permanent residents. Many shuttled between Japan and China regularly for trade or study. The Sino-Japanese traffic was relatively free and it was not difficult for them to return to China if anything went wrong in Japan. Although national sentiments were high among Chinese residents in Japan, it was unsafe for them to express these sentiments explicitly. Returning to China was the way to express their anger and mistrust.

The identity of Chinese in prewar Japan as temporary residents can be seen from the kind of Chinese education they received. The Chûka dôbun gakkô (and later Kôbe chûka dôbun gakkô) adopted the Chinese educational system. Unlike Japanese schools that started their new academic year in April and ended it in March, the school year of the Chûka dôbun gakkô and other Chinese schools in prewar Japan was from

September to July. The Chûka dôbun gakkô adopted the same curriculum and textbooks as public schools in China. Its Chinese education aimed at helping Chinese residents in Kobe return to China rather than to settle in Japan. Many of its graduates went back to China to study or work.

Mandarin was the only language used at the Chûka dôbun gakkô. Almost all teachers were recruited in China and could not speak Japanese. Most of the students were first or second-generation immigrants and they could speak Mandarin and at least one Chinese dialect, although Japan-born second or third generations were bilingual, speaking Japanese and Chinese fluently. Students were not allowed to speak Japanese at school under penalty of being fined. Gradually, Mandarin replaced Cantonese as the common language used in Chinatown.

Torn between Two National Identities in Early Postwar Japan

National identity among Chinese residents in Japan was further strengthened after the war. Regarded by the Occupation as citizens of an allied country, they enjoyed better social and economic status than before. The change in the ratio among different Chinese sub-ethnic groups after the war also helped to dilute regional identities.[4]

However, the confrontation between Communist China and Nationalist Taiwan spilt the Chinese community in Japan and caused a crisis in national identity among the Chinese residents. Two rival overseas Chinese organisations were founded in Kobe: the pro-Communist Kôbe kakyô sôkai (Association for Overseas Chinese in Kobe) and the pro-Guomindang Ryû-Nichi Kôbe kakyô sôkai (Kobe Association for Overseas Chinese Studying in Japan). Guomindang authorities founded the Ryû-Nichi Kôbe kakyô sôkai in 1946 to unite all Chinese in Kobe. In 1957, some pro-Communist elements left this pro-Guomindang organisation and founded the Kôbe kakyô rengikai (Association for Promoting Friendship among Overseas Chinese in Kobe, later renamed as the Kôbe kakyô sôkai in 1976). The Kôbe kakyô sôkai had more members than the Ryû-Nichi Kôbe kakyô sôkai.[5]

This spilt had a great impact on Chinese education in Kobe, since both pro-Communist and pro-Guomindang forces wanted to use Chinese education to increase their influence in the Chinese community in Kobe.

Before the War, the Chûka dôbun gakkô, like other Chinese schools, was basically pro-Guomindang, although it also employed some leftists as teachers. During and after the War, the Chûka dôbun gakkô gradually fell into the hands of the leftists. Leaders of the Kôbe kakyô sôkai and administrators of the Chûka dôbun gakkô were basically the same group of people. For instance, Li Wenzhi, the principal of the school, was the first president of the association. The second president, Lin Tongchun, is also the chairman of the school's executive board.[6]

In the 1950s, Taiwan's Guomindang authorities attempted unsuccessfully to take the Kôbe chûka dôbun gakkô over from the pro-Communist forces. The issue of building a new campus became their battleground. The old campus was destroyed in June 1945 and the school rented a Japanese primary school in 1946 as the temporary campus. In 1954, Chûka dôbun gakkô submitted its application for building a new campus to the Kobe municipal government. The Taiwanese Guomindang authorities lobbied Japanese politicians and bureaucrats to block this plan. Due to Taiwanese's intervention, the new campus plan was not approved until 1958.

Taiwan's Guomindang authorities also tried to sabotage the school's fund-raising campaign. For example, a group of Japanese founded a support group of the Chûka dôbun gakkô and planned to donate four and a half million yen to the school. Taiwan's Guomindang authorities warned that if the support group donated the money, their business interests in Taiwan would suffer and they would not even be able to get a visa to visit Taiwan. The support group was forced to disband. The Guomindang government in Taiwan promised to provide funds (30 million yen) for the construction of the new campus on the conditions that Li Wenzhi and some pro-PRC administrators resign and the size of the school's executive board be expanded from 25 to 70. Whether the Chûka dôbun gakkô should accept Taiwan's financial assistance or not was debated hotly among school administrators and Chinese community leaders in Kobe.[7] After many twists and turns, the school decided not to accept Taiwanese assistance but to raise the funds itself. Pro-Taiwanese members were expelled from the school's executive board. When the school wanted to get a 50 million yen loan from the Bank of Tokyo, Taiwan tried to block this loan in vain. The lion's share of the fund came from the Chinese community in Kobe itself. For instance, the pro-PRC entrepreneur, Lin Tongchun, donated five million yen or 40 percent of his wealth to the school. The PRC government secretly remitted 17 million yen to support the school.

Despite all of these difficulties, the new campus was completed in September 1959. The Chûka dôbun gakkô remained a pro-PRC school. It received financial support from the PRC government until the 1960s. PRC leaders like Liao Chengzhi in 1973 and Deng Xiaoping in 1978 visited the school during their visit to Japan. The school held memorial services for deceased PRC leaders. In 1969, the PRC national table tennis team visited Kobe as a part of its sports diplomacy tour and had a tournament with the table tennis team of the Chûka dôbun gakkô.

Although the Chûka dôbun gakkô became pro-Chinese in the early postwar period, it did not discriminate against students from Taiwan or students who had a pro-Taiwanese background. Shortly after the War, the number of Chinese in Japan increased tremendously mainly due to the influx of Taiwanese. The Taiwanese became new Chinese residents in Japan (shinkakyô). The Chûka dôbun gakkô created special classes for Taiwanese students who made up about 20 percent of its enrolment. Nowadays, administrators and teachers of the Chûka dôbun gakkô are all pro-PRC. They visit mainland China regularly, but cannot get visas to Taiwan. The school adopts Chinese official textbooks published in the PRC and teaches simplified Chinese characters. It has connections with government organisations and schools in mainland China and pro-PRC organizations in Japan, but seldom communicates with the pro-Taiwan Ôsaka chûka gakkô (Osaka Chinese School), the other Chinese school in the Osaka-Kobe area.

The Chûka dôbun gakkô has played an important role in shaping the political orientation of Chinese residents in Kobe, turning the majority of its population pro-PRC. The rivalry between mainland China and Taiwan, however, also alienated some Chinese in Japan and promoted their localisation.[8]

The Making of a New Identity in Contemporary Japan

The Chûka dôbun gakkô, like the other four Chinese schools in contemporary Japan, is a whole-day private school that is not a part of the regular Japanese educational system. The school includes a six-year primary school section (thirteen classes) and a three-year secondary (or junior high) school section (six classes). It does not receive subsidies from the Ministry of Education, Culture, Sports, Science and Technology of Japan and thus has the autonomy to decide its own curriculum and textbooks. The school constantly runs in the red. About 60 percent of its revenue comes from school fees and the rest from donations. As the largest Chinese school in Japan and overseas, the Chûka dôbun gakkô has more than six hundred students and forty-some teachers in a campus of about six thousand square feet. It serves as the center of Chinese education for overseas Chinese in Western Japan or the Kansai area. It has a dormitory mainly for students from the Kansai region. Of these forty-some teachers, only two or three are Japanese. The rest are overseas Chinese whose grandparents or parents came to Japan from different Chinese provinces.

The Chinese community in postwar Japan has undergone great changes. It has been transformed from a foreign community to a localised ethnic community. The new generation of Chinese has developed a new national and cultural identity.

Before the establishment of diplomatic relations between Japan and the PRC in 1972, it was difficult for Chinese residents in Japan to go to mainland China or for Mainland Chinese to come to Japan. This had a tremendous impact on the identity and psychology of Chinese in Japan. Since they were cut off from mainland China, they began to establish their identity as *kajin* (permanent Chinese residents) in place of *kakyô* (temporary Chinese residents). Going back to mainland China was no longer an option or a dream and they had to settle permanently in Japan.[9] Localisation accelerated in the 1960s mainly due to economic growth in Japan and the Cultural Revolution in China. The living standard gap between mainland China and Japan widened and the Cultural Revolution alienated overseas Chinese. Regardless of the difficulties, even until the early 1960s, some graduates of the Chûka dôbun gakkô went back to mainland China to work, study, or settle. This trend stopped after the persecution of returning overseas Chinese during the Cultural Revolution.

In response to the localisation of Chinese residents in Japan, the Chûka dôbun gakkô has also modified its educational goals, curriculum, textbooks and school system. Regarding the goals of the Chûka dôbun gakkô in the postwar period, Li Wanzhi said:

"Our goal is to promote the consciousness [among overseas Chinese] of being Chinese and to know our motherland [China]. We are not promoting narrow-minded national education. We must cultivate people with an international sense to promote Sino-Japanese friendship" (Kôbe 1987, p. 79).

Chen Shunchen, a popular writer and a former member of the executive board of the Chûka dôbun gakkô, emphasizes the value of Chinese education to Japan. He has written that:

"The existence of people who know Chinese culture and language in Japan helps to enrich Japanese culture. People with different talents can cover Japan's weak spots. Our goal is to cultivate this kind of people" (Kôbe 1987, p. 86).

From the above-mentioned citations, we can understand that the localisation of the school is quite obvious. The importance of the Chûka dôbun gakkô, as they put it, is to train talents for Japan in an age of internationalisation rather than for the PRC in its modernisation drive.

This transformation is also reflected in the new curriculum of the Chûka dôbun gakkô. In 1954, the school abandoned the Chinese academic year and adopted the Japanese system in which the new academic year starts in April instead of September.

The main objective of its primary school section (six-year system) is to teach the Chinese language for Chinese children in Japan. In order to have more time to teach Mandarin, the teaching hours are slightly longer than in Japanese public primary schools. Primary school students study Mandarin for ten to twelve hours a week and study Japanese for only one to three hours a week. By contrast, its secondary school section (three-year system) aims at relocating its students within the Japanese educational system so that they can enter Japanese high schools and then universities to become full members of mainstream society. Secondary school students spend five to six hours a week on Mandarin and four to five hours a week on Japanese. The main language used in the secondary school section is Japanese instead of Mandarin. The curriculum is more like a Japanese secondary school and the only major difference is that students have to study Mandarin and some subjects about China. Besides

Mandarin, Chinese history and Chinese geography are offered in both primary school and secondary school sections to increase students' knowledge of China. The school uses Chinese textbooks published in China and teaching materials compiled by its own teachers. Students study Chinese folk songs in the music class and Chinese calligraphy and painting in the art class. Many extracurricular activities are also related to Chinese culture, such as Chinese opera, Chinese dancing, the lion dance, etc.

Many students of the Chûka dôbun gakkô take the Chinese language proficiency test, a qualification examination open to everyone in Japan. Very few are able to pass the level two or above. For the new generation of overseas Chinese, Japanese is their mother tongue and Mandarin is their second language. Most cannot communicate with their parents in Chinese dialects.[10] Hence, Japanese is the family language in overseas Chinese families in Japan today. In the past, Chinese students were only allowed to speak Mandarin at school and for speaking Japanese they would be fined and punished. Now, since Japanese is the mother tongue of teachers and students, they speak both Mandarin and Japanese at school. Some Japanese is used even in the Mandarin class (Kôbe 1987, pp. 73–74).

The Chûka dôbun gakkô no longer recruits teachers from mainland China and has turned to overseas Chinese in Japan. The Chinese background of these locally recruited teachers (many are former graduates of the school) is not very strong, but they know how to make the Chûka dôbun gakkô more compatible with Japanese education and society.

Many young overseas Chinese in Japan face an identity crisis. Now, more than half of Chinese youths in Kobe consider themselves as Chinese residents in Japan rather than as Chinese or as Japanese.[11] The Chinese identity of the Chûka dôbun gakkô students is also weakening. They belong to the third to fifth generations and some have become naturalised Japanese. Almost all students of the Chûka dôbun gakkô are ethnic Chinese. Seventy percent of them hold Chinese passports (PRC and/or Taiwanese) and 30 percent have Japanese passports (Zhu 1996, pp. 84 & 157). The high percentage of naturalised Chinese is mainly due to the revision of the nationality law in 1985, which gives children of mixed marriage between a Japanese and a foreigner Japanese nationality. It also makes it easier for Chinese residents to apply for naturalisation. In the lower classes at the Chûka dôbun gakkô, there are more Japanese passport holders than Chinese passport holders.

For those who do not hold a Japanese passport, many use a Japanese first name in their Chinese passport, such as Chen Fujiko. In the name list of the Chûka dôbun gakkô's graduates, the number of Chinese residents with a Japanese first name increases from the upper grades to the lower grades. This is clear evidence of changing identities from *kakyô* to *kajin* among Chinese in postwar Japan. Chinese parents often do not choose a Chinese first name for their children, lest their children be subject to discrimination. Since their children will have to live their whole life in Japan, a Japanese first name is a natural choice, at the expense of ethnic identity.

In the early postwar period, more than 70 percent of Chinese families in Japan sent their children to Chinese schools. Now, it has dropped to less than ten percent (Zhu 1996, p. 152). The majority of Chinese families in Japan send their children to Japanese schools. This is another barometer of the localization of overseas Chinese in Japan. The number of students at the Chûka dôbun gakkô has declined considerably from its peak of over 900 in the late 1970s and early 1980s to around 600 in the late 1990s. Now 70 percent (or about 420) of its students come from Kobe City. It is obvious that more Chinese children study at Japanese schools than at the Chûka dôbun gakkô. Kobe has the largest Chinese community in Japan (about 11 thousand). About one-third or 3,700 are students. In other words, only about 14 percent of young people of Chinese origins in Kobe attend the Chûka dôbun gakkô and the rest go to Japanese schools.

Intermarriage between overseas Chinese and Japanese is very common, a fact that further dilutes the national and cultural identity of overseas Chinese in Japan. In the past, Chinese residents tended to marry Chinese. The Kôbe chûka seinenkai (Kobe Chinese Youth Association) was founded in 1945 with the main objective of promoting marriage among young Chinese in Kobe. Now the Chinese community is less exclusive and intermarriage between overseas Chinese and Japanese has become the rule rather than the exception. Eighty to 90 percent of young Chinese marry Japanese (Guo 1999, pp.78, 183). Their children will hold a Japanese passport and become Japanese. Children of mixed marriages, no matter whether the father or mother is Chinese, will lose their Chinese identity.

They will adopt a Japanese name and usually go to a Japanese school (especially when the father is Japanese). Young Chinese in Japan are very similar to young Japanese in their looks, language, values and social life. They have more Japanese friends than Chinese friends.

The older generation of overseas Chinese experienced discrimination in their choice of careers. Very few could work for the government or big companies and many engaged in trade, the restaurant business, or real estate. The new generation of overseas Chinese have a better opportunity to advance in their careers than their parents, who had engaged in the so-called "three knives business" (*sanbadao*) — cooks, tailors, and barbers. Education is the key to climbing the social ladder. However, the Ministry of Education does not recognise the qualifications given by Chinese schools. For graduates of the Chinese school, they have to enter prestigious high schools and universities to have a promising future. The Chûka dôbun gakkô runs no high school. The majority of its graduates go to Japanese high schools and then universities. If the graduates want to enter the Chinese high school, they have to go to the Tôkyô chûka gakkô (Tokyo Chinese School) or Yokohama chûka gakuin (Yokohama Chinese Academy). This is very unlikely because the Japanese government does not recognise the qualifications of Chinese high schools and the two Chinese high schools are pro-Taiwan with no connection to the Chûka dôbun gakkô.

Ironically, young overseas Chinese feel that they are Chinese only when they are discriminated against in jobs and marriage. Although Japan-born overseas Chinese hold permanent residentship, they have to apply for an "Alien Registration Card" (*gaikokujin tôroku*) and renew it once every three years. They cannot vote or work for the central government. Thus, Chinese origin is a burden to them. While some are proud of being Chinese, others want to hide this identity. Now, the majority of overseas Chinese dream of living in Japan like a Japanese rather than returning to China as a home-coming queen.

Problems in student enrolment and finance have forced some Chinese schools to close.[12] In order to survive, the Chûka dôbun gakkô should carry out reforms to cater to the needs of new generations of Chinese residents and the age of internationalisation (*kokusaika*). While the size of the Chinese community is diminishing due to naturalisation, the Chûka dôbun gakkô should open itself up and actively recruit two groups of people: the first-generation Chinese in Japan and the Japanese.

While fewer Chinese families and families of mixed marriage send their children to the Chûka dôbun gakkô or other Chinese schools, many "overseas Chinese candidates" (jûnkakyô) including Chinese students, researchers, trainees, and professionals in Japan send their children to Chinese schools. The number of Chinese students in Japan alone is around 17 thousand (Ichikawa 1988, 1.69). Some of them will eventually settle in Japan and become first-generation Chinese immigrants. They are the new blood and hope for the shrinking and localising Chinese community.

In recent years, due to the government's promotion of internationalisation, the number of Japanese parents who want to send their children to study Mandarin at the Chûka dôbun gakkô has increased, since they believe that mastering a foreign language will give their children more opportunities in their future. However, the Chûka dôbun gakkô tries to discourage them and only accepts their applications on a case-by-case basis (Sugawara 1979, p. 282). It should be open to all Japanese and foreign nationals in Japan to study Mandarin and Chinese culture, which can serve as a kind of melting pot for international exchange.

The financial assistance from the Japanese government is needed to revive the Chûka dôbun gakkô. The school should make the government understand its unique contribution to Japan, such as training diplomats, China specialists, and interpreters.[13] The Chûka dôbun gakkô is taking some initiatives to seek the cooperation of six other foreign schools (five are American and European and one is Korean) in Kobe to lobby the Japanese government to recognise their contribution to Japan in this age of internationalization (Yasui & Chen 1996, pp. 8, 10).

Conclusion

Through this historical overview of the Kôbe chûka dôbun gakkô, from its founding in 1899 to the present, we can see that the national and cultural identities of Chinese in Japan has undergone several major changes in the last century. Chinese in prewar Japan saw themselves as kakyô or temporary Chinese residents. Chinese identity was transformed from regional to national, or from Cantonese/Fujianese to Chinese in Kobe.

After the war, Chinese identity changed from temporary Chinese residents to permanent residents or from *kakyô* to *kajin*. The Chinese community has been localised. In recent years, due to the naturalisation of overseas Chinese in Japan, the identity of the new generation of overseas Chinese is gradually changing from overseas Chinese to Chinese Japanese or from *kajin* to *Chûgokukei Nihonjin*. It seems that the weakening of the Chinese community in Japan is inevitable. The Chûka dôbun gakkô must reform to serve the needs of a changing Chinese community and Japanese society in order to survive.

Notes

[1]The Chûka dôbun gakkô was the third oldest Chinese school in Japan, founded two years later than the Daidô gakkô (Grand Peace School) in Yokohama and a few months later than the Tôkyô daidô kôtô gakkô (Tokyo Grand Peace High School) in Tokyo.

[2]The Shinhan chûka kôgaku was the result of the merger of the Kakyô gakkô and Chûka kôgaku in 1932. Teachers and students were mainly Sanjiangese and Fujianese. The merger is the best example of the emergence of a national consciousness that overcame regional differences.

[3]Dead bodies (in the case of northern Chinese) or bones (in the case of Southern Chinese) were shipped back to China from Kobe in the prewar period. However, this practice was discontinued after World War II (Kôyama 1979, pp. 104–108).

[4]Before World War II, the Cantonese were the largest Chinese sub-ethnic group in Japan and the Cantonese dialect was the main language used in the Chinese community. After the war, the composition of the Chinese community in Kobe became more complicated. While the Taiwanese and Cantonese are the largest sub-ethnic groups, the Fuqing Fuzhou people who came from Northern Fujian have become the most powerful Chinese sub-ethnic group. Chinese community leaders and administrators of the Chûka dôbun gakkô speak the Fuqing (also called the Minbei dialect instead of Cantonese or Mandarin).

[5]Now, the Kôbe kakyô sôkai has about 7,000 members, whereas the Ryû-Nichi Kôbe kakyô sôkai has about 5,000 members. Many overseas Chinese in Kobe have registered as members in both organisations (Kôbe 1987, pp. 151–53).

[6]Another example of this close affinity between the Kôbe kakyô sôkai and Chûka dôbun gakkô is that after the Kobe Earthquake of 1995, the Kôbe kakyô sôkai used the school as its headquarters to carry out relief measures (Zhu 1993, pp. 196–203).

[7]For a first-hand account of the tug-of-war between pro-PRC administrators and pro-Taiwan groups over this issue, see Lin 1997, pp. 161–70 & Min 1997, pp. 123–29.

[8]In recent years, the relationship between pro-PRC and pro-Taiwan schools has improved considerably. For example, after the Kobe Earthquake, the Ôsaka chûka gakkô sent a donation to the Chûka dôbun gakkô and its chancellor attended the memorial held at the Chûka dôbun gakkô (Yasui & Chen Laixing 1996, p. 45).

[9]Overseas Chinese live and die in postwar Japan. An example to show the difference in identity between Chinese residents in Kobe before and after World War II is that of how the body of the chairman of Kôbe kakyô rengikai, who died in Beijing during his visit in 1975, was sent back to be buried in Kobe (Kôbe 1987, p. 282).

[10]Usually, brothers and sisters talk to each other in Japanese. Parents talk to their children in their Chinese dialects and the children reply in Japanese (Kôbe 1987, p. 114).

[11]According to a survey conducted by the Kôbe chûka seinenkai (Kobe Chinese Youth Association) on 110 young Chinese in Kobe and Osaka, more than half identified themselves as Chinese residents in Japan and not as Chinese or as Japanese (Kôbe 1987, pp. 116–17).

[12]For instance, the Kakyô jichû shôgakkô (Zhizhong Chinese Primary School), an old Chinese school in Nagasaki, closed in 1988.

[13]For instance, the Chinese interpreter for Tanaka Kakuei and Zhou Enlai at the normalisation meeting was a graduate of the Chûka dôbun gakkô.

CHAPTER 6

Chinese Education in Prewar Singapore: A Preliminary Analysis of Factors Affecting the Development of Chinese Vernacular Schools

Wee Tong Bao

Much has been written about Chinese education in Singapore, both in Chinese and in English, and both have contributed to the understanding of the subject in their own ways. While some writings present a chronology of the development of the Chinese vernacular education in Singapore and Malaya, others have provided descriptive accounts of the history of selected Chinese vernacular schools, as seen in the works of Koh Soh Goh (Koh 1950, pp. 23–56), Tan Yeok Seong (Tan 1983, pp. 228–34), and others. Works in English includes those by David D. Chelliah (Chelliah 1948, pp. 79–84), Lee Ting Hui (Lee 1957, pp. 1–266), and others who analysed the topic within a political framework.

The Literature

Generally, studies on the topic written in Chinese have involved a great deal of research using primary sources. One of the earliest writings on this topic, Koh Soh Goh's *Chinese Education in Singapore* (in Chinese), gives a rather comprehensive narrative of the development of Chinese schools in Singapore from the earliest known school until the time of publication. Koh Soh Goh refers to the school systems, curricula, administration of the schools, and teachers' associations. He also includes two listings containing about 300 defunct and existing schools. He only provided, however, a brief history of only 31 schools and had no citations (Koh 1950, 4, pp. 23–56). Hence, while such genre allows for a quick overview of the subject, it does not allow for verification to aid further searches. There was also no attempt to "weave" the knowledge of all these schools into one simplified story or thesis.

Only descriptive accounts of the development of Chinese vernacular education have been presented in works by Wang Shiow-Nam (Wang 1970, pp. 115–40; Wang 1974, pp. 2–16) and Tan Yeok Seong (Tan 1983, pp. 221–36). Both writers having been in the education profession, their writings are based on personal observations and involvement.

Wang Siow-nam divided the development of the Chinese vernacular education into two periods in his work published in 1970 (Wang 1970, pp. 115–40). The first period, from 1819 to 1904, was that of old-style schools and reading clubs. The second period, from 1904 to 1941, saw the growth of modern education. However, in a later work on the development of Chinese vernacular education in Singapore, Malaya and Brunei, written in 1974, his periodisation differed from that in his earlier writing. He described the period from 1800 to 1870 as having been a culturally "barren" period while describing the next period, stretching from 1870 to 1941, as the period when the Chinese vernacular schools received support from the British Government (Wang 1974, pp. 2–16). In Tan Yeok Seong's analysis, the pre-war development of Chinese vernacular education has three periods, namely: 1854 to 1900 — the beginning of old-style schools, 1900 to 1920 — the period of growth of the modern schools and 1920 to 1957 — the period of turmoil and achievements (Tan 1983, pp. 221–36).

Essentially, works in English are generally discussions of how bureaucratic and political changes affected Chinese vernacular education. Most writings in English thus tend to contextualise their studies on the development of Chinese vernacular education using political markers and perspectives. While T. R. Doraisamy's *150 Years of Education in Singapore* contains a good historical account (in English) of the milestones and events which took place in the development of Singapore's education, his time markers follow Singapore's political development rather than the shifts inherent in the subject. As for the section on the development of Chinese education in Doraisamy's compilation, contributed by Gwee Hwee Hian, the development of Chinese vernacular education was divided into six periods, with the first three periods before World War II. The 1800s are considered the beginning of Chinese education in Singapore. The period from 1900 to 1919 is seen as the phase of rapid expansion and the period between 1920 to 1941 is seen as a period of conflict (Gwee 1969, pp. 82–98).

Also following political time-markers, H.E. Wilson studied the education policies of the four ruling governments in Singapore's history (Wilson 1978, pp. ix–xii). Such studies have been carried out by Kiong Beng Huat and Kok Loy Fatt in their studies of "Educational Progress in Singapore, 1870–1902" (Kiong 1953, pp. 10–20) and "Colonial Office Policy Towards Education in Malaya, 1920–1940" (Kok 1978, pp. 68–86), respectively. However, all these analyses excluded the other social-economic elements influencing the development of education.

In studies by Lee Ting Hui and Ong Her Yen (Ong 1974, pp. 138–144), political events in China are considered paramount to the development of the local Chinese vernacular schools. Lee Ting Hui sees the development of Chinese vernacular schools as having been shaped and influenced by political events in China, such as China's defeat in the first Sino-Japanese War (1894), the Wuchang Revolution (1911), early Republican education policies (1919), the re-organisation of the Kuomintang (KMT) in 1924, the success of the Northern Expedition (1928), the KMT's first official education policy formulation (1930), the end of the Northern Expedition (1938), and the outbreak of the second Sino-Japanese War, also in 1938 (Lee 1957, pp. 1–266).

Admittedly, much has been revealed about Chinese vernacular schools using the institutional-political approach, but there remain gaps in our knowledge of the subject. Local socio-politico-economic factors, which constituted the local environment that allowed for the development of modern Chinese education in Singapore, have yet to be fully examined. Local Chinese schools in the prewar days were also communal institutions and were not merely a product of policies and politics, whether local or foreign.

From the mid-1980s, some writers have begun to incorporate social analysis into their works. In the article, "Development of Chinese Education in Malaya before the Second World War" (in Chinese) published in *Chinese Culture in Malaysia and Singapore*, Tay Lian Soo employed first-hand primary information. The writer based his writing on various vernacular sources like school magazines and the vernacular press. Thus, he was able to provide insights into the organisation of the school's managing committees, funding of the schools, the school system, the syllabus and problems faced by the teaching staff of the schools. The writer is also one of the few to provide evidence that Chinese vernacular schools proliferated even after the passing of the School Registration Ordinance in 1920 (Tay 1986, pp. 102–114). However, Tay's insights on the various aspects of Chinese vernacular schools were not framed into a focused thesis but instead stand in isolation on their own (Tay 1986, pp. 128–79). In Chen Li Ren's academic exercise, "The development of Chinese Education in Singapore in the early 20th century", a narrative account of Chinese education in the late 19th and early 20th centuries is provided. Unlike earlier studies, Chen examined other factors that affected Chinese vernacular education, such as the nature of early modern Chinese schools, the girls' schools and vocational schools, the impact of China's politics on local education, the *huiguans'* involvement in education, the significance of the founding of the Chinese High School, and the 1920 School Registration Ordinance. Although Chen looks beyond a chronological study of the subject, as in Tay's study, each of Chen's various sections appears as an isolated discussion (Chen 1987–88, pp. 22–142). In both of these works, the discussions about the nature of the school did not reflect the effects of China's politics, the impact of the 1920 School Registration Ordinance, or the *huiguans'* role. Rather, the writer has chosen to discuss each of them in separate sections.

Considering Other Variables

Modern Chinese vernacular schools were social institutions where cultural values were perpetuated alongside the teaching of a modern curriculum. Their existence was not merely dependent on political factors, but on the interplay of social and economic factors as well.

The modern Chinese vernacular schools that eventually replaced the old-style schools were not too different from the latter at the beginning. Like the old-style schools, the venues for conducting lessons were either at shophouses, temples, or even in the residences of some of the sponsors. Sometimes, rent had to be paid for the use of these premises, but in some cases, the owners provided free use of the place.

In studies on the development of modern Chinese vernacular schools as described above, scholars have generally emphasised political aspects more than other aspects. The years 1911 and 1919, for example, have often been regarded as "significant" years in the development of Chinese education in Malaya. In the years before 1911, the spurs of modern Chinese vernacular schools had been attributed to the visits of Liang Qichao, Sun Yat Sen, Zhang Bishi, Liu Shiji, and other prominent personalities from China. Similarly, the 1919 May Fourth Movement and China's Nationalistic Government had been credited too. In reality, the growth and development of modern Chinese vernacular schools in Singapore in the first decade of the 20th century was by and large led by the dialect-*bangs* that set up modern schools for their own children. Whatever policies or politics had anything to do with the rise of these modern *bang* schools, the *bang raison d'être* should not be glossed over in the study of this topic.

In a corresponding manner, many studies have "politicized" the 1920 School Registration Ordinance of the British government. They concluded in their studies that the development and growth of Chinese schools were retarded by the Ordinance. As a result of the various regulations the schools had to comply with, fewer schools were established. While it is true that the Ordinance was implemented to curb the subversive nature of some schools, the government had also done much for the general improvement of the schools (SSGG 1920, No. 21).

These political time markers only explain some of the factors affecting the development of Chinese vernacular education in Singapore. Demand for education, and thus schools, and eventually modern schools, did not just simply appear overnight because of the impetus of external political events or local policies. Other socio-politico-economic factors had also played a part in the development of modern Chinese vernacular schools. By contextualising the study within the socio-politico-economic milieu of the period, we will be able to gain a better understanding of the subject. Such an analysis will require more in-depth study of the changing social milieu as well as the sources on Chinese vernacular education, including mapping out the correlation among them.

The Chinese Community in Singapore

The number of females and children immigrating to Singapore had increased greatly from the late 19th century until the outbreak of the Second World War. The number of female arrivals increased from 3820 in 1890 to 30,958 in 1934 (Figure 6.1). In the context of the gender ratio imbalance in nineteenth-century Singapore, it would be understandable that there was a lack of progress of Chinese vernacular schools. Hence, with more Chinese women in Singapore, and consequently more families formed and rooted, the demographics for school-going children would also increase. An increased communal need would correspond with a community response. Between 1895 to 1934, the number of Chinese children born locally rose steadily (Figure 6.2). Likewise, the number of child immigrants, though fluctuating between the period 1890 to 1934, also increased over time (Figure 6.3). It is interesting to note that the population of female and child immigrants (Figures 6.1 and 6.3) in Singapore experienced highs and lows at about the same points in time. The population figures in themselves may not say much, other than that more had settled and more were born locally over time. However, such a trend does strongly indicate that there was an increase in Chinese families in Singapore in the pre-war years. With the increase of families and hence, the size of the Chinese sub-committees, the need for communal institutions such as temples, clan associations, guild houses, and schools also increased. Chinese vernacular schools in Singapore were also such institutions shaped by the increases in the arrivals of Chinese female immigrants and child immigrants, and in the rise in the birth rate among the Chinese community. The overall impact of these social processes was the creation of more indigenised communities that sought the creation of, among other things, local schools in which to educate their children.

Education and Society

The Chinese community in Singapore, before the Second World War, did not just consist of immigrants from China. There were also the Straits-born Peranakan Chinese, many of whom were English-educated, who had also established schools for the education of their children. In Singapore, there were the Cheang Wan Seng School at Telok Ayer (1875), the Gan Eng Seng Free School (1886), the Cheang Jim Hean

Figure 6.1: Female Arrivals from China, 1890–1934

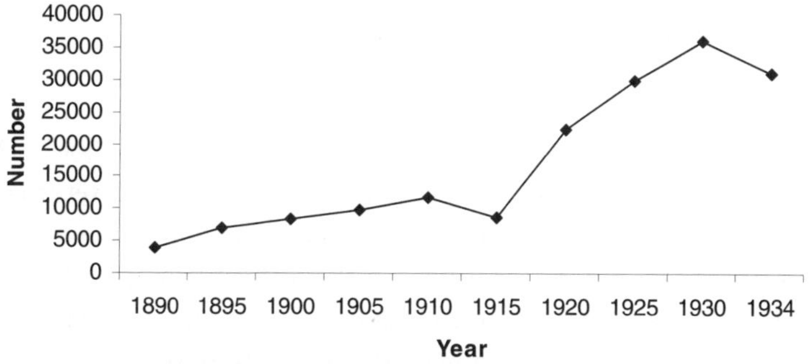

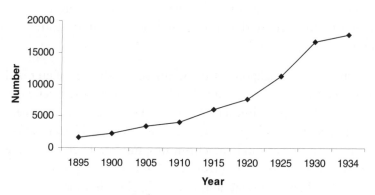

Source: *Straits Settlement Annual Reports*, 1861–1938. **There were fluctuations in the growth of Chinese female immigration throughout this period.**

Figure 6.2: Birth of Chinese in Singapore, 1895–1934

Source: *Straits Settlement Annual Reports*, 1861–1938.

Figure 6.3: Children Arriving from China, 1890–1934

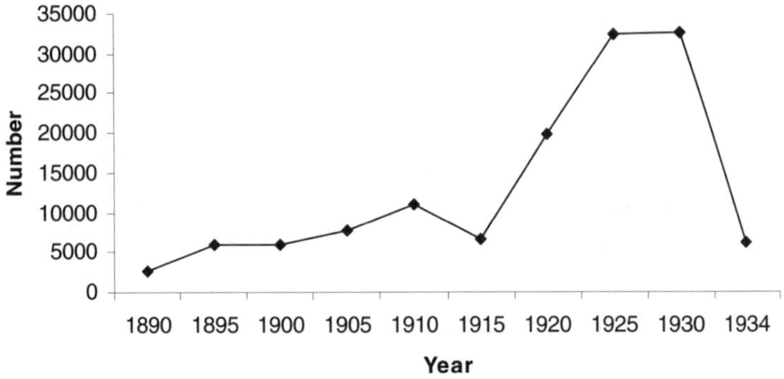

Source: *Straits Settlement Annual Reports*, 1886–1938.

Free School (c.1890), and the Singapore Chinese Girls' School (1899). In addition, there were also other English language schools set up either by the government or by missionaries, which accepted Chinese children as their students. Thus, long before the establishment of Chinese vernacular schools, many Chinese children were taught in English schools founded by various groups. Although, the instruction in these schools was in English, Chinese lessons were sometimes also part of their curricula, just as in the government schools. There arose a fear in some quarters that Chinese children attending these "modern" schools would eventually became anglicised and alienated. In a 1922 report by the local Catholic bishop, it was noted that some Chinese Catholic children were being anglicised to the extent that they could not use their mother tongue anymore:

> "In the city of Singapore, at the Chinese parish of Sts Peter and Paul, Fr Mariette encountered difficulties during the religious instruction of the children. Many of them are sent, at a very young age, to the English schools. It is a real problem to make them learn prayers and catechism in Chinese. There are some for whom it becomes impossible. Moreover, the priest has to create for them, a special division, the English division" (*Compte Reude* 1922).

Therefore, it could be possible that, to counteract this "threat" arising from the English schools, the various *bangs* of the Chinese community began to set up schools for their own children to aid the perpetuation of their own Chinese culture. Perhaps, on this level, the proliferation of the *bang* schools was a "concerted" effort of the entire Chinese community and not just a move to fulfill the interests of individual *bangs*. If the young, the future of any community, were not imbued with the cultural knowledge of their own communities, but with one that was considered alien, then it is certain that the future leadership of the respective community would pass on to members with different cultural orientations.

Aside from the social-cultural aspects of Chinese vernacular education in Singapore, one must also consider to what ends that education led. The Chinese were just as aware as the Europeans and Eurasians that education made it easier for a person to find a job. In British Singapore, learning English or a practical skill such as book keeping, was important for socio-economic advancement. Such a "modern" curriculum was not only implemented in the English schools but was offered in the schools set up by the Chinese immigrants. English was taught in the afternoons at Toh Lam School. It is apparent that the Chinese schools started English classes to provide the skills necessary for economic relevance. However, being acquainted with English was about more than just gaining employment, since one's social status was also dependent on acquiring the English tongue.

Another Look at British Policies

As mentioned earlier, policies of the British government did not always work against the Chinese schools. The role of the British colonial government was not simply to clamp down on subversive Chinese schools. On the contrary, the progress of the Chinese schools was a concern of the government, and attempts were made to achieve that goal. In 1925, an Education Conference attended by the island's educationists and directors of the Education Department was held in Singapore (SSAR 1925, p. 208). In this "business" conference, the practical problems of education in the Malay Peninsula were discussed (Conference 1925, p. 1).

During this conference, several issues on the teaching of Chinese in English schools and the teaching of English in Chinese vernacular schools were brought up. To the latter, the meeting discussed various practical ways of accommodating it in the current education system. Increasingly, many Chinese parents wanted their children to learn both languages, with a working knowledge of one and a more solid grounding in the other. In response to this, the Education Department started a class for the training of Chinese vernacular teachers. This was the more preferred way as the Department was not able to supervise the teaching of English directly due to financial constraints. In any case, the Chinese schools preferred to engage their own teachers. In addition, the meeting proposed a special English class to be formed in English schools whenever there were sufficient numbers of Chinese students joining the schools. Other proposals included starting night classes to teach simple English for business purposes at a fee (Conference 1925, pp. 5–7).

Additional evidence of government involvement to ensure suitable environs for schools can be found in the official working records of the British government. In 1924, when the Tuan Mong School wanted to build a three-storey building as a branch school at Minto Road, the Inspector of Schools (Chinese) reported that:

> "It is a good neighbourhood for a large school; there are several
> small private schools near and only one public school [Hokkien].
> If we can get the pupils from the private into the public schools,
> so much the better" (SIT 58/25).

Approval for the branch school was granted and the school committee went ahead to acquire the necessary land. When it ran into some problems in the process, it approached the Municipality for help. The Municipal Assessor then wrote a letter with the following paragraph to the owner of the land, Abdul Gaffar Bin Kassim:

> "I (Municipal Assessor) am of the opinion that his offer ($0.50 a
> foot) is a fair one and unless you can see your way to accept the
> same, the Commissioners will have to apply for powers to
> purchase it by Compulsory Acquisition in order that the building
> may not be held up … " (SIT 221/25).

Similarly, when the lining of a stretch of Outram Road would bring traffic too close to the school, the Senior Executive Engineer of Public Works Department wrote to the Singapore Improvement Trust on 1 November 1928 enquiring on the possibility to "take the road a little further away from the corner of Outram Road School ... (as) the Inspector of Schools has called my attention to the probability of the end rooms being rendered useless as class rooms" (SIT 1214/28).

The above are examples of the British Municipality and Inspectorate intervention directly on behalf of the Chinese schools. Other insights to the development of Chinese vernacular education in Singapore may well be possible if one incorporates other sources other than the traditional political and policy documents. By adopting a social perspective in examining British colonial policies, we would also gain a wider understanding of the role of the colonial administration and understand more of the social dynamics that shaped and influenced the development of Chinese schools.

The Schools and the Bang Communities

Between 1900 and 1910 several modern vernacular schools were established by the various dialectal *bangs* — Yeung Ching School in 1905, Yin Sin School in 1905, Tuan Mong School in 1906, Toh Lam School in 1906, Khee Fatt School in 1907, Yock Eng School in 1910, and others. However, to date, there are no known accounts of the rise of the big *bangs* in relation to the rise of the modern vernacular schools.

A look at the founders and financiers of the schools would also reveal that dialect group affiliation was the main factor in the establishment of these schools. Yin Sin School and Yeung Ching School were both established by the Cantonese *bang*, while the Teochews, Hokkiens, Hakkas and Hailams founded Tuan Mong School, Toh Lam School, Khee Fatt School, and Yock Eng School respectively. These schools were developed along *bang* lines. In the case of Yeung Ching School, it was first founded by a group of Cantonese merchants as the Guangzhao Xuetang on 3 June 1905. Later in that year, various Cantonese clan associations (mostly from the Guangdong and Zhaoqing areas in China) came together to raise funds to buy eleven houses at Park Road, nos. 13 to 23 (near Majestic Theatre) to house the school. The school was later renamed Guanghuizhao Yangzheng Xuetang in 1907. The amount raised to buy the houses came to 30 thousand dollars, and five of the houses, that cost ten thousand dollars, were donated by Look Yan Kit (Kreta 1993, p. 74; Koh 1950, p. 24; Yeung 1957, pp. 27, 31).

It is interesting to note that merchants from the various Cantonese clan associations pooled their resources to establish the school. Was such an act done merely out of the need to optimise financial resources, or was it a sign that a "modern" unified *bang* had risen? There were obvious advantages for these dialect *bangs* to set up schools for their own sub-committees, and, on a larger front, help establish schools to be shared by all in the Chinese-speaking community. If a more holistic approach was not adopted in the studies of the development of the Chinese schools in this topic, such social dynamics would have been overlooked.

Conclusion

From the various variables discussed above, one may conclude that local variables were also critical to the development of the local Chinese vernacular schools, besides the blossoming ideological developments in China. Most Chinese vernacular schools started off with mere enrolment of more than a dozen students, and over some years, expanded to hundreds of students, with a few schools even setting up branch schools. All of these developments certainly reflect a communal institution in transition and thus, a study of the development of these schools should include an examination of the wider context of change in society in order that a deeper understanding of the development of that topic may be attained.

While the changing political and bureaucratic environs, in Singapore and abroad, were important bricks in the evolution of the modern Chinese schools, there were other local catalysts for change. It was evident that changes had already taken place before the founding of the Republic of China and before the Nationalist Government issued any policies or regulations on the Chinese vernacular schools overseas. Clearly, there is still a rich story about the development of the Chinese vernacular schools waiting to be told. By simply viewing educational development as a function of political changes and policies, a whole wealth of knowledge about the social milieu and character of the Chinese vernacular schools in Singapore will be overlooked.

CHAPTER 7

Hokkien Immigrant Society and Modern Chinese Education in British Malaya, 1904–1941

Yen Ching-Hwang

Late Qing education reform had the biggest impact upon the rise of modern Chinese education in British Malaya. Humiliated by Japan in the First Sino-Japanese war (1894–95) and impressed by Japanese modernisation, some Qing high-ranking officials, such as Zhang Zidong, saw educational reform as an effective means of self-strengthening. But the reform had to be conducted within overall institutional reform that his predecessors in the Self-Strengthening Movement failed to grasp (Ayers 1971, pp. 152–95). Zhang's plan for the educational reform was contained in his famous treatise — Quanxuepian (*Exhortation of Education*) published in 1898 (Zhang 1963: 6.3702–50), and its publication had an impact on some senior bureaucrats. Zhang's work later provided a theoretical basis for Qing education reform after 1901.

Qing institutional reform at the turn of the 20th century was made possible by rapidly changing political circumstances and the dwindling fortune of the court. The Empress Dowager Cixi, the *de facto* ruler of the court, fled Beijing for Sian in October 1900 as the result of the occupation of the capital by the Allied forces following the disastrous Boxer Uprising. Obligated under the peace treaty as well as to recover the support for the crumbling dynasty, the Empress Dowager accepted the memorial presented by Zhang Zidong and Liu Kunyi, another high-ranking official, to carry out educational reform. In September 1901, an edict was issued to that effect. Provincial governments were instructed to convert old private academies and community schools into modern schools. The reform-minded of the officials were more active in carrying out the edict. Zhang Zidong, for instance, established at least eleven new schools of various kinds between 1901 and 1902 in Hunan and Hubei provinces, where he was the governor-general. When he took charge of Jiangsu and Jiangxi, he established more modern schools in these two provinces in 1903 and 1904 (Zhu 1963, pp. 5426–27). By 1904, the Qing dynasty had already established a modern education system based upon the Japanese model. It had an integrated structure, from primary schools up to high schools and universities. To control and manage the new education system, a Ministry of Education was established in 1905 (Zhu 1963, pp. 5426–27).

The impact of Qing educational reform was transmitted overseas to Chinese immigrant communities through Qing diplomats and immigrant leaders who had close relations with the court. In the case of British Malaya, the person who was instrumental in the establishment of the first modern Chinese school in the region was none other than Zhang Bishi (Chang Pi-shih, also known as Zhang Zhenxun, or popularly known in the West as Thio Thiau Siat). Zhang, a Hakka, was a Chinese community leader in Penang and Batavia, and a wealthy tycoon with a variety of businesses to his credit (Godley 1981). He was made first Chinese vice-consul in Penang in March 1893 (Yen 1985, p. 171). He rose rapidly in Qing official hierarchy, and was made, in 1905, China's Imperial Commissioner to promote business in Southeast Asia. Zhang's dual positions as an immigrant community leader and a Qing official enabled him to play the leading role in bringing modern Chinese education to the region. In 1904, with the support of a group of wealthy Chinese merchants, he founded the Zhong Hua School, the first of its kind in the Chinese immigrant communities in Southeast Asia (*Penang Sin Poe* 1 July 1904; *Lat Pau* 30 December 1904). The founding of this modern Chinese school was a great success. It attracted a number of students. It started with 240 students when the school was officiated in May 1904, and they were organised into eight classes. A headmaster and twelve teachers, all recruited from China, ran the school (Penang Chinese Vice-Consulate Records, 'Despatches' Vol. 6). It was placed under the control of a management board with 14 directors. They were further classified into two superintendents, six directors and six deputy directors, and all of them were elected to the board among wealthy Chinese merchants in Penang (Xuebu 1906; Penang Chinese Town Hall Minutes Vol. 2). The curriculum of the school was a combination of traditional and modern syllabi and the integration of Chinese and Western learning. Traditional Chinese subjects such as 'self-cultivation' (*xiushen*) and 'the study of the Confucian classics' (*dujing*) and modern subjects such as Chinese language, history and geography, plus Western subjects such as foreign language (English), mathematics, and physics were made compulsory for students (Y. S. Tan 1963, pp. 136–37; Y. S. Tan 1984, 2.242–44; Tay 1998, 1.101–02).

It is significant to note that this first modern Chinese school in British Malaya was to serve as a beachhead for the modernisation of the Chinese immigrant society. The study of modern subjects helped open the eyes of young ethnic Chinese who would see the world differently than had their parents generation. The modern contents of the subjects were not yet linked to meaningful nation-building, but a vague idea of educating children to be modern persons who had to understand history, geography, mathematics, and physics emerged. What should be noted further is that the school acquired strong community support as well as the endorsement of the Chinese government. The former was important because the school could not sustain its growth without strong financial backing; while the latter ensured the supply of teachers and teaching materials for the running of the school.

The founding of the Zhong Hua School had a profound impact upon the Chinese immigrant community in the region. From 1905 to 1911, a number of modern Chinese schools were founded in British Malaya. These included the Ying Sin Primary School (May 1905) (Xie 1965, p. 15), the Yang Zheng, Duan Meng, and Dao Nan primary schools (all founded in 1906) in Singapore (Yang Zheng xuexiao 1956, p. 31; *Lat Pau* 19 April 1906; Li & Lin 1936; Lin 1966, pp. 25–8); and the Confucian Primary School and the Kuen Cheng (Kun Zheng) Girls' School (both founded in 1907) in Kuala Lumpur (Sili Zun Kong Zhongxue 1965, p. 6; Zheng 1968, p. 11). Different Chinese dialect groups founded the majority of these schools (Xie 1965, p. 15; Yang Zheng xuexiao 1956, p. 31; *Lat Pau*

19 April 1906; Li & Lin 1936; Lin 1966, 25–8). Belonging to the major dialect group in Singapore, the Hokkiens were aware of the importance of modern education for their children in competition with other dialect groups. They were financially more powerful than their counterparts in Malacca and Penang. This was partly due to the rise of Singapore as a leading international port in the region since the second half of the 19th century (Wong 1978, pp. 50–84). More importantly, Singapore had a number of high profile Hokkien leaders who were also the leaders of the entire Chinese community on the island. Their lead in the quest for modern Chinese education guaranteed success. Under the leadership of Goh Siew Tin (Wu Shouchen), the Hokkien community founded in 1906 the Dao Nan Primary School (Daonan xuetang) that was opened in April 1907 (*Lat Pau* 16 & 23 April 1907; 2 May 1907). The preparatory committee for the establishment of the school was set up in 1906 with its first meeting convened on 8 November. The committee comprised of some influential wealthy merchants whose support was crucial for the success of this project. It raised a sum of 40 thousand dollars for initial expenses with pledges of monthly contributions from Hokkien shops and companies (Lin 1966, p. 25). Renting the Siam House on North Bridge Road as premises, the school started its classes in April 1907 with 90 students. Ma Zhengxiang, a Hokkien scholar, was appointed first headmaster together with eleven other teachers in the same year. All of the teachers, except one, were native Hokkiens, and most of them appeared to have been recruited from China (Lin 1966, pp. 46–47). With the strong financial support of the Hokkien community and the small student to teacher ratio, the early results of the school were excellent. This gave confidence to Hokkien parents who might otherwise have sent their children to local English schools. The popularity of the school was reflected by the rapid growth in student numbers that increased to 182 in 1908 and to 296 in 1909; and by 1911, the school had 304 students (Lin 1966, p. 44).

The school was placed under the control of a Management Board with 40 directors who were elected to their positions by the Hokkien community. Most of them were rich merchants who possessed social status as well as financial power. Goh Siew Tin, for instance, was elected the first chairman of the Management Board. He was a wealthy merchant

with high social status and political influence, and was the first president
of the newly-founded Chinese Chamber of Commerce of Singapore (Yen
1995b, pp. 142 & 155). Two other known merchants involved in the
founding of the Dao Nan School were Lee Cheng Yan (Li Qingyan) and
Teo Sian Keng (Zhang Shanqing). Both of these men were wealthy export
and import merchants. Lee was the leader of the Eng Choon (Yongchun)
sub-Hokkien dialect group in Singapore, while Teo was a director of the
Singapore Chinese Chamber of Commerce (Su 1948, pp. 59 & 63;
Singapore Chinese Chamber of Commerce Minutes 1.1–2; Yen 1986,
pp. 183 & 208). The involvement of wealthy Hokkien merchants in the
founding of first modern Hokkien school set the example of active
involvement of merchant class in the promotion of modern Chinese
education. With wealth, status, and community spirit, the merchants were
in the best position to undertake such a task. In return, they acquired
additional recognition of their leadership status in the Chinese immigrant
society. This pattern of active merchants' participation in education
continued throughout the period, and ended with Tan Kah Kee's founding
of Xiamen (Amoy) University in 1921 and Tan Lark Sye's founding of
the Nanyang University in 1953 in Singapore.

Republican Educational Reforms in China

The founding of the Republic in early 1912 brought a new education
system to China. Although late Qing educational reform had brought
changes in the structure of the school system and in curricula, the reform
was not thorough. Further, education was still geared to the preservation
of the dynasty, and the ideas of loyalty to the emperor and respect for
tradition were still alive. The founders of the new Republic were
revolutionaries who were more exposed than their predecessors — the
scholar-gentry — to foreign influence. They witnessed the rise of the
Western powers, the emergence of Japan which they had credited in part
to the result of introduction of modern education. In their eyes, education
was the instrument for nation-building, the key to wealth and power for
a new China. When Dr. Sun Yat-sen was inaugurated as the provisional
president of the new Republic, one of the early tasks he undertook was
the establishment of a new Education Ministry. He appointed Cai

Yuanpei, a known educationist, to be the first education minister (Li 1989, p. 354). Cai's achievements as education minister rested with his new ideas and his consolidation of a modern education system introduced in the late Qing period. He pointed out the traditional 'loyalty to emperor' and 'respect for Confucius' were no longer compatible with the spirit of the new Republic. They should be replaced by new values of "morality of citizens, militant nationalism, utilitarianism, globalism and aestheticism". Cai's views were incorporated into the government's education principles announced in September 1912 (Li 1989, p. 355). Cai's achievements included the promulgation of the educational ordinance in May 1912 in which the inadequacies and imbalance of the Qing educational reform were corrected. It consisted of the change of the name of school from '*xuetang*' to '*xuexiao*' and the title of headmaster from '*jiandu*' to '*xiaozhang*'; the replacement of Qing textbooks with new republican textbooks; the abolishment of the subject of 'study of Classics' from the curriculum; the abandonment of the link between education and bureaucracy; the introduction of co-education at the primary level; and the setting of high school education as general education (Li 1989, pp. 354–55; Peake 1970, pp. 75–76). The change in the nomenclature of the schools and personnel may seem trivial, but it nevertheless gave a sense of newness, the image of creating something new and a departure from traditional China. The abolition of the study of Classics and the replacement of Qing textbooks with new ones were designed to free Chinese children from the old frame of mind that encouraged students to look back to the past rather than forward to the future. The introduction of co-education was intended to remove gender barriers and ease traditional discrimination against females in the Chinese society. To set high school education as general education was aimed at lifting China's education and literacy standards. A popular belief among the Republicans at the time was that literacy was the key to national strength and democracy.

An outstanding achievement of the early Republican period was the promulgation of the "1912–13 School System" known as "Renzi Kueichou" school system (Renzi was the year of 1912 in the Chinese calendar, while Kueichou was the year of 1913 in the Chinese calendar). The new initiatives formalised the structure of the education system. The entire length of education was 18 years, divided into three different stages: primary education (seven years), secondary education (four years), and tertiary education (seven years).

Both primary and tertiary were sub-divided into two different phases: junior primary and senior primary education; and preparatory and normal tertiary education. In addition, two ancillary systems relating to vocational and teachers' training were attached. The former was divided into elementary and secondary schools; and the latter was subdivided into medium and higher normal schools (Li 1989, p. 356).

Even more significant was the reform of school curricula. In September 1912, the Ministry of Education promulgated the new curricula for all schools. In the junior primary schools, subjects of 'self-cultivation' (*xiushen*), 'Chinese language' (*guowen*), mathematics (*xuanshu*), 'handicraft' (*xougong*), drawing (*tuhua*), music (*gechang*) and 'physical education' (*tichao*) were offered. Extra 'sewing' (*fongren*) class was added for female students. At the senior primary level, Chinese history and geography were added with extra subject of 'agriculture' (*nongye*) for male students. In the secondary schools, in addition to those subjects taught at the senior primary, new subjects such as foreign languages, advanced mathematics (*suxue*), physics, chemistry, legal system (*fazhi*) and economics were introduced. For girls' schools, horticulture (*yuanyi*) and 'home economics' (*jiashi*) were added (Li 1989, p. 358).

Two important points need to be noted in this curriculum reform. Firstly, the removal of 'the study of classics' from both primary and secondary education freed the young minds from profound influence of Confucianism and some feudal values. It helped to prepare Chinese to accept new Republican values in order to build a new nation. Secondly, the introduction of natural science and technical subjects helped to create a modern civil society where its citizens could participate rationally in the moulding of the future of a new China.

Another major step in the Republican educational reform took place in 1922, a decade after the first major reform. The main thrust of the reform was in the structure of education. The length of overall education was shortened from 18 to 16 years. Primary education was reduced by one year from seven to six years. Secondary education was increased from four to six years. Tertiary education was restricted to four years for liberal arts and teachers' training degrees, and five years for professional degree such as law and medicine. Primary education was sub-divided into four years junior primary and two years senior primary. Secondary education was sub-divided into junior and senior with three years each. The new system was promulgated by the president of the Beijing government that was under the control of the Beiyang warlords (Mao & Shen 1988, pp. 79–83). Political instability and chaos at that time did not seem to have deterred reform initiatives. Perhaps the warlord regime in Beijing had also shared with the Republicans the idea of using education to strengthen the nation.

What motivated the reform was also partly due to the social and economic needs of the time. The post-war (the First World War) China saw the return of Western economic influence and the rise of Chinese modern industry. The need for literate workers in industry was greatly felt. The reduction of primary education from seven to six years facilitated the spread of literacy in society. Workers with six years education were able to perform their jobs satisfactorily in modern factories. This change helped pave the way for the development of modern Chinese industry.

The division of the secondary education into two stages served different purposes. Those students who were not inspired to pursue academic studies at the university could switch to technical education after completing three years in junior secondary school. The new system provided this flexibility. The 1922 educational reform, known as 'Renshu System' (Renshu was the year of 1922 in the Chinese calendar), became the cornerstone of the modern Chinese educational system. It was later retained and practised in China by the Nanjing government that came into power in 1927. The system appeared to have been adopted by the ethnic Chinese, including those in British Malaya.

Strong support for Southeast Asian Chinese for the 1911 Revolution predestined their close educational ties with China (Yen 1976; L.T. Lee 1987). After the founding of the Republic, the government, both central and provincial, was interested in promoting ethnic Chinese education. The governments in Fujian and Guangdong, the two provinces that provided most of the ethnic Chinese migrants to Southeast Asia, sent officials to tour the region for that purpose. In 1913, the Beijing government also involved Chinese diplomats for the protection and promotion of ethnic Chinese education. Since the founding of the

Nanjing regime in 1927, China further strengthened its educational ties. In 1929, an 'Ethnic Chinese Education Planning Committee' was established within the bureaucratic structure of the Ministry of Education. The committee was charged with the responsibility of planning and consultation over the ethnic Chinese education (Mao & Shen 1988, p. 366). Due to its close political ties with the ethnic Chinese, the Guomindang (Kuomintang, the Nationalist Party) which established the Nanjing regime, broadened its base of support by recruiting a number of ethnic Chinese leaders into its party structure — the Ethnic Chinese Affairs Committee (*Qiaowu weiyuanhui*). Some leading ethnic Chinese leaders such as Deng Zeju and Tan Kah Kee of British Malaya, and Xiao Focheng of Thailand, were recruited into the committee (Chang & Shen 1987, 1.282). They were able to provide up-to-date information that would help the Guomindang and its government to formulate a correct policy and strategy in handling ethnic Chinese education.

The Development of Modern Chinese Education in British Malaya, 1912–41

Modern Chinese education in British Malaya achieved its most remarkable growth during the Republican period between 1912 and 1941. It would not be an exaggeration to claim that without the developments that took place during this period, modern Chinese education would not have taken off and achieved what it has achieved in the region today. Three factors were responsible for such a rapid growth. Firstly, the founding of the new Republic in 1912 raised hopes that China would emerge as a rich and powerful state. Modern education was a means of achieving modern statehood. Secondly, the Republican government, particularly the Nanjing regime, had integrated ethnic Chinese education into its education system. The Chinese government was able to help solve the problems of the supply of teachers and textbooks, and to provide necessary advice. Thirdly, the new cultural movement unleashed by the May Four Movement in 1919 emphasised the importance of education as a means of salvation for China. This theme received good exposure in the Chinese newspapers in British Malaya. It inspired and encouraged people to take action to found modern Chinese schools (Mao & Shen 1988, pp. 15–53; *Nanyang Siang Pau*, 11 February, 14 March 1924).

The development of modern Chinese education during this period can be divided into two phases: the first phase, from February 1912 to February 1919, and the second, from March 1919 to December 1941. The former was characterised by rapid growth in the number of primary schools, while the introduction and growth of secondary education marked the latter. The euphoria of the founding of the new Republic combined with the efforts of Republican educational missions and resulted in the flourishing of modern primary schools in British Malaya. In the first phase, at least 19 main schools were founded in the region. This included six schools in Singapore and 13 in the Malay Peninsula (Xu 1949, pp. 19, 29–31; Tay & Gwee 1975, pp. 6, 12, 15, 173, 181, 186 & 247). What should be noted is the spread of Chinese schools to small towns such as Kampar, Sungei Patani, and Province Wellesley where Chinese children had access to modern Chinese education. It helped to bridge the gap between city and town in the area of educational services.

Compared with the late Qing period, modern Chinese schools in British Malaya during the Republican period were financially stronger. General awareness of the importance of education encouraged rich Chinese merchants to donate generously to Chinese schools. Most late Qing schools had to rent their premises and the basic equipment for teaching were inadequate, while the schools during this period were better equipped, and some of them had built their own premises (Xu 1949, pp. 25–27; Li & Lin 1936, p. 14). This meant that these schools could undertake long-term planning which would lead to improvement and expansion. Secondly, the curricula of the schools had also been modernised due to the impact of China's new education. The study of the Chinese Classics was removed and new subjects were introduced. Republican ideas and nationalist feelings were nurtured in the classrooms.

But the most important progress during this first phase of the Republican period (1912–19) was the growth of female education. In 1900, Dr. Lim Boon Keng in Singapore founded the first Chinese girls' school. But the school, Singapore Chinese Girls' School, used the medium of English and thus catered mainly for the Straits-born Chinese (Song 1967, p. 305). Huang Dianxian, the daughter of Wong Ah Fook

(Huang Yafu), a famous Cantonese business tycoon in Singapore and Johore, founded the first Chinese language girls' school in 1905 (Xu 1949, p. 46; Tay 1997, p. 48). We know almost nothing about this school except that it was named Hua Qiao Nu Xiao (Overseas Chinese Girls' School). With the impact of the activities of the Reformists led by Kang Yuwei and the Revolutionaries led by Dr. Sun Yat-sen, four other Chinese girls' schools were founded in British Malaya during the late Qing period, two each in Singapore and the Malay Peninsula (Xu 1949, p. 46; *Nanyang Zonghui Bao* 13 February 1909; Penang Sin Poe 8 January 1909; Kun Zheng nuxiao 1968, p. 76). The founding of the Republic in China lifted the status of women in Chinese society and gave female education in the Chinese communities a boost. At least five in Singapore and eight in the Malay Peninsula were founded during this period (Tay 1997, pp. 52–56; Xu 1949, pp. 48–50). What should be noted is that many of the founders of the girls' schools in British Malaya were merchants and intellectuals who were directly or indirectly associated with Sun Yat-sen's revolutionary movement (Tay & Gwee 1975, pp. 247–48; Yen 1976, 91–94). The success of the Republican revolution in China gave them special encouragement in the founding of these girls' schools, for they had shared with some revolutionaries' progressive ideas of equality of sexes in access to modern education.

The second phase of the Republican period (1919 to 1941) saw great advancement in modern Chinese education in the region. The importance of this period did not just rest with the increase in the number of the Chinese schools, but also with the strengthening of Chinese education as a viable alternative for Chinese children — the introduction of secondary education. Without Chinese secondary schools, modern Chinese education would have remained at a primary level, and it would probably have faded away *vis-à-vis* competition with English education. The founding of the Hua Qiao Zhong Xue (The Chinese High School) in Singapore on 21 March 1919 marked the beginning of this new phase. The school was to provide a much-needed secondary education for Chinese-educated students. Chinese students who completed six years of education and wished to pursue further study had to go back to China for that purpose. Of course, the distance and cost prevented many of them from doing so. The founding of the school was due partly to the efforts of the some far-sighted leaders such as Tan Kah Kee who were deeply committed to the idea of using education to strengthen China and Chinese race. With the support of a group of different dialect group leaders, he succeeded in founding the school in March 1919. Its classes commenced on 21 March with 73 students who came from different parts of Southeast Asia. Another 18 students were added in September. At that time, the school had 91 students with ten teachers (Nanyang Hua Qiao zhongxue 1969, p. 11; Xu 1949, pp. 50–51; Tan 1993, 1.30).

The founding of the Singapore Chinese High School was a major step towards the construction of a viable modern Chinese education system in the region. It was a significant step that set the example for others to follow. In addition, the founding of the school broke down the dialect barrier and promoted inter-*bang* (a dialect and geographical entity) co-operation in education. Since the second half of the 19th century, the Chinese community in British Malaya was plagued by the inter-*bang* rivalry and conflict (Yen 1986, pp. 194–98). Most of the modern schools founded during the late Qing period were very much *bang*-oriented with restrictions in enrolment. Although this restriction was gradually lifted after the founding of the Republic, the Chinese community had never had any real co-operation in the founding of schools. Tan Kah Kee's success in acquiring support from various *bang* leaders to found the first Chinese secondary school was a major breakthrough in modern Chinese educational endeavours.

Following the footsteps of the Singapore Chinese High School was Zhong Ling High School which was founded in Penang in 1923. It was built on the campus of the Zhong Ling Primary School, founded in 1917 by the Penang Philomatic Society (Ping Cheng Yeshu Baoshe), a reading club closely affiliated with Sun Yat-sen's revolutionary movement (Yen 1976, pp. 140, 260–64).

The leaders of the Philomatic Society were mostly staunch supporters of Dr. Sun Yat-sen and shared many of his aspirations. They were well aware of the importance of modern education and its potential contribution to the modernisation of local Chinese society. Under the leadership of Koh Seng Li (Xu Shengli) and Ong Keng Seng (Wang Jingcheng) a meeting was convened and they founded the Zhong Ling High School. The school was inaugurated on 20 January 1923 and it was the first Chinese high school in the Malay Peninsula (Tay & Gwee p. 1975, 164). Following the example of Zhong Ling, six other Chinese high schools were established in British Malaya in the 1920s, all of them on the Peninsula except for one in Singapore (Tay & Gwee 1975, p. 164; Wang 1963, p. 20; Tay 1999, 2.288).

The 1930s formed the peak decade for the development of Chinese secondary education in British Malaya. It not only witnessed the sustained growth of schools, but also an extension of secondary education. At least seven high schools were founded, three in Singapore and four in the Malay Peninsula. But the most important development during this decade was the introduction of the senior secondary education. All of the high schools founded in the 1920s were confined to junior secondary, providing students with three years education after completion of six years of primary school. It was comparatively easy to provide teachers and resources for junior secondary students, but senior secondary education that involved more intensive teaching and specialisation in subjects required better qualified teachers and equipment. Without the introduction of senior secondary education, Chinese-educated students would not have been able to pursue their tertiary education in China. To meet such a need, Au Boon Haw (Hu Wenhu), a Hakka community leader and a Chinese medicinal tycoon in Singapore, took the, lead to introduce senior secondary classes in the Nanyang Girls' High School in Singapore. He donated five thousand Singapore dollars as the basis of the school's development fund, and a preparatory committee was established in 1930 to co-ordinate the work. A fund-raising campaign was successfully launched with strong community support. The school was physically extended to accommodate new senior classes. New equipment was purchased and a new library was established (Xu 1949, p. 55). The example set by the Nanyang Girls' High School was soon followed by other high schools in the region. In the period between 1930 and 1941, there were at least ten high schools offering senior secondary classes (Tay & Gwee 1975, pp. 9–10).

There were many problems with Chinese secondary education. Two notable ones were small enrolments and shortage of funds. Many Chinese high schools started with a small number of students, and enrolments stagnated. For instance, the Pei Yuan High School in Kampar, Perak, started with a dozen students in 1941. The Kuen Cheng Girls' High School in Kuala Lumpur only had 20 students when it started its secondary classes. The Zhong Hua High School in Seremban started with 26 students (Tay & Gwee 1975, p. 13). Student numbers either stagnated or declined. Even the first high school, the Singapore Chinese High School, had a rather poor record of growth. In its slightly more than one decade from 1919 to 1929, student numbers only doubled from 91 to 180 (*Nanyang Siang Pau* 1 January 1929). Small enrolment meant a small sum of fees collected from students and school coffers suffered the shortfall of income. In turn, the schools were unable to appoint more staff, and the need for specialisation in teaching was not met. As a result, the standard of education dropped. Worse of all, the dwindling enrolments, plus the impact of the downturn of the economy of the Chinese community, took their toll in the Chinese high schools in British Malaya. For instance, the Duan Meng (Tuan Mong) High School in Singapore started a junior secondary class in January 1924 with a small number of students. It was forced to discontinue in the following year as the enrolments declined (Li & Lin 1936, pp. 21–22).

The shortage of funds was the second major problem facing Chinese high schools. The problem was an inherent one. All of the Chinese high schools were either supported by a particular bang or by the entire Chinese community, and this support was subject to the fluctuations of the fortunes of the *bang* and the community. When the prices of rubber and tin — two mainstays of the Malayan economy — were good and the community witnessed an economic boom, the support for Chinese high schools was strong; but the financial support dissipated when the community was hit by economic recession. Although government grants-in-aid for Chinese schools were introduced in 1923, the amount received from the government per student was little in comparison with the aid given to the English school students (L. E. Tan 1997, p. 21). The stable income of a Chinese high school derived mainly from tuition and auxiliary fees charged on students; and also the monthly contributions promised by shops and trading companies. If these incomes were proven to be insufficient, the school had to raise funds from the general public by way of staging drama performances or concerts. Increasingly, the schools had to depend upon fund-raising for their survival and expansion (*Nanyang*

Siang Pau, 9, 13, 18 & 21 February 1924; 22 March 1924; 3, 14 & 30 April 1924; 1 & 20 May 1924; 26 & 27 February 1929; 5 & 18 April 1929; 27 December 1929). To overcome the financial problems of the Chinese high schools, a contemporary observer in early 1929 suggested a levy on the commodities traded by the Chinese. The levy was to be based upon the volumes and values of the goods exported and imported, and it was to be taken charge by *gonghui* (public associations) (*Nanyang Siang Pau* 1 January 1929). The suggestion sounded good but impractical, and it was not enforcable. The Chinese community in the late 1920s was still divided into *bangs* though inter-*bangs* difference had narrowed. Further, not all businessmen were enthusiastic about Chinese secondary education although a minority of them were converted believers. Without the full support of the business community, the scheme would not have worked. The Chinese community had no power to impose a levy and enforce it successfully. Therefore, the proposal was never taken up.

Hokkien Community and Modern Chinese Education in British Malaya

The Hokkien community was the earliest ethnic Chinese community established in British Malaya. It first took roots in Malacca, an international entrepot, in the 15th century. Hokkien traders formed the backbone of a small Chinese community in Malacca in the 16th and early 17th centuries (Yen 1993, p. 681; de Eredia 1930, p. 19). The numbers of Hokkien grew rapidly after the founding of Penang in 1786 and Singapore in 1819 (Mak 1995, pp. 100 & 120). The Hokkiens, being the earliest Chinese settlers in the region, entrenched themselves in trade, and had a lion's share of some important lines of business. With their economic power, the Hokkiens played an active role in the promotion of modern education. In Singapore, the founding of the Dao Nan School in 1907 was the first step taken by the Hokkien community. It was among the best of the early 20th-century Chinese schools, characterised by a sufficient number of teachers, small class teaching, and good teaching facilities. Stimulated by the founding of the Republic in early 1912, the Hokkien community in Singapore founded two more modern Chinese schools: Ai Tong School in 1912 and the Chong Fu Girls' School in 1915.

The founding of the Chong Fu Girls' School was of some significance. The first modern Chinese girls' school in Singapore was the Hua Qiao Girls' School founded in 1905 by Huang Dianxian, the daughter of a rich Cantonese merchant, Huang Yafu (Wong Ah Fook). But the school appeared to have used Cantonese as the medium of instruction (Xu 1949, p. 46; Tay 1997, pp. 47–58). Dialect barriers and social rigidity of the time barred the Hokkien girls from entering this school. The founding of the Chong Fu Girls' School was thus intended to meet an urgent social need of the community. The founder of the school was Wang Huiyi (Wang Hui-i) who was the Educational Superintendent of the Hokkien Association (Hokkien Huay Kuan) of Singapore holding a concurrent position as the acting principal of the Dao Nan School. With his influence over educational matters, he was able to gain support from the Hokkien Association to found the Chong Fu Girls' School. The school started its classes in April 1915 with over 30 pupils and a headmistress, Lin Shuqin, appointed from Xiamen, China (Xu 1949, p. 48). Wang was a progressive intellectual, a reformist who supported Kang Yuwei's reform movement. He was also a journalist working for *Jih Shin Pau* and *Thien Nan Shin Pao* (both the reformists' mouthpieces in Singapore) and was actively involved in the Confucian Revival movement in Singapore (Yen 1982, pp. 404 & 422). He was probably influenced by Liang Qichao's attitude toward female education, and became a fervent advocate for female education in Singapore.

Dao Nan, Ai Tong and Chong Fu were the three main Chinese schools financed and controlled by the Hokkien Association in Singapore during the Republican and post-war periods. In addition, at least another eight private and public Hokkien schools existed around 1929 in Singapore and they received financial subsidies from the Hokkien Association. All of these schools were in financial straits, and had to depend upon monthly and special contributions from the community for their survival. As a result, the number of teachers and students declined and the standard of education slipped (*Nanyang Siang Pau*, 3,10 & 24 April 1924). In February 1929, the change in leadership in the Hokkien Association in Singapore altered the priority of the Association and an educational committee was established to oversee Hokkien education. The result was a financial subsidy given to these needy Hokkien schools (*Nanyang Siang Pau* 4 & 13 February 1929; 5 August 1930).

During the Republican period, the Hokkien community in the Malay Peninsula founded a number of Chinese schools. In Kuala Lumpur, for instance, there were at least four Hokkien schools before 1932, and one of these was a girls' school (Selangor Hokkien Association Minutes 1930–32, 149). The recession of the Malayan economy in the early 1930s as a result of the world economic depression took its toll on Chinese education. One of the four Hokkien schools in Kuala Lumpur was closed, while the remaining three were in financial straits. Since 1936, the Selangor Hokkien Association helped the three schools survive the financial crisis by providing monthly subsidy as well as allowing them to use the Association's premises for school activities (Selangor Hokkin Association Minutes 1930–32, p. 131 & 145; 1934–37, p. 21; Guo 1986, p. 56).

The founding of the Zhong Hua High School in Kuala Lumpur in 1939 was a major step taken by the Selangor Hokkien community in promoting Chinese education. Inspired by burgeoning ethnic Chinese nationalism and the preparation for the reconstruction of China after the Second Sino-Japanese War (1937–45), a group of wealthy Hokkien merchants in Kuala Lumpur led by Chen Rener, Huang Zhongji and Hong Qidu founded the school in July 1939. A known Hokkien educationist, Liang Lingguang, was appointed as the school's first principal (Xuelane Zhong Hua zhongxue 1946).

An important contribution of the Hokkien community towards modern Chinese education in British Malaya was the promotion of Mandarin as the medium of instruction and the weakening of the dialect barrier. Dr. Lim Boon Keng (Lin Wenqing), a well-known Hokkien community leader, was the first to promote Mandarin in Singapore. Believing in language as a useful tool for nurturing Chinese identity and national unity, he started the first Mandarin class in his house as early as 1898 for Straits-born Chinese (Khor 1958, p. 28; G.K. Lee 1990, pp. 64–65). In 1906, he convened a meeting of clan leaders and exhorted them to introduce Mandarin as a subject in the 'temple schools' (*Straits Budget* 18 July 1907). His campaign for popularising Mandarin in Singapore helped contribute to the breakdown of dialect barriers in education (Yen 1976, p. 289).

The popularisation of Mandarin in Chinese schools received a tremendous boost after the founding of the Republic in 1912. The Republic gave ethnic Chinese (including the Chinese in British Malaya) a new identity and a new confidence in being Chinese. The 1919 May Fourth movement in China further injected into ethnic Chinese a new vigour of nationalism that was expressed partly in the use of Mandarin and the breakdown of dialect barriers. In this regard, the Hokkien community in Singapore appeared to have taken the lead. In 1916, The Dao Nan School, the flagship of Hokkien education in Singapore, took steps to phase in the use of Mandarin as the medium of instruction by appointing a non-Hokkien principal, Xiong Shangfu, who was a native of Hunan province (Lin 1966, p. 46). From 1920, Dao Nan School also recruited a number of non-Hokkien teachers from China to strengthen the use of Mandarin in the school (Lin 1966, pp. 47–48).

The effort of the Dao Nan in promoting Mandarin as the teaching medium in Chinese schools in British Malaya was exemplified in its constructive proposal put forward to the conference on ethnic Chinese education in Southeast Asia sponsored by Jinan University of Shanghai held in June 1929. This conference was well attended by Chinese and overseas Chinese delegates numbering about 97 (*Nanyang Siang Pau* 27 June 1929; 2 & 3 July 1929). Dao Nan's proposal was constructive and relevant, and had attracted the attention of the participants. In the proposal, three points are worth noting. Firstly, the Chinese government was to send experts to tour Southeast Asia to promote Mandarin in schools and help to train Mandarin teachers. Secondly, night schools attached to existing Chinese schools were to be established in Southeast Asia to promote Mandarin speaking. Thirdly, effort was to be made to weaken dialect and regional differences in education (*Nanyang Siang Pau* 20 May 1929).

For the knotty problems of dialect and regional barriers in the Chinese schools, the Dao Nan proposal also suggested the establishment of an umbrella organisation named Jiaoyu zonghui (Educational Association) in every city or territory in Southeast Asia. The proposed association was to be supported and financed by entire Chinese community. The association was then to distribute funds to various schools according to their needs (*Nanyang Siang Pau* 20 May 1929). We do not know how much of the Dao Nan proposal was adopted by the Chinese government. But it nevertheless had contributed to the idea of promoting Mandarin in the Chinese schools in the region.

Tan Kah Kee and Modern Chinese Education in British Malaya

Tan Kah Kee is an important name in modern ethnic Chinese history. He is appropriately dubbed by Yong Ching Fatt (C.F. Yong) who produced the best biography of him, as an 'Overseas Chinese legend' (Yong 1987). Tan was an entrepreneur, a business tycoon, a community leader, a philanthropist, an education promoter, and a Chinese patriot. His non-profit-making educational enterprises in Southern Fujian province (including the famous Xiamen University) at the cost of much of his personal wealth, set a good example for the promotion of modern Chinese education in China and in the Ethnic Chinese communities. His deeds are widely known throughout South China and Southeast Asia and have inspired other wealthy ethnic Chinese to follow his example.

Many academic works on Tan Kah Kee were published in both mainland China and overseas in the 1980s to honour his great contributions to modern Chinese education. These works include Wang Zengbing & Yu Gang's *Chen Jiageng Xingxue ji* (*Tan Kah Kee's Contributions to Modern Education*) (1981), Chen Bisheng & Yang Guochen, *Chen Jiageng zhuan* (*A Biography of Tan Kah Kee*) (1983), *Huiyi Chen Jiageng* (*Reminiscences of Tan Kah Kee*) (1984) and Chen Bisheng & Chen Yimin, *Chen Jiageng nianpu* (*A Chronology of Tan Kah Kee*) (1986). Outside of China, Dr. Yong Ching Fatt of the Flinders University of South Australia, Adelaide, first published his Chinese work on Tan Kah Kee in Singapore entitled *Zhanqian de Chen Jiageng yanlun shiliao yu fenxi* (*Tan Kah Kee in Pre-war Singapore: Selected Documents and Analysis*) (1980) and his English biography of Tan Kah Kee entitled *Tan Kah Kee: The Making of an Overseas Chinese Legend* (1987). Yong had spent more than ten years exhausting much of the original materials and produced a definitive work on Tan Kah Kee. These academic works shed much light on Tan's life, his business and community activities, his political aspirations, and his contributions to the promotion of modern Chinese education.

Tan Kah Kee was born on 21 October 1874 in Jimei, a seaboard village, in Tong An district, Fujian province. Most of the villagers were both farmers and fishermen. The geographical location and its proximity to Xiamen (Amoy), an early international port in Southeastern China, moulded the attitudes and aspirations of Tong An folks, encouraging seafaring and overseas ventures. The Tong An people spread widely throughout Southeast Asia, pursuing trade and wealth (Chen & Chen 1986, pp. 1–3). Tan Kah Kee's father, Tan Kee Peck (Chen Qibai), migrated to Singapore and had early success in business. Tan Kah Kee received some traditional Confucian education in his home village and later joined his father in Singapore where he worked as an apprentice in his father's shops.

What Tan learned from his father's business layed the foundation for his future success in business (K. K. Tan 1993, 2.479). Tan started his own business in 1904 and, step-by-step, was actively involved in plantation, manufacturing, and shipping, and he emerged as one of the most successful businessmen in Southeast Asia. At the peak of his business in 1923 and 1925, he possessed a wealth of an estimated 10.8 million Singapore dollars and a large number of employees; in 1925, his rubber manufactory in Singapore alone employed over 14 hundred workers (K. K. Tan 1993, 2.505; Yong 1987, pp. 44–57). With his enormous wealth, Tan Kah Kee was able to pursue his non-profit educational enterprise in Southern China. He began by founding a primary school in his home village as early as February 1913. His business success in later years propelled him to commit more of his personal wealth to the promotion of secondary and tertiary education in Southern Fujian. In 1917, he founded the famous Jimei High School, and then the Jimei Normal College and the Jimei Marine and Navigation College between 1918 and 1921. But his most famous educational enterprise was the founding of Xiamen (Amoy) University in April 1921. His personal wealth sustained the University for about 16 years until 1937 when it was taken over by the Nationalist government (Wang & Yu 1981, pp. 24–25; K. K. Tan 1993, 1.13–28; Chen & Chen 1986, pp. 20–50). His deep commitment to non-profit educational enterprise contributed to the collapse of his business empire in Southeast Asia in the 1930s.

Tan Kah Kee's involvement in promoting Chinese education in British Malaya appears to have been secondary to his entire non-profit educational enterprise. But he did it with equal enthusiasm. In 1906, only about two years after he had started his own business, Tan had already begun to show interest in modern Chinese education in Singapore. In that year when the Hokkien community in Singapore began to found a modern Chinese school, the Dao Nan School, he was one of its 110 founding members and a member of the preparatory committee. He donated one thousand dollars towards the cost of establishing the school. After the school was opened in 1907, he was elected a director of School Board, and later became one of the two auditors. In 1911, he began to demonstrate his leadership and enthusiasm in education that saw him elected as the chairman of the School Board. He served in that capacity for ten years intermittently between 1911 and 1929 (Lin 1966, p. 45; Yong 1987, p. 87). Apart from his commitment to Dao Nan in terms of his time and money, he was also generous in donating a large sum of money to support the Ai Tong School and Chong Fu Girls' School (Xu 1949, p. 29). In 1929, when he was elected to the position of the president of the powerful Hokkien Association of Singapore, he began to restructure the association and altered its priorities. The emphasis on the promotion of modern education saw the injection of a large sum of the association's funds into the running of the Hokkien schools. It took over control and directly financed the Ai Tong School and Chong Fu Girls' School and provided subsidies to eight other lesser Hokkien schools that were in financial straits (Xu 1949, pp. 29 & 48; *Nanyang Siang Pau* 4 & 13 February 1929).

Tan Kah Kee's most important contribution to the promotion of modern Chinese education in British Malaya was his leadership role in the founding of the Singapore Chinese High School (Hua Qiao Zhong Xue) in March 1919 (Tay & Gwee 1975, pp. 260–61). The high school, the first of its kind in the region, set the example for others to follow and had a profound impact upon the introduction of Chinese secondary education into the region.

What motivated Tan Kah Kee to take such significant step? What we need to take into account is the fact that his educational activity in British Malaya, though secondary to his efforts in Southern Fujian, was an integral part of his entire non-profit educational enterprise. It was not motivated by personal gains, but by a lofty idea of using education as a means for strengthening China and the Chinese race (Yong 1980, p. 27). This is his famous dictum of "jiaoyu jiuguo" (rescuing the nation through education).

An enquiry into the motives and aspirations of Tan Kah Kee's promotion of modern Chinese education would not only shed light upon the relationship between immigrant society and modern education, but also the relationship between immigrants and their deep commitments to the well-being of their mother countries. Tan Kah Kee was an ethnic Chinese nationalist and a Chinese patriot. Although he was not a political activist responding to Dr. Sun Yat-sen's call for anti-Qing revolution, he was nevertheless a committed Chinese nationalist ready to help safeguard the sovereignty of his mother country. Tan's deep involvement in the anti-Japanese movement in British Malaya as a result of the Jinan (Tsinan) Incident (Yen 1988, pp. 1–22; Yen 1995a, pp. 306–329) and his leadership in the Anti- Japanese and Relieve China Movement in Southeast Asia between 1938–45 (K. K. Tan 1993, 1.64; Yong 1987, pp. 213–16; Ren 1989, p. 63; Yen 1998a, 155–56) demonstrated his clear political stance. Being a Chinese patriot, he was elated by the founding of the Republic of China in 1912, but was later saddened by Yuan Shikai's usurpation of power and the plunge of China into political turmoil and military chaos after Yuan's death in 1916.

It was against this background that Tan Kah Kee expounded his theory of "jiaoyu jiuguo". This lofty idea was clearly revealed in Tan's speech to the community meeting organised for the purpose of raising funds for the proposed Chinese High School in Singapore in June 1918. In a rather emotional tone, Tan called upon his compatriots to donate generously to Chinese education, for education could indirectly strengthen the nation, and "preserve our cultural essence and to expound our national spirit" (*Guomin Ribao* 18 & 20 June 1918; Yong 1980, pp. 26–27). Drawing a contrast with Japan and Europe, he lamented the fact that there was 96 percent illiteracy in China against 30 percent in Japan and ten percent of European and American countries such as Britain, the United States, Germany, and France. He also lashed out at the Chinese government (the warlord government in Beijing) for its negligence of education and its preoccupation with internal fighting for power and personal gains. He urged wealthy ethnic Chinese to donate a small portion of their assets (three percent to five percent) to education which he believed would not in anyway diminish their wealth (Yong 1980, p. 27). In this sense, Tan Kah Kee had discovered a meaningful role for the Chinese immigrants to play in relation to their mother country. Many of the ethnic Chinese were financially better off than their compatriots in China, and had the capacity to undertake such an important role.

Another less obvious but equally important intent of Tan Kah Kee's involvement in promoting modern Chinese education was his belief that education would improve the competitiveness of the Chinese in business. Being a far-sighted ethnic Chinese entrepreneur (Yen 1998b, pp. 1–13), Tan was at the forefront of competition with other foreign businessmen. He was keenly aware of the weakness of the traditional Chinese business and believed strongly that ethnic Chinese businessmen had to improve their competitiveness for future survival and growth. This line of thought was clearly revealed in his declaration for the inauguration of the *Nanyang Siang Pau*, the Chinese daily newspaper in Singapore founded by him in September 1923. Tan pointed out that the merchants of advanced nations were well equipped with the knowledge of economics and commerce and were able to deal with different types of businesses such as natural resources, manufacturing, navigation and transport, and banking and insurance. They also possessed a broad world-view. These gave them competitive advantage and placed them in a leadership position in world business (*Nanyang Siang Pau* 6 & 7 September 1923; Yong 1980, p. 35). He also deplored the ignorance of the Chinese (including ethnic Chinese) merchants. He said that " … they are at the loss of the principles of commerce, and are poor of common knowledge of doing business … and they are at the mercy of God and fate … " (Yong 1980, p. 35). Therefore, he believed that the promotion of education was the best way of overcoming the ignorance of Chinese merchants and would indirectly improve their competitiveness in doing business.

These two noble motives undoubtedly shaped Tan Kah Kee's attitude towards the promotion of modern Chinese education both in China and in the ethnic Chinese communities. What prompted him to start taking the lead in the founding of the Chinese High School in Singapore was a social need for Chinese secondary education. Prior to the founding of the School in 1919, there was no Chinese high school that could admit those who had completed six years of primary education. Some wealthy parents were able to send their children back to China for further study, but secondary education was denied to most of the Chinese children in British Malaya. Thus, the founding of a Chinese high school was to meet an urgent social need of immigrant society. Tan Kah Kee was also concerned with the future of Chinese education in the region. The absence of Chinese secondary education would have rendered primary education ineffective and would have driven it into oblivion. Thus, the founding of the Chinese High School would stimulate its development and make it viable in immigrant society (*Guomin Ribao* 18 & 20 June 1918). Again, using advanced nations as examples, Tan Kah Kee warned his compatriots of the futility of just having Chinese primary education which would have failed to equip the younger generation with the necessary knowledge and skills to earn a living (Guomin Ribao 18 & 20 June 1918).

Tan Kah Kee's idea of founding a Chinese high school in Singapore went much earlier than 1919. In 1913, after he had successfully founded a primary school in his home village in Fujian (Jimei), he began to float the idea of founding a Chinese high school in Singapore. He wrote from Xiamen to the Singapore Chinese Chamber of Commerce and asked for support. But the Chamber turned down his idea on the grounds that education matters were not within its jurisdiction (Singapore Chinese Chamber of Commerce Minutes 1913–16, 8.19). When Tan arrived in Singapore in the spring of the same year (1913), he raised this idea again, but found no favourable response (*Sin Chew Jit Poh* 7 June 1980). His idea became more concrete in 1917 when a feasibility study was conducted by Xiong Shangfu, the headmaster of the Dao Nan School, showing that at least over one hundred students were eligible for entry into high school (*Guomin Ribao* 10 April 1917). Although this finding was encouraging for Tan Kah Kee, the community response was still feeble.

In May 1918, with the twist of events, Tan Kah Kee was called upon by the representatives of the Tong De (T'ung Teh) Reading Club, a front organisation of the Guomindang (or Kuomintang, Nationalist Party) in Singapore, to take the lead in the founding of a Chinese high school in Singapore. With the support of the presidents of 16 Chinese schools,

Tan Kah Kee convened a public meeting on 15 June 1918 held at the premises of the Singapore Chinese Chamber of Commerce. Fifty-five representatives of various groups attended the meeting, chaired by Tan Kah Kee. He made a rousing and emotional speech appealing for support and enunciated his objectives for founding the proposed Chinese high school as a strategy to help modernise China and to preserve the Chinese cultural essence and spirit (Yong 1987, p. 89).

The meeting endorsed Tan's proposal to set up a Chinese high school with the official name of "Xinjiapo Nanyang Huaqiao Zhongxue" (The Nanyang Overseas Chinese High School of Singapore) and Tan was unanimously elected the provisional president, with Lim Ngee Soon, a leader of Teochew community in Singapore, as his deputy. A board of directors of the school was also formed from representatives of various dialect groups and Chinese primary schools (Tay & Gwee 1975, p. 260). Under the leadership of Tan and Lim, two five-man committees were set up to raise funds and to purchase a site for the school. Tan Kah Kee donated a sum of 30 thousand dollars out of a total of 675,262 dollars raised. He continued as president of the school intermittently from 1918 to 1934 when he was replaced by Lee Kong Chian (Li Guangqian), his son-in-law (Yong 1987, p. 89).

What should be noted in Tan Kah Kee's leadership in the founding of the Singapore Chinese High School was his non-sectarian approach. Although he was a leader of the Hokkien *bang* and was to some extent restricted by the *bang's* sectarian interests, he was struggling to break the dialect barrier in education. He was a nationalist and a patriot, and held a bigger picture for China and ethnic Chinese communities. As education was a means for strengthening China and the Chinese race, the effort of promoting Chinese education, especially the introduction of Chinese secondary education, should not be restricted to one particularly dialect group. A united ethnic Chinese society perhaps was a first step towards the creation of a modern and powerful China. Further, a non-sectarian approach to education would broaden the social base of modern Chinese education, and would guarantee the success of this first Chinese high school in the region. In pursuance of this non-sectarian approach, he had contacted the presidents of the 16 Chinese schools belonging to various *bangs*, and invited them to join in as the founders for the proposed high school. At the same time, the election of Lim Ngee Soon (Lin Yisun), a Teochew *bang* leader in Singapore as his deputy, and the election of various *bang* representatives to the board of directors of the school, projected a positive image of *bang* co-operation in this important community endeavour.

Tan Kah Kee's less well-known educational initiatives were also of some significance to modern Chinese education in British Malaya. These included the founding of a marine and navigation school and a teachers' training college in Singapore. In May 1938, as a result of the Japanese occupation of Xiamen port and the neighbouring areas of Southern Fujian, Tan Kah Kee's educational institutions were greatly affected. The Jimei Marine and Navigation College founded by Tan was forced to move into the interior of Fujian; and the enrolment and standards of the college were badly affected. Tan Kah Kee proposed to found another Marine and Navigation school in Singapore to continue his efforts in the areas of fishery and navigation (Yeap 1990, p. 150). In November 1938, Tan made the official proposal. With the support of the Singapore Hokkien Association, the Singapore Marine and Navigation school came into being on 2 February 1939 with 32 students (20 of them came from Singapore, while the rest came from other parts of Southeast Asia). A former principal of the Jimei Marine and Navigation College was appointed as the first principal of the school and seven teachers were recruited (Yeap 1990, p. 153). The school only existed for three years due to the Hokkien Association's financial difficulties and it was closed in 1942.

Tan Kah Kee's founding of a teachers' training college in 1941 was another one of his educational enterprises in British Malaya. The supply of teachers for the Chinese schools in the region in the pre-war period was mostly dependent on the teachers trained in China. The Pacific war had cut off that important supply. The need for qualified teachers prompted Tan Kah Kee to start raising funds in February 1941 for a teachers' training college in Singapore. An enthusiastic response from the Chinese community raised a sum of 360 thousand dollars (*Nanyang Siang Pau* 18 April 1941). The college was opened on 10 October 1941 (the national day of China) with 230 students (Wang & Yu 1981, p. 69). It was closed after a few months' operation due to the Japanese occupation of Singapore in 1942. After the war, the college was re-opened as the Nan Qiao Girls' High School in March 1947.

The impact of Tan Kah Kee's non-profit educational enterprise on Chinese immigrant society in British Malaya can be discussed at three different levels: through his close relatives and fellow district men; through his friends and business associates; through his employees and graduates of Jimei colleges and Xiamen University and fellow Hokkiens. Tan Kah Kee was a traditional type of leader characterised by his paternalism and dedication. Not only had he set a good example for others to follow, but he was also prepared to put pressure on others to comply. His son-in-law, Lee Kong Chian, closely followed his footsteps in promoting Chinese education. Lee first worked for Tan Kah Kee and later came out to start his own business. He proved to be a shrewd entrepreneur and succeeded in building a business empire in British Malaya, gaining him the nickname, 'king of rubber' (Lim 1995, pp. 183–226; Zheng 1997). In 1934, when Tan resigned from his presidency of the Singapore Chinese High School, he encouraged Lee to step into his shoes (Yong 1987, p. 111). In 1936, Lee donated a sum of 50 thousand Singapore dollars as a partial contribution to the purchase of 400 acres of rubber estate. The income from this rubber estate was used as Xiamen University's operation funds (Tan 1993, 1.28). In 1941 when Tan raised a large sum of money for the founding of the Singapore Marine and Navigation School, Lee also donated a sum of 110 thousand dollars (Yong 1987, p. 111). Lee continuously supported Tan's non-profit educational enterprises in Southern Fujian. In a period between 1950 and 1961, he and Tan Lark Sye were reported to have contributed a sum of 8.8 million (Renminbi) to the rebuilding of Jimei Colleges and Xiamen University. He also donated generously towards the University of Malaya in Singapore and to the Nanyang University (ten percent of total collections, a sum over one million Singapore dollars). He also set up his Lee Foundation which gives generously to education and cultural and welfare activities.

Apart from Lee Kong Chian, Tan Lark Sye was another person who was profoundly influenced by Tan Kah Kee's deeds. Tan Lark Sye, the founder of the Nanyang University, Singapore, was Tan Kah Kee's fellow district man. He was born in Tong An district, Fujian in 1897. He came to Singapore in 1916 and worked for Tan Kah Kee's factory as a foreman.

Later, he was joined by his brothers and started their businesses. He made millions in rubber trading, and later built up his vast business empire in Singapore and Malaysia (Lim 1995, pp. 227–63). Tan Lark Sye was profoundly influenced by Tan Kah Kee's dedication to the promotion of modern Chinese education and was prepared to donate generously to the maintenance of Jimei Colleges and Xiamen University. He, together with Lee Kong Chian, contributed a sum of 8.8 million (Renminbi) towards the rebuilding of Jimei Colleges and Xiamen University in the period between 1950 and 1961 (Yong 1987, p. 111). In 1950, when the University of Malaya was founded in Singapore, Tan Lark Sye donated a sum of 300 thousand Singapore dollars to the university [*Nanyang Siang Pau* (Malaysia) 6 January 1990]. Tan Lark Sye's most important contribution to Chinese education in the region was his founding of the Nanyang University in 1953. In January 1953, He proposed to found a Chinese university in Singapore, the first of its kind among the Chinese communities in Southeast Asia, and he had donated a huge sum of five million Singapore dollars as building funds for the new university (Xinjiapo Nanyang wenhua chubanshe 1956, p. 26). At the same time, the Singapore Hokkien Association, under his influence as the president, also donated 500 acres of land in the Jurong area as the site for the university (Xinjiapo Nanyang wenhua chubanshe 1956, p. 32). Undoubtedly, Tan Lark Sye's action was inspired by Tan Kah Kee's example in the founding of Xiamen University in Southern Fujian.

The second group of people who were influenced by Tan Kah Kee's deeds consisted of his friends and business associates. Of course, many of them were wealthy Chinese businessmen and were able to donate generously to Chinese education. They included Oei Tiong Ham (Huang Zhonghan), the renowned 'king of sugar' of Java, Zeng Jiangshui, a wealthy Hokkien merchant of Malacca, and Lim Ngee Soon (Lin Yisun), a wealthy merchant and a leader of the Teochew community in Singapore. They were not only Tan Kah Kee's friends and business associates, they were also his relatives through marriages. Zeng was particularly supportive of Tan Kah Kee's endeavours. He donated ten thousand Singapore dollars to the funds for the medical faculty of Xiamen University in 1926. In 1931, he donated another large sum of 150 thousand Singapore dollars to the library and operation funds of the University. In 1941, Zeng came up with another 20 thousand Singapore dollars for Tan's project for the founding of the teachers' training college in Singapore (*Lat Pau* 23 February 1926; *Nanyang Siang Pau* 20 November 1931; Tan 1993, 2.372). While both Oei Tiong Ham and Lim Ngee Soon contributed financially to the founding of the Singapore Chinese High School, the former donated a sum of 100 thousand Singapore dollars for the construction of the main hall of the school. The hall was later named after Oei Tiong Ham (Tay & Gwee 1975, pp. 261–62).

The third group of ethnic Chinese who were influenced by Tan Kah Kee included his former employees, graduates of Jimei Colleges and Xiamen University, and fellow Hokkiens. Many of them had seen and heard of Tan Kah Kee's educational deeds, and were inspired by him to contribute to the promotion of Chinese education in the region. This influence has been sustained for many generations. In the 1970s, when Chinese education faced an unprecedented crisis in Malaysia, some of the Hokkien leaders came out to defend it and contributed significantly to the revival of Chinese education in Malaysia. They included Li Zhengfeng (Lee Seng Png) in Kuala Lumpur, Yang Jindian in Ipoh, and Dato Tan Say Eng (Chen Shiyong) in Seremban, Negri Sembilan.

Li Zhengfeng was elected as the president of Zhong Hua High School in Kuala Lumpur in 1974. Under his leadership and with his generous donation, a huge sum of money was raised for the rebuilding of the high school. A new majestic building gave the school new life that marked the revival of the school with fast increased enrolments. Li had worked as the Kuala Lumpur branch manager of the Lee Rubbers Pty. Ltd., and was inspired by both Tan Kah Kee and Lee Kong Chian's deeds in education [*Nanyang Siang Pau* (Malaysia) 8 February 1990; Zeng *et al.* 1993, pp. 80–85].

Like Li Zhengfeng, Yang Jindian was a dedicated promoter of Chinese education. As a Hokkien community leader in Perak, he had been active in promoting Chinese education in the state. In 1955, he raised a large sum of money for the construction of the Pei Nan High School in Ipoh of which he was the president. In the 1970s, when the Chinese education revival movement was launched in Malaysia, he came out to lead a fund-raising drive for the new building of the Yu Cai (Yuk Choy) Independent High School in Ipoh. He served as the chairman of the fund-raising committee that had been targeted to raise a sum of five million Singapore dollars. In 1984, at the age of 70, he was made chairman of the construction committee, and succeeded in building a majestic new building for the independent school. Yang had attributed his enthusiasm in Chinese education to the influence of Tan Kah Kee [*Nanyang Siang Pau* (Malaysia) 1 July 1990; Zeng *et al.* 1993, pp. 128–29].

Dato Tan Say Eng (Chen Shiyong) in Seremban was another Hokkien leader who was inspired by Tan Kah Kee's deeds. Born in Eng Choon district, Fujian province, in 1909, he came to British Malaya at the age of 18 and later became a successful businessman. His enthusiasm in promoting Chinese education in the state of Negri Sembilan was reflected in his deep involvement in the running of Chinese schools. He had been chairman and deputy chairman of the Managing Board of Chinese Schools in the state. He had also been the president, deputy president, and treasurer of the Zhong Hua High School in Seremban, a leading Chinese high school in the state of Negri Sembilan (Malaixiya huaxiao dongshi lianhehui zonghui 1987, 1.102–03). He was also active in the Chinese educational revival movement in Malaysia in the 1970s. When Dato Tan first arrived in Seremban, he worked as junior clerk in the Seremban branch of the Tan Kah Kee Company Pty. Ltd. Greatly impressed by Tan Kah Kee's spirit of "promoting education at the sacrifice of personal wealth", he took Tan Kah Kee as his role model in his efforts to promote modern Chinese education [*Nanyang Siang Pau* (Malaysia) 11 May 1990; Zeng *et al.* 1993, pp. 168–70].

Conclusion

Several concluding remarks can be made from the above study. Like many other immigrant societies, Chinese immigrant society in British Malaya retains strong cultural and emotional ties with China. The rise of modern Chinese education in British Malaya between 1904 and 1941 was the result of such strong ties. The Chinese immigrant society developed its independent attitude and shouldered the burden of educating its young without seeking much government help. Modern Chinese education in British Malaya grew by leaps and bounds with the community's financial support, but sectarian division weakened its efforts. Being the earliest dialect community and with a strong financial position, the Hokkien community played a leading role in the promotion of Chinese education in the region. Tan Kah Kee, a Hokkien community leader, an entrepreneur, and an ethnic Chinese nationalist, played a significant role in the promotion of Chinese education. His deeds in the non-profit educational enterprise, both in southern Fujian and in Singapore, set an important example for the Chinese in Singapore and Malaysia to follow. Tan's work has inspired many generations of Chinese (in South China and Southeast Asia) in the promotion of modern Chinese education.

CHAPTER 8

The Search for Modernity: The Chinese in Sabah and English Education

Danny Wong Tze-Ken

The Chinese community in Sabah, East Malaysia, emerged in the closing years of the 19th century at a time when Chinese began to emigrate from Southeastern China to various parts of Nanyang (Southeast Asia) and beyond. Sabah began to receive its first batch of Chinese immigrants in 1881. Since then, a Chinese community was established and has undergone significant transformation over the years, including the field of education.[1]

This paper will examine several issues. The response of the Chinese in Sabah towards English education and how it gained prominence for a section of the community, particularly the Hakkas, while remaining alien to others will be examined. As a significant number of Hakkas were Christians, this may have made them more receptive to English education. It is no coincidence that the majority of Chinese civil servants and professionals in Sabah are Hakka Christians. The role of Christian missionaries, the prime initiators of English education in Sabah, will also be looked at. Finally, this paper seeks to establish whether or not the Chinese in Sabah saw English education as the key to modernisation. The focus of this paper will be on the period between 1882, the first year in which the Chinese entered Sabah in large numbers, and 1963, when Malaysia was formed.

Historically, Sabah was part of the Brunei and Sulu sultanates until 1878 when the North Borneo Chartered Company established Western rule in the territory. It ruled Sabah from 1881 until 1942. Between January 1942 and August 1945, the Japanese Army occupied Sabah. After the war, Sabah was at first administered by the British Military Administration from September 1945 until July 1946, when it was declared a Crown Colony. In September 1963, Sabah joined Malaysia and became the second largest state in the Federation.

Early Education for the Chinese

During the first 40 years of their presence in Sabah, the Chinese of Sabah did not have a very strong educational tradition. This can be attributed to the class of Chinese who came to settle in Sabah. Unlike Singapore and the Malay States where some Chinese scholars had congregated, most of the Chinese immigrants who first came to Sabah were either labourers or people with little formal education.

In 1881, the newly-established British North Borneo (Chartered) Company[2] started to recruit Chinese into the state as labourers and settlers. Between 1881 and 1900, various immigration schemes were introduced for this purpose.[3] Among them was the pioneering Medhurst scheme introduced in 1882 by Sir Walter Medhurst. It managed to bring in labourers as well as traders from Hong Kong and China. This was followed in succession by efforts of other agents appointed either by the North Borneo Company or by the estates, both European and Chinese owned, and European business enterprises in Sabah. Out of these schemes came the Chinese labourers who worked mostly in the plantations on the east coast of Sabah. Most of these labourers were engaged on indenture arrangements, serving through their contracts with the option for renewal. There was also, among the Chinese immigrants, a different class of people who were more concerned with the prospect of settling in Sabah. They were mostly Hakka Christians. The majority came to Sabah via a separate arrangement made between the British North Borneo Company and the Basel Missionary Society which was working among the Hakkas in Guangdong Province (Basel 1983).

It was this latter group who started the first Chinese school in Sabah in 1886 in Kudat. This was followed by the common school set up at the premises of *San-Sheng Kung* of Sandakan, a temple built in 1887 through contributions from the four dialect communities which had originated from the province of Guangdong, namely, the Cantonese, the Hakkas, Teochius, and the Hailams. The Hokkiens were not involved, as they were from another province.

Chinese Education in Sabah at the turn of the century remained very diverse. Most Chinese schools were set up through the efforts of those in the community who had hoped to educate their young with a view to preserve Chinese culture and its tradition of focusing upon learning. Many Chinese businessmen became founders and proprietors of schools. Apart from the businessmen, Chinese dialect groups also began to establish schools of their own. Some of the names of these schools suggest that these places were actually reading clubs instead of schools. However, it is difficult to determine whether these 'reading clubs' were of similar background as those started in Singapore and Malaya after 1907. The latter were originally cradles for anti-Qing activities (Yen 1976, p. 265). All the Chinese schools maintained the traditional syllabus, emphasising the learning of the classics. Elementary English was later taught at the Basel Mission schools and the North Borneo Chinese Primary School (SR 1911). Throughout the Chartered Company rule, government assistance was not given to any of the Chinese schools, except those that introduced English into their syllabus.[4] In 1911, the number of Chinese schools in the state was small, with 12 in Sandakan and one each in Jesselton and Kudat, both of which were set up by the Basel Mission. Nonetheless, this does not reflect the actual overall enrolment of Chinese children in schools. This is because Chinese students also made up the majority of the student population in the nine Englishs medium schools in the state.

Apart from individuals, Chinese organisations began to play a part in supporting Chinese education. In Sandakan, the Chinese Chamber of Commerce started the Chung Hwa School (also known as North Borneo Chinese Primary) in 1908. The school was housed in two shop lots at No. 55 and No. 56 Jalan Tiga. The first schoolmaster was Loong Thou, assisted by Loo Fun Chong. In 1910, there were 47 students in the school, making it the largest among the 12 Chinese schools operating in Sandakan at that time (ERS 1911).

In 1917, the Jesselton Chinese Chamber of Commerce started a similar school, also named Chung Hwa.[5] Thirty students enrolled in its first year. The school was also situated in a shophouse at the entrance of the town. However, unlike its Sandakan counterpart that had started with the Cantonese dialect as the medium of instruction (Sandakan Chinese Chamber of Commerce 1991, p. 31), the Chinese school in Jesselton adopted the current policy of China in the use of Mandarin in all its classes, and teachers were recruited from China. The founding of the Chung Hwa School in Jesselton marked the apex of the introduction of early Chinese education in Sabah. For the first time, a reformed Chinese syllabus was introduced with effect from 1918 onward. It included the 'Thoughts of Dr. Sun Yat-Sen' conceptualised in the San-Min-Chu-i (Three Principles of the Republic).

Another Chinese organisation that began to be actively involved in Chinese education was the Hakka Association of Sandakan. This association placed emphasis on providing education to the offspring of members of its community. In 1910, Lam Man Ching, the Kapitan Cina for Sandakan and the east coast, was elected chairman of the Yan Foh Fui Kwon (the new name for the Ngo Chen Hui Khon). Lam, who was educated both in Chinese and English, saw the importance of promoting education in line with the changes that were taking place in China. Prior to this, Lam Man Ching was the main supporter for another Chinese school named Lam See Hok Hau (Lam Clan School), situated at 16 Lorong Ampat, Sandakan (ERS 1911). Together with Liau Nyuk Kui, another Hakka leader, Lam started the Chi Hwa Primary School for 30 students on the premises of the Tan Kung Tsu-Miao Chinese temple. The school was first started as a traditional Chinese school with the instruction of the four Books and five Classics until it was taken over by the Chinese Chamber of Commerce a few years later. Under the sponsorship of the Chamber, the school became a branch of the North Borneo Chinese Primary School (Chung Hwa School, Sandakan) (ibid), and the new republican curriculum was introduced, replacing the learning of the classics. The school ceased operation some time in the 1920s because it lacked of funding, but was later revived by Lam Man Ching and the Hakka Association, and was renamed Chi Hwa (Chi Hwa 1989, p. 4).

The 1920s saw an increase in the number of Chinese schools from 22 in 1917 to 37 in 1925. The total enrolment of students in these schools had also increased from 470 in 1917 to 977 in 1925. This expansion of Chinese schools was very much due to the modernisation programme in education that was taking place in China. In China, the renaissance of the Chinese language in the modern colloquial manner through the efforts of Professor Hu Shih began to spread to the state. New schools were opened in Sabah in places wherever there was a sizeable Chinese community. In line with the changes in China, some of the traditional reading clubs and Chinese schools in Sabah also underwent some reform in the form of a new and modern syllabus. For the first time, many small towns had a Chinese school of their own, including Kota Belud (Chung Hwa–1920), Tuaran (Chi Chi–1923), Tenom (Mien Nan–1925), Weston (Chi Hwa–1927), and Membakut (Pei Ying–1927).

Chinese education, however, did not start in Tawau until 1920 when the Hakka community opened the Hin Wah School that year. The school was actually mooted in April 1919, but was only fully operating in 1920. The late development of Chinese education in Tawau, the third largest town in Sabah, was not due to the lack of a Chinese population. On the contrary, by 1921, the town's Chinese population numbered 4,368, or 40.51 percent of the town's total population. Reporting in 1924, the District Officer for Tawau attributed the failure for the Chinese in Tawau to start a Chinese school in the town to the "lack of co-operation between the various races of Chinese" (TAR 1925).

Despite the increase in the number of schools, the actual situation did not really reflect a significant improvement in the overall development of Chinese education. This was due to the fact that the average student population of these schools was very small. This was because the number of Chinese children in the state remained small compared to the adult population. In 1931, the total number of Chinese children was 13,699, representing only 27.36 percent of the total population, or a ratio of almost three adults to a child.

The number of Chinese children who attended Chinese schools represented only half of the total Chinese children in schools altogether, with the other half attending mission schools. In 1925, the total enrolment in the 39 mission schools in Sabah stood at 1,472 students. Out of this figure, almost one thousand were Chinese. As in other parts of Southeast Asia, this trend of having Chinese children enrolled into two major streams of education would have future consequences for the community. The existence of two different streams of education inevitably produced two different groups of Chinese in the state. The first group would identify with everything Chinese, fervently supporting Chinese education in the state. The second group consisted of the Chinese who were more English-inclined and, in most cases, became Christians.

English Education through Mission Schools

Being a company that looked to profit as its main consideration, the British North Borneo Chartered Company administration did not have a clear programme to provide education to the population. The Company's apathy in providing education can be seen in the fact that the Company did not appoint any school inspector until the 1920s. Thus, the initiative of starting English education in Sabah was very much left to the efforts of the various missionary societies.

There were three major missionary societies that provided the people of Sabah with English education. These were, namely, the Roman Catholics, the Society for the Propaganda (SPG), and the Basel Missionary Society.

The Roman Catholics were the first to start a formal school in Sabah. In 1883, St. Mary's School was started in Sandakan with an enrolment of five boys. It was closed two years later due to a shortage of staff but was revived in 1887. The SPG did not lag behind. In 1888, the SPG opened St. Michael's School. Rev. William Elton, the SPG priest, fully subscribed to the idea of providing education for girls. In 1889, St. Monica's School was built. After that, new schools were opened at Inobong, Penampang. Nearly all the students who attended these schools were Chinese (George 1987, p. 27).

Even though the Basel Church had started a school in Kudat in 1886, it was a Hakka school. In 1912, the Basel Church started a school in Sandakan known as Sung Siew School, with Rev. F. Fritz, a Basel Missionary of Austrian origins, as its first schoolmaster. A Chinese schoolmaster, Rev. Yap Hien Mu, assisted him. The school was the first Chinese-based school that included English in its curriculum. The Basel Church also started another school in Papar that offered instruction in English. That school, Anglo-Chinese School, was started some time after 1922 under the leadership of Chin Chung Tat.

The two decades between 1900 and 1920 formed a significant period in the development of Christian churches in Sabah. Alongside this development was the development of English education. By 1905, the Roman Catholic Church had six schools, situated in Sandakan (two), Jesselton, Papar (two), and Putatan. A total of 231 students were enrolled in the Catholic schools, out of which, 60 were girls. The SPG also had six schools, situated in Sandakan (two), Kudat (two), Jesselton, and Labuan. These schools had a total enrolment of 152 students, 24 of whom were girls. The students who were enrolled in these mission schools were almost entirely Chinese (George 1987, p. 27), allowing the community a head start in education compared to other communities.

There is reason to believe that most of the Chinese who went to the Mission English schools were Hakkas. This was due to the fact that apart from the Roman Catholic Church, the membership in the other Christian churches, the Basel Church, and the Anglican Church was predominantly Hakka. Additionally, the fact that most of the Mission schools' students were from families of their church members lends support to this development. The fact that most Hakka students attended the English-medium mission schools meant that these schools had a significant impact on the social development of the Hakka people. Even though the Hakka people had begun to engage in business and other fields of economic activities prior to the Second World War, the majority still engaged in land-related activities, either as farmers or labourers in the estates. Thus, until the outbreak of the Second World War, the primary economic activities of the Hakkas remained agriculture-based.

This strong tie with the land meant that the community was more rural-based compared with other Chinese dialect groups. Nevertheless, social transformation did take place within the Hakka community. The high number of Hakka children enrolled in the English schools would inevitably result in a major shift in the economic inclination of the community. This shift involved their break wth their traditional ties to landholding and their venturing into other vocations. This shift was most apparent in the government services in which the Hakkas clearly dominated by the 1920s. During the earlier days of Chartered Company rule, Hokkien and Teochiu domination of the civil service was almost complete as most of them were recruited from the Straits Settlements. The trend began to change in the 1920s when more and more Hakkas were taken in to serve as government servants (Establishment List 1922–28 & 1931–37). In 1922, for instance, out of the 225 Chinese employed in the government, 135 were of Hakka origin (Establishment List 1922). Apart from that, though no statistical evidence exists, the Hakkas also began to dominate the clerical and white collar supporting staff sectors of the European business enterprises operating in Sabah at that time.

The eventual domination of the civil services and the white collar supporting positions in the European business enterprises by the Hakkas was not merely a result of the fact that Hakkas had become the largest dialect group in Sabah. It was also, in many ways, a reflection of their inclination for English education, seeing it as the means for social mobility. A survey of the occupations listed by those who were married in the Hakka-based Basel Churches of Sandakan, Kudat, Jesselton, Inanam, Papar, Beaufort, Tenom, and Telipok, between 1921 and 1930, also yielded results that supported this argument. Out of the 128 couples, there were 27 clerks, six teachers, three wireless operators, three hospital dressers and one apothecary (MCBSEC n.d.). This represented a departure from the traditional, agricultural, occupations of the Hakkas. This development persisted even after the Second World War.

The stronger inclination of the Hakkas in Sabah towards Western education and education in general can be attributed to at least two historical reasons. The first is the Hakkas' initial contacts with the Christian religion and, secondly, the nature of Hakka migration to Sabah which had a higher percentage of women folk compared to other dialect groups.

Contacts between the Hakkas in southern China and the Christian religion can be traced to as early as the 1840s following the First Opium War (1839–42). At that time, Christian missionaries began to propagate the Christian faith among the Chinese in the treaty ports. Among the missions working among the Hakkas in Guangdong province were the Rhenish Mission and the Basel Mission, both of the Protestant faith. The Hakkas looked upon this initial contact positively, as they benefited from the missionaries' zeal in providing education to the community (Lutz & Lutz 1998, pp. 6–7). Like other Christian missions in China at that time, both the Rhenish and the Basel missions also started schools for the Hakka children. The Basel Mission also started a theological college and a teacher's training college at Lee Long (Lilang) allowing further education. The outbreak of the Taiping Rebellion and its subsequent defeat (1850–64), saw the Hakkas being persecuted by the Qing Government, and prompted a migration process that eventually brought many to Sabah. Even though the persecution against the Taiping covered the Hakkas in general, many of those who came to Sabah were in many ways connected with the Taiping Rebellion and some were even related to Hong Xiuquan, the leader of the Taiping Rebellion (Lee n.d.). Once in Sabah, the Hakka Christians revived their educational links with the Basel Missionary Society through the guidance of the missionaries who had accompanied them to Sabah.

Among all the dialect groups of Chinese who came to Sabah, the Hakkas had the largest number of women, migrating with their families, whereas most of the others consisted of single males. The Hakkas had benefited from the various immigration schemes that aimed at bringing Chinese settlers to Sabah, particularly the agreements made between the Chartered Company with the Basel Missionary Society and through the implementation of the Free Passage Immigration Scheme, introduced in 1921. While others were more transient in nature, hoping to earn enough to return to a comfortable life in China, many of the Hakkas intended to settle in Sabah. This was mainly due to the political hardships of the Qing period and the desire to escape economic hardship after 1911. It was mainly due to these considerations that the Hakkas migrated in family units. While there are no statistics that provide a breakdown of the children-adult ratio of new immigrants, it is assumed that the large number of Hakka women in Sabah as compared to women from other dialect groups would also, in itself, reflect a larger number of Hakka children as compared to other dialect groups (Jones 1953, p. 112). It is based on this assumption that Hakka children made up the majority of

Table 8.1: Number of Female Chinese in Sabah According to Dialect Group, 1921–1951.

Dialect Group	1921	1931	1951
Hakka	6,168	11,330	20,610
Cantonese	2,413	3,621	4,995
Hokkien	1,213	1,735	3,074
Teochew	424	710	1,562
Hailam	124	333	1,347

Source: Jones (1953: 112)

school children during the first few decades of the 20th century (see Table 8.1).

In 1915, English education development in Sabah received a boost from the setting up of the Chee Swee Cheng Scholarship fund, compliments of Chee Swee Cheng, the wealthy Chinese businessman of Jesselton and Singapore (Lee & Chow 1996, pp. 19–20). The scholarship would be awarded to a single scholar from Sandakan every year, and was worth 60 dollars for one year. The winner would be determined by an examination in which candidates would be tested in arithmetic, general geography, general knowledge, essay writing, and dictation. The first scholarship was awarded to Lo Feng Chung from the Basel Mission School.[6]

Even though the scholarship was open to all boys and girls residing in Sandakan regardless of race, the majority of the candidates were Chinese students from the three mission schools in Sandakan. In the first examination for the scholarship, for instance, there were only three students who were of non-Chinese in origin, all of whom were students of the Roman Catholic Mission School, St. Mary's.

Two scholarships were offered in the 1917 Chee Swee Cheng Scholarship examination. Kong Fung Bo of the Basel Mission won the contest followed by H. August Peter from the Roman Catholic Mission. The scholarship was extended to Jesselton in 1918 when Chee Swee Cheng donated two thousand to set up a similar scholarship fund for schools in Jesselton. Since then, two scholarships were offered annually

(GPC 1918). At a glance, the number of candidates who presented themselves for the scholarship examination showed that Chinese students dominated the lists.

Chinese Education versus English Education

The 1930s can be considered the most active years in the development of Chinese education in Sabah. There were at least three significant developments. First, more Chinese schools were established in the state during this period than in any other. Second, there was a major dispute over syllabus and texts books used in Chinese schools. Third, the founding of the Chung Hwa Secondary School in Sandakan in 1938 brought the beginning of secondary Chinese education to Sabah.

At least 18 new Chinese schools were started in Sabah throughout the 1930s. Apart from those founded in the major towns such as Sandakan, Jesselton, and Tawau, others were started in smaller towns where the Chinese population was small but growing. In 1931, the northern Chinese started their second school at Kinarut, after a large number of the community had moved to the vicinity of the town from their initial settlement at Penampang. Along the railway line, three schools were opened in Beaufort (the Third and Fourth Kung Ming Schools in 1934 and 1938, respectively, and Lok Yuk in 1938). In Tenom, the Hwa Chiao School was started in 1931. In 1933, two Chinese schools were started in the Kudat area, including one started by the Basel Church. In Semporna, the Hwa Chiao School was started in 1934, and in Tawau Lama, a Chung Hwa school was opened in 1934.

Except for the series of Lok Yuk Schools, which were started by the Basel Church in different locations, various Chinese associations established most Chinese schools through public subscription. Prior to 1938, secondary education was only available in the English medium through the mission schools. Chinese secondary education had to be obtained elsewhere. This meant having to travel to Singapore, Hong Kong or even China. Due to the financial constraints to study abroad, or failure to gain entry into the local English-medium secondary schools, many Chinese youths left school at an early age.

In 1938, the Chinese Chamber of Commerce of Sandakan decided to sponsor a secondary school for those who had completed their primary education. This effort marked a departure in Chinese education in Sabah. Under the sponsorship of the Chinese Chamber of Commerce, the school managed to produce its first batch of nine lower secondary graduates before the beginning of the Japanese occupation (SCCC 1991, p. 90).

Just as the Chinese community was organising their Chinese Secondary School, two other individuals decided to introduce English into the syllabus of their schools. The first to do so was Chan Fook, a Hakka Christian landowner from Beaufort, and a member of the Basel Church, who started a Chinese school in that town which included English as part of its curriculum. For this, Chan Fook's school was the first Chinese School to be given capitalisation aid by the Chartered Company Government.

Another individual who had introduced English into the syllabus of his school was Tsen En Fook, a Hakka and former catechist in the Seventh Day Adventist who later joined the Basel Mission as the schoolmaster in Jesselton during the 1920s. By the 1930s, he started a school known as Ping Ming School in Jesselton, and introduced English as one of the subjects in the school syllabus. However, Tsen's school was not given government aid until 1939. This was mainly due to his enmity toward the Chartered Company administration. Tsen was the English Secretary for the Chinese Chamber of Commerce, West Coast, which was very vocal against Government policy towards the Chinese in the 1930s. Both Chan Fook and Tsen En Fook's efforts to introduce English in the school syllabus again demonstrated how the Hakka Christians were being more receptive to English education compared to others.

The start of the Chinese secondary school came very late compared to the achievements of the mission schools. Chinese involvement in English education through the mission schools came to a temporary end between 1942 and 1945. The invading Japanese Administration disallowed the teaching of the English Language and the schools remained closed throughout most of the war, except when used by the Japanese to teach Japanese lessons.

Postwar Development

After three and a half years of Japanese occupation, many Chinese were anxious to have their children back in schools to make up for the time lost during the war. The British Borneo Civil Affairs Unit (BBCAU), the organisation responsible for administering civil affairs in Sabah during the immediate postwar period, reported a marked enthusiasm for education among the locals, which was especially true of the Chinese. Between the end of the war and May 1946, a total of 40 Chinese schools and about 25 mission schools were reopened. This represented half of the total number of such schools in pre-war Sabah. By May 1946, a total of 8,543 school-aged children in Sabah and 705 in Labuan attended schools. The number represented 85.4 percent of the 1941 school attendance figures (RBMAB 1946).

One very interesting development in post-war education in Sabah was the attention given by the British Military Administration (BMA) to Chinese education. For the first time, there was some realisation among the administrators in Sabah of the possibility of using education to mould the Chinese into permanent residents of the state. In outlining his five-year Education Plan for Sabah, R. E. Parry, the Acting Director of Education stated:

> "Chinese Schools Communities are at present too self-centred in outlook, and the present policy of non-financial assistance in Government tends to emphasize this tendency. The fact that China has already developed an active policy of mass education, must be utilized towards the conception of a common citizenship within the Colony of North Borneo" (Parry 1946).

Parry also expressed concern for the Chinese Government's campaign to attract the Chinese residing overseas to return and rebuild post-war China. He feared that such campaigns, which were aimed at getting skilled artisans or traders, might jeopardise Sabah's own efforts to reconstruct the state. Such concerns acknowledged the importance of the Chinese population in the development of the state, and the acceptance of the community as part of Sabah's population. As part of the efforts to gain Chinese support to the state's efforts for reconstructing the country, Parry proposed an extension of government grant-in-aid to the Chinese public schools (*ibid*).

The granting of aid to non-mission schools by the government provided the Chinese schools with a significant boost, allowing them to develop further. However, this did not mean that English education suffered. In fact, for the first time, the government took the initiative to establish a secondary school known as the Sabah College in Jesselton in 1952, marking the first direct government initiative in promoting English education by the Government. Apart from that, grants-in-aid were continued for the mission schools. Enrolment at these schools had also increased.

Another postwar development in education was the increasing awareness by Chinese of other dialect groups of the importance of English education, not only as the gateway to higher education abroad but also as a prerequisite to Government service or white-collar jobs. In many ways, this new awareness was probably prompted by the political change that was taking place in China, with the Communist Party taking power since October 1949. With the severing of the cultural links with China, many Chinese had no choice but to turn to English education. This development had inevitably challenged the Hakkas' predominant position as the dialect group that was most receptive to Western education. This, in turn, also began to pose a threat to their predominant position in the civil service and their hold on white-collar jobs.

Han Sin Fong, one of the earliest researchers of the Chinese in Sabah, opined that due to their strong links with Western Missionaries, the Hakkas in Sabah were indeed more receptive to English education than were other dialect groups. However, Han Sin Fong also pointed out that though the Hakkas had a head start in English education, making them the most progressive group among the Chinese community, especially in terms of social mobility, they rarely went beyond secondary education. According to Han Sin Fong,

> "… even though they [the Hakkas] were the first and the most numerous Chinese to receive a Western education, very few continued beyond the secondary school level. They seem to be satisfied with the middle level white-collar jobs that they can

obtain with their high school diplomas. This explains why today they are not represented in professional occupations such as law, medicine, engineering, and architecture, despite their earlier and closer association with Western education" (Han 1976, p. 158).

Han's observation however, did not take into consideration the fact that though the Hakkas were the pioneers in English education among the Chinese community in Sabah, they were economically weaker when compared with those from other dialect groups, particularly those from the stronger business class. A survey of the 1963 Report of the Hakka-dominated Basel Church for instance, yielded a total of 64 members who were pursuing tertiary education abroad, especially in the Commonwealth countries (Basel 1963). The figure should be seen as the beginning of the emergence of a new Hakka professional group that Han Sin Fong had failed to detect.

Conclusion

During the 60 years of Chartered Company rule, the perception of the Chinese of Sabah towards English education varied. The Hakkas took the lead among the various Chinese dialect groups to seek English education, and in some cases, to provide such education through their own initiatives. In this regard, the role of the various Christian churches, especially the Basel and the Anglican churches, was extremely important. Their better grasp of the English language placed them in favourable position to seek government employment, white-collar jobs, and, after the Second World War, higher education in Western countries.

Postwar development also saw Chinese from other dialect groups putting greater emphasis on English education. This trend inevitably challenged the Hakkas' dominant position in the civil service and in gaining white-collar jobs. Despite having a head start, as well as being the most numerous of the dialect groups in Sabah, the Hakkas' dominance in the ranks of the civil service and white-collar jobs slowly eroded. It remained unassailable at least until the early 1970s. Since then, especially with new government policies, including the introduction of the Malay language to replace the use of English in Government departments, the advantage of English language facility among the Chinese has become increasingly irrelevant.

Notes

[1]To date, there are several works on the Chinese of Sabah. Among them are Purcell (1980, pp. 357–82), Han (1976), and Wong (1998 & 2000, pp. 382–406).

[2]'North Borneo Company' and 'Chartered Company' shall be used interchangeably in this paper.

[3]Several studies are available on the immigration of Chinese into Sabah, among them is Oades (1961), Niew (1993, pp. 187–195), and Wong (1999).

[4]The Chartered Company government began to grant financial assistance to the Mission Schools in 1910 with a budget of $1.50 to $2.00 per student, per annum.

[5]There is a problem in dating the beginning of Chung Hwa School in Jesselton. Whereas the Chamber's sources give 1917 as the date, the Chartered Company papers give 1918, which is actually the official date of its inauguration by the Resident, West Coast.

[6]Lo Feng Chung actually came in second to Charles Kong, also of the Basel Mission, who was disqualified as he did not meet the stringent two years in-school requirement, having been employed under Darby & Co. as a participant in the course of his studies. See AIS 1915.

PART THREE

Fitting in:
Social Integration in the Host Society

CHAPTER 9

Language, Education, and Occupational Attainment of Foreign-Trained Chinese and Polish Professional Immigrants in Toronto, Canada*

Li Zong

There are many barriers to foreign-trained immigrants obtaining their professional occupations in Canada. Some of these relate to individual factors such as a lack of Canadian work experience and inadequate command of English (Ornstein & Sharma 1983; Basavarajappa & Verma 1985). Many immigrants face an initial adjustment period as they establish contacts in Canada, learn one of the official languages, and adapt to a new environment. Beyond this, they also face the difficulty of getting their education and professional credentials recognised by Canadian employers and professional organisations (Badets 1999; Basran & Zong 1998). The purpose of this paper is to use survey data to highlight some of the individual and structural barriers, and to examine how foreign-trained Chinese- and Polish-Canadian professionals perceive the devaluation of their foreign credentials. This study illustrates that the systemic barriers relating to devaluation of foreign credentials may affect foreign-trained professionals in accessing professional jobs and that

*Research for this paper was supported by a grant from the Department of Canadian Heritage in Canada. The author is solely responsible for the analysis, interpretation, and views expressed in the paper.

individual barriers cannot be seen in isolation from social conditions or structural arrangements.

Individual versus Systemic Barriers

There are two perspectives on occupational attainment of foreign-trained professional immigrants in the literature. The first one focuses primarily on individual barriers experienced by foreign-trained professional immigrants and argues that immigrants who wish to work in Canada must acquire equivalence in terms of Canadian standards. Individual barriers include the inability to meet occupational entry requirements, a lack of Canadian work experience, and an inadequate command of English (Ornstein & Sharma 1983). For instance, Basavarajappa and Verma argue that the period of residence in Canada has a crucial impact on the ability of Asian immigrants to receive returns for their high educational attainments. They also suggest that a lack of Canadian experience and failure to meet Canadian professional standards may cause problems for professional immigrants (Basavarajappa & Verma 1985).

Although the individual approach has elucidated some personal difficulties, it has not explained how the structural factors pertaining to policies, criterion, and procedure of evaluation also contribute to occupational disadvantages for foreign-trained professionals. Failure to locate individual barriers in social conditions and structural arrangements tends to blame immigrant professionals themselves for failing to acquire professional jobs in Canada.

The second perspective stresses systemic barriers in the recognition of the foreign credentials of professional immigrants. It suggests that control of entry to the professions has caused systematic exclusion and occupational disadvantages for professional immigrants (Boyd 1985; McDade 1988; Trovato & Grindstaff 1986; Rajagopal 1990; Ralston 1988; Beach & Worswick 1989; Basran & Zong 1998). For instance, Boyd provides an analysis of differences between Canadian-born and foreign-born workers in the acquisition of occupational status. Boyd argues that the Canadian-born receive a greater return for their education compared to the foreign-born because of "difficulties of transferring educational skill across national boundaries" (Boyd 1985, p. 405). Several studies use census data to demonstrate the difficulties in translating educational achievements into occupational advantage that are faced by selected cohorts of immigrants (Trovato & Grindstaff 1986; Grindstaff 1986). Pendakur and Pendakur's research (1996, p. 26) suggests that even when controlling for occupation, industry, education, potential experience, CMA, official language knowledge, and household type, visible minorities earn significantly less than native-born white workers.

Two approaches have been used to study structural barriers. The first one focuses on policies, regulations, and procedures, which are evident in government reports concentrating on specific components of the accreditation process (Abt. Associates of Canada 1987; Task Force on Access to Professions and Trades in Ontario 1989; Alberta Task Force on the Recognition of Foreign Qualifications 1992; Manitoba Working Group on Immigrant Credentials 1992; Employment and Immigration Canada 1993). Access to information on accreditation procedures, agencies involved in the assessment, and the nature of the evaluation itself are some of the aspects that have been studied by this approach.

Another approach focuses on experience and perceptions. Foreign-trained professionals were typically asked in a survey to describe their own perceptions of credential problems and occupational disadvantages (Ontario 1980, 1984; Basran & Bolaria 1985; Fernando & Prasad 1986; Taylor 1987; Szado 1987). Based on such an approach, for example, Fernando and Prasad report that among professional immigrants interviewed, particularly doctors and engineers, 71 percent had perceived barriers to full recognition (Fernando & Prasad 1986).

It is sometimes difficult to separate individual barriers from structural barriers, especially for visible minority foreign-trained professionals who may perceive racial discrimination. For example, lacking Canadian experience is an individual attribute, but it is related to employers refusing to recognize foreign credentials and to hire immigrants in jobs suited to their training. From the vantage point of foreign-trained professionals, it would not be accurate to consider their occupational disadvantages as resulting from two types of barriers in isolation.

Previous surveys have frequently dealt with foreign-trained professional immigrants in general. Studies that focus on visible minority foreign-trained professionals are lacking. As visible minority foreign-trained professionals have a distinctive cultural background and experience that differs from white foreign-trained professionals, they may be more disadvantaged in the Canadian labour force. Richmond, for example, suggests that despite high levels of education, visible minority immigrants from Third World countries appear to be particularly vulnerable in the Canadian labour market (1984, p. 253).

This paper emphasizes the importance of personal experience and perceptions in understanding individual and structural barriers. In particular, this study inquires into the experiences and perceptions of foreign-trained Polish- and Chinese-Canadian professionals and compares their level of occupational attainments.

Source of Data

The data of this analysis is derived from a survey conducted in Toronto in 1998. Using the snowball sampling method, 302 foreign-trained professionals were surveyed, including 128 professionals originally from Mainland China and 174 professionals from Poland. "Foreign-trained professionals" refers to those who received their professional training outside of Canada and who entered this country as immigrants and resided in Toronto at the time of the study.

All the respondents in the study have obtained Canadian citizenship. The respondents had the following characteristics: 49 percent were male and 51 percent were female; 96 percent arrived in Canada in the 1980s and 1990s, and four percent in the 1960s and 1970s. In terms of age, two percent were under 30, 93 percent were between 30 and 55 years of age, and five percent were over 55. About 91 percent of the respondents had at least a bachelor's degree and 57 percent had a Master's or Ph.D. degree. The professions among the respondents were primarily medical doctors, engineers, and school/university teachers. Table 9.1 also shows similar characteristics of foreign-trained Polish- and Chinese-Canadian professionals.

The data were obtained by self-administered questionnaires. The questionnaire, 19 pages long, included 71 questions on credentials, work experience before and after immigration, personal difficulties and perceived structural barriers in accessing professional jobs in the Canadian

Table 9.1: Sample Characteristics

	Chinese		Polish		All	
	N	%	N	%	N	%
Gender						
Male	60	47	89	51	149	49
Female	68	53	85	49	153	51
Total	128	100	174	100	302	100
Age						
>30	2	2	4	2	6	2
30–55	120	94	162	93	282	93
55<	6	4	8	5	14	5
Total	128	100	174	100	302	100
Marital Status						
Married	107	84	134	77	241	80
Single	10	8	16	9	26	9
Other	11	8	24	14	35	11
Total	128	100	174	100	302	100
Number of Years Living in Canada						
>4	4	3	1	0.5	9	3
4–6	27	21	12	7.0	35	12
6<	97	76	161	92.5	258	85
Total	128	100	174	100.0	302	100
Year of Arrival						
1960s–70s	2	2	11	6	13	4
1980s–90s	126	98	163	94	289	96
Total	128	100	174	100	302	100

labour force, opinions on policy issues, and general respondent information. Well-trained research assistants personally delivered the questionnaires to prospective respondents who were willing to participate in the survey.

Since the total target population in Toronto is unknown, it is difficult to assess statistically how representative the sample is. Considering the fact that most respondents (96 percent) came to Canada in the 1980s and 1990s, the sampled respondents are probably more representative of recent foreign-trained Chinese- and Polish-Canadian professionals who came to Canada in these two decades. They are less representative of those who immigrated in the 1960s and 1970s.

Findings and Discussion

Table 9.2 shows that 73 percent of respondents reported having worked as professionals (doctors, engineers, school/university teachers, and other professionals) in their country of origin before immigrating to Canada. However, only 33 percent of them said that they worked or had worked as professionals in Canada. Although 15.5 percent of the respondents became proprietors, managers, supervisor, and administrators in Canada, 49 percent of them had lower social status in non-professional jobs and two percent never worked in Canada.

Table 9.2 also shows that compared with Polish-Canadian professionals, Chinese-Canadian professionals have lower levels of occupational attainment in Canada, although their occupational attainment in their country of origin seems better than that of Polish-Canadian professionals. Eighty-five percent of Chinese-Canadian professionals reported having worked as professionals in China before immigrating to Canada, which was 21 percent higher than for Polish-Canadian professionals. However, only 23 percent of Chinese-Canadian professionals said that they worked or had worked as professionals in Canada, which was 20 percent lower than for Polish-Canadian professionals.

Tables 9.3.1 and 9.3.2 present the transition matrix of occupational mobility showing the change between the last occupation in the country of origin and the respondents' current occupation in Canada. Tables 9.3.1

Table 9.2: Occupational Attainment in Country of Origin and in Canada for Foreign-trained Polish- and Chinese-Canadian Professionals

| | Polish-Canadian Professionals | | | | Chinese-Canadian Professionals | | | | Polish- & Chinese Canadian Professionals | | | |
| | in Poland | | in Canada | | in China | | in Canada | | in origin country | | in Canada | |
	N	%	N	%	N	%	N	%	N	%	N	%
1. Professional												
Doctor	11	6.3	12	7.0	14	11.0	0	0.0	25	8.3	12	4.1
Engineer	52	29.9	25	14.5	35	27.6	12	9.7	87	28.9	37	12.5
School/university teacher	34	19.5	10	5.8	43	33.9	2	1.6	77	25.6	12	4.1
Other professionals	15	8.6	23	13.4	16	12.6	15	12.1	31	10.3	38	12.8
Sub-total	112	64.4	70	40.7	108	85.0	29	23.4	220	73.1	99	33.4
2. Non-professional												
Proprietary	3	1.7	10	5.8	0	0.0	13	10.5	3	1.0	23	7.8
Managerial	11	6.3	12	7.0	1	0.8	5	4.0	12	4.0	17	5.7
Administrative	7	4.0	3	1.7	7	5.5	3	2.4	14	4.7	6	2.0
Clerical	3	1.7	9	5.2	0	0.0	5	4.0	3	1.0	14	4.7
Sales	2	1.1	7	4.1	1	0.8	9	7.3	3	1.0	16	5.4
Operative	5	2.9	16	9.3	1	0.8	18	14.5	6	2.0	34	11.5
Service	1	0.6	13	7.6	1	0.8	6	4.8	2	0.7	19	6.4
Unskilled	1	0.6	8	4.7	0	0.0	10	8.1	1	0.3	18	6.1
Farm	1	0.6	0	0.0	0	0.0	3	2.4	1	0.3	3	1.0
Other	12	6.9	23	13.4	4	3.1	18	14.5	16	5.3	41	13.9
Sub-total	46	26.4	101	58.7	15	11.8	90	72.6	61	20.3	191	64.5
3. Never worked	16	9.2	1	0.6	4	3.1	5	4.0	20	6.6	6	2.0
Total:	174	100.0	172	100.0	127	100.0	124	100.0	301	100.0	296	100.0

Table 9.3.1: Mobility Matrix for Foreign-trained Polish Professional Immigrants: Outflow Percentage (N=174)

Last Occupation in Poland	Current Occupation in Canada													Total	
	1		2		3		4		5		6				
	N	%	N	%	N	%	N	%	N	%	N	%		N	%
1. Professional	54	48.6	14	12.6	30	27.0	12	10.8	0	0.0	1	0.9		111	100.0
2. Proprietary, Managerial & Administrative	4	20.0	7	35.0	5	25.0	4	20.0	0	0.0	0	0.0		20	100.0
3. White-collar*	3	16.7	0	0.0	12	66.7	3	16.7	0	0.0	0	0.0		18	100.0
4. Blue-collar**	1	16.7	1	16.7	1	16.7	3	50.0	0	0.0	0	0.0		6	100.0
5. Working in farm	0	0.0	0	0.0	0	0.0	1	100.0	0	0.0	0	0.0		1	100.0
6. Never worked	8	50.0	3	18.8	4	25.0	1	6.3	0	0.0	0	0.0		16	100.0
Total	70	40.7	25	14.5	52	30.2	24	14.0	1	0.0	1	0.6		172	100.0

Notes: *clerical, service, sales, and others
        **operative and unskilled

Table 9.3.2: Mobility Matrix for Foreign-trained Chinese Professional Immigrants: Outflow Percentage (N=128)

Last Occupation in China	Current Occupation in Canada													
	1		2		3		4		5		6		Total	
	N	%	N	%	N	%	N	%	N	%	N	%	N	%
1. Professional	26	24.8	18	17.1	30	28.6	26	24.8	2	1.9	3	2.9	105	100.0
2. Proprietary, Managerial & Administrative	1	12.5	3	37.5	4	50.0	0	0	0	0.0	0	0	8	100.0
3. White-collar*	1	16.7	0	0.0	4	66.7	0	0.0	1	16.7	0	0.0	6	100.0
4. Blue-collar**	0	0.0	0	0.0	0	0.0	1	100.0	0	0.0	0	0.0	1	100.0
5. Working in farm	0	0.0	0	0.0	0	0.0	0	0.0	0	0.0	0	0	0	0.0
6. Never worked	1	25.0	0	0.0	0	0	1	25.0	0	0.0	2	5.0	4	100.0
Total	29	23.4	21	16.9	38	30.6	28	22.6	3	2.4	5	4.0	124	100.0

Notes: *clerical, service, sales, and others
         **operative and unskilled

Table 9.3.3: Occupational Mobility for Foreign-trained Polish and Chinese Professional Immigrants (N = 302)

	Chinese		Polish		All	
	N	%	N	%	N	%
Upward mobility	4	3	27	16	31	10
Remain the same	36	29	76	44	112	38
Downward mobility	84	68	69	40	153	52
Total	124	100	172	100	296	100

Missing = 6

and 9.3.2 show that downward mobility (numbers to the right of the diagonal) is more prevalent than upward mobility (numbers to the left).

In total, 52 percent of respondents experienced downward mobility, 38 percent held the same type of job after immigration, and ten percent experienced upwardly mobility (see Table 9.3.3). Table 9.3.3 also shows that 68 percent of Chinese-Canadian professionals and 40 percent of Polish-Canadian professionals experienced downward occupational mobility.

In this survey, 44 percent of respondents reported that they experienced difficulties in terms of their command of English and 15 percent also experienced difficulties in their adaptation to Western culture. Table 9.4.1 shows that among those who answer "difficult" or "very difficult" in command of English, 69 percent have experienced downward occupational mobility. For those who answered "difficult" or "very difficult" in their adaptation to Western culture, 50 percent have experienced downward occupational mobility (Table 9.4.2). Data does show the effect of linguistic abilities and cultural adaptation on downward mobility. However, they also indicate that "linguistic abilities" and "cultural adaptation" alone cannot fully explain the downward mobility of foreign-trained professional immigrants. As a matter of fact, among those who answered "no difficulty" or "less difficult" in their command of English and their adaptation to Western culture, 40 to 54 percent reported having experienced downward mobility.

Table 9.4.1: Mobility between the Last Occupation in Country of Origin and Current Occupation in Canada by Linguistic Abilities as Reported by Foreign-trained Polish- and Chinese-Canadian Professionals (N = 302)

	Command of English					
	No difficulty/less difficult			Difficult/very difficult		
	Polish	Chinese	All	Polish	Chinese	All
	%	%	%	%	%	%
Downward mobility	35	50	40	53	81	69
Remain the same	47	48	47	37	14	24
Upward mobility	17	2	13	10	5	7
Total	100	100	100	100	100	100

Table 9.4.2: Mobility between the Last Occupation in Country of Origin and Current Occupation in Canada by Level of Adaptation to Western Culture as Reported by Foreign-trained Polish- and Chinese-Canadian Professionals (N = 302)

	Adaptation to Western Culture					
	No difficulty/less difficult			Difficult/very difficult		
	Polish	Chinese	All	Polish	Chinese	All
	%	%	%	%	%	%
Downward mobility	41	71	54	41	59	50
Remain the same	44	28	37	41	27	34
Upward mobility	15	1	9	18	14	16
Total	100	100	100	100	100	100

In this survey, most of the foreign-trained professionals considered the non-recognition or the devaluation of their foreign credentials as the most important factor contributing to their inaccessibility to professional occupations and downward mobility. 63 percent of the 302 respondents reported that they experienced difficulties in having their foreign credentials recognised in Canada.

Table 9.5.1 shows foreign-trained professionals' opinions on how foreign education is evaluated in Canada. Based on their experiences and observations, 36 to 49 percent of respondents reported that their foreign education was not fairly recognised by provincial government agencies, professional organisations, and educational institutions, and 42 percent of respondents did not believe that "the foreign education of foreign-trained professionals is compared to Canadian standards fairly".

Non-recognition of foreign work experience is also a problem. In our survey, over 90 percent of foreign-trained professionals reported that they had professional work experience in their country of origin before immigrating to Canada. Among them, 32 percent had four to nine years of professional work experience and 37 percent had ten or more years of professional work experience.

Table 9.5.2 shows that over 40 to 55 percent of respondents thought that foreign work experience is not fairly recognised by provincial government agencies, professional organisations, and educational institutions, and 48 percent of respondents do not believe that "the foreign work experience of foreign-trained professionals is compared to Canadian standards fairly".

Most foreign-trained professionals believed that they could not enter into professional occupations in which they are trained because their foreign credentials and work experience were devaluated. Table 9.6 shows that 79 percent of respondents reported that their occupations in their home country matched their professional qualifications well, while approximately 37 percent reported that their current (or last) occupation in Canada matched their professional qualifications. 59 percent of respondents reported that they were overqualified for their current occupations in Canada.

The respondents were asked if colour of their skin, national or ethnic origin, and speaking English as second language were factors in the evaluation of their credentials and recognition of foreign experience. 60 percent of Chinese-Canadian professionals and 17 percent of Polish-Canadian professionals perceived discrimination on the basis of their skin colour, while 26 percent of Chinese-Canadian professionals and

Table 9.5.1: Opinions on Evaluation of Foreign Education (N=302)

Professionals: (in %)	Polish-Canadian			Chinese-Canadian			Polish- & Chinese Can.		
	Agree	Disagree	Don't know	A	D	Dk	A	D	Dk
1 "Provincial government agencies recognise fairly the foreign education of foreign-trained professionals."	30	46	24	14	32	54	24	40	36
2 "Professional organisations recognise fairly the foreign education of foreign-trained professionals."	18	62	20	20	30	50	19	49	32
3 "Educational institutions recognise fairly the foreign education of foreign-trained professionals."	39	42	19	31	27	42	36	36	28
4 "The foreign education of foreign-trained [pros] is compared to Canadian standards fairly."	32	48	20	22	32	46	28	42	30

Table 9.5.2: Opinions on Evaluation of Foreign Work Experience (N=302)

Professionals: (in %)	Polish-Canadian			Chinese-Canadian			Polish- & Chinese Can.		
	Agree	Disagree	Don't know	A	D	Dk	A	D	Dk
1 " Provincial government agencies recognise fairly the foreign work experience of foreign-trained [pros]."	17	57	26	8	40	52	13	50	37
2 " Professional organisations recognise fairly the foreign work experience of foreign-trained [pros]."	8	65	27	19	39	42	13	55	32
3 " Educational institutions recognise fairly the foreign work experience of foreign-trained professionals."	29	48	23	31	28	39	30	40	30
4 " Foreign work experience of foreign-trained [pros] is compared to Canadian standards fairly."	22	55	23	22	39	39	22	48	30

Table 9.6: Occupational Match to Professional Qualification for Polish-Canadian Professionals before and after Immigration to Canada (N = 302)

| | How did your occupation in your home country match your professional qualifications before immigrating to Canada? | | | How does your current (or last) occupation in Canada match your profesisonal qualification? | | |
	Polish	Chinese	All	Polish	Chinese	All
	%	%	%	%	%	%
Perfectly matched	72	87	79	42	27	37
Overqualified	13	6	10	54	66	59
Underqualified	2	2	2	1	5	2
Never worked	13	5	9	3	2	2
Total	100	100	100	100	100	100

Table 9.7: Perceived Discriminations (N = 302)

| | Do you think the following statements are true or not true? (Professionals) | | | | | | | | |
| | Polish-Canadian | | | Chinese-Canadian | | | Polish- & Chinese-Canadian | | |
	True or Partially True %	Not True %	D'ont Know %	True or Partially %	Not True %	Don't Know %	True or Partially %	Not True %	D'ont Know %
In my experience of foreign work Experience and qualifications Overall are not fairly recognised By licensing bodies or regulatory Agencies because of									
Discrimination based on:									
1. Colour	17	54	29	60	9	31	35	35	30
2. National or ethnic origin	52	32	16	26	13	61	41	24	35
3. Speaking English as a second language	64	22	14	53	12	35	60	18	22
4. Gender	25	52	23	38	18	44	30	38	32

52 percent Polish-Canadian professionals mentioned that national or ethnic origin was a factor that influenced the evaluation of their credentials and recognition of foreign experience. Respondents also indicated that speaking English as a second language and gender were important factors (see Table 9.7).

Based on their own experiences and observations, 83 percent of respondents reported that "the difficulty in having their foreign qualifications or credentials recognised" was a major factor that affected (53 percent) or might have affected (30 percent) their chances to practise in their chosen professions. 82 percent of respondents think that "unequal opportunity to be hired in the professional jobs" was another major factor that affected (58 percent) or might have affected (24 percent) their chances to obtain professional jobs in the Canadian labour market.

Foreign-trained professionals encounter a difficult situation in the Canadian labour market. On the one hand, non-recognition of their foreign professional work experience disqualifies their entry into professional jobs leaving them no chance to get Canadian work experience. On the other hand, the emphasis on Canadian work experience as a requirement for professional employment makes it difficult for them to be recognised as qualified for professional jobs. As indicated in our survey, 68 percent of respondents reported having "actually experienced difficulties in obtaining professional work experience in Canada".

Survey findings indicate that there are some similarities between Polish- and Chinese-Canadian professionals in terms of occupational disadvantages and perceived discriminations. It demonstrates that foreign-trained professionals, whether from Poland or China, perceive similar systemic barriers in accessing professional occupations in the Canadian labour force, and experience similar downward occupational mobility. However, being visible minority members, foreign-trained Chinese-Canadian professionals are more disadvantaged.

Conclusion

This study suggests that foreign-trained professionals, especially visible minority professionals, perceive that they face systemic barriers to their entry into their respective professions. The problem of transferring educational equivalencies and work experience across international boundaries results in professional immigrants taking jobs for which they are overtrained, resulting in downward occupational mobility relative to their occupations held before their immigrating to Canada. It is evident that professional immigrants bring significant human capital resources to the Canadian labour force. However, a better understanding of how these human resources are actually used after the immigrants' arrival in Canada is needed. It is essential for federal, provincial governments, and professional organisations to understand how highly educated foreign-trained professional immigrants establish themselves in the labour force and what systemic barriers they encounter. The study suggests that in order for Canada to fully benefit from international human capital transfer, a policy is needed to ensure that the credentials of foreign-trained professional immigrants are properly and fairly evaluated.

CHAPTER 10

Career and Family Factors in Intention for Permanent Settlement in Australia

Siew-Ean Khoo & Anita Mak

During the second half of the 20th century, Australia's postwar immigration programme brought some 5.7 million migrants to the country, making immigration a vital component of both population growth and a productive labour force (Department of Immigration and Multicultural Affairs 1999a). Since the immigration programme emphasises permanent settlement, how well immigrants adjust after their arrival is an important issue. Immigrants who do not adjust are likely to return to their home country, representing a loss of their human capital to Australia after its investment in their recruitment and selection.

Studies of immigrant adjustment, especially in terms of participation in the labour market, have been a major component of immigration studies in Australia (Wooden et al. 1994). However, there has been little systematic research on the relationship between immigrants' employment outcome and their likelihood for permanent settlement. The longitudinal study reported in this chapter aimed to investigate both career and family factors in skilled Asian immigrants' intention for permanent settlement. The Asians studied were mainly ethnic Chinese from Hong Kong, China, Malaysia, Taiwan, and Singapore, but the study also included people originally from India, Sri Lanka, and Korea.

Skilled Asian Immigration to Australia

Significant changes to Australia's immigration policy since the 1970s have resulted in a new wave of migration of Asian, especially ethnic Chinese, skills and capital to Australia (Baker *et al.* 1994; Inglis & Wu 1992). Since the adoption of a racially non-discriminatory immigration policy by the Whitlam Labour Government in 1973, Australia has accepted a dramatically increased number of immigrants from various parts of Asia.

Then, in 1979, the Numerical Migrant Assessment System (NUMAS), commonly known as the points system, was introduced, selecting applicants on the basis of various observable characteristics, including educational background and occupational skills (Parcell *et al.* 1994). Since the mid-1980s, NUMAS has brought large numbers of highly educated and skilled independent immigrants to Australia. Sponsored immigrants selected under the Concessional Family Migration category were also screened by the points system, and so invariably were highly educated and/or possessed desirable occupational skills. In its report in 1988, the Committee to Advise on Australia's Immigration Policies, more so than any previous major policy review committees, also argued for an increased skill focus in Australia's immigration programme.

As a result of these important changes to Australian immigration policy, large numbers of skilled Asian men and women have immigrated to Australia since 1986. The number of Asian-born immigrants to Australia between 1986 and 2000 totalled more than half a million and they made up close to 40 percent of all settler arrivals during that period. During the same period at least five of the top ten sources of immigrants to Australia were Asian countries (Department of Immigration and Multicultural Affairs 1997a; 2000d). Asians also made up a significant proportion of skilled immigrants, comprising as high as 55 percent of all independent skilled immigrants and 93 percent of business migrants in 1991–92 (Kee *et al.* 1994). Since 1995, between ten and 15 thousand business and skilled immigrants have arrived each year from Asia.

As the major sources of immigrants to Australia since the mid-1980s include Hong Kong, China, Malaysia, Vietnam, Singapore, and Taiwan, a large proportion of the Asian newcomers are ethnic Chinese. The 1996 Census showed that 90 percent of Australian residents born in China and

89 percent of those born in Hong Kong spoke Chinese at home (Department of Immigration and Multicultural Affairs 2000a; 2000b). Cantonese was the fourth most commonly spoken language in Australia in 1996 while Mandarin, the official Chinese language spoken in China and Taiwan, was the eighth most commonly spoken (Department of Immigration and Multicultural Affairs 1997a). The number of people speaking Chinese at home had increased from 130,800 in 1986 to 343,200 in 1996. China (excluding Hong Kong and Taiwan) was ranked sixth in 1996 in terms of its contribution to the foreign-born population in Australia, a jump from fifteenth place in 1986. The number of Australian residents born in China, Hong Kong, or Taiwan totalled 199,000 in 1996, an increase from 67,700 ten years earlier (Department of Immigration and Multicultural 1997a).

Unfortunately, the increasing presence of the Asian-born in Australia since the 1970s has not been welcomed by all segments of the Australian community. There were heated debates about reducing levels of Asian immigration in 1984, 1988, and 1996–97 (Mak & Nesdale, in press). As visibly different minority members from a culturally different background, ethnic Chinese and other Asian-born immigrants are particularly susceptible to becoming targets of racial stereotypes and discrimination (Ip *et al.* 1994).

There is research evidence (e.g. Hawthorne 1994; Ip 1993; Iredale & Newell 1991; Mitchell *et al.* 1990) that Asian entrepreneurs and professionally-qualified Asians may encounter various barriers in transferring their occupational skills to the Australian workplace. However, the extent of employment and underemployment depends on occupational grouping, country of origin, length of residence in Australia, and Australian economic conditions (Birrell & Hawthorne 1997; Bureau of Immigration, Multicultural, and Population Research 1996; Khoo *et al.* 1994; Mak 1996). Watson (1995) found that not all skilled Asian immigrants suffer from disadvantaged employment outcomes. He actually identified an over-representation of individuals born in Hong Kong, Malaysia, India, and Sri Lanka in Australian managerial positions in finance, property, and business services. As the period of residence increased, Asian immigrants' English proficiency and rates of labour force participation and employment also increased (Khoo *et al.* 1994).

Attrition of Settlers

A reality of skilled immigration programmes is that not all of the arrivals would stake it out long enough to reap the benefits of linguistic and cultural familiarity and satisfactory employment outcomes. Indeed, the earliest studies of immigrant adjustment in Australia were motivated by concerns of settler loss among British immigrants in the 1950s and 1960s (Appleyard 1962a; 1962b; Commonwealth Immigrant Advisory Council 1967). These studies focused on the reasons for return migration and found that the returnees had not adjusted to living in Australia, felt homesick, and wished to return to their family and friends. A quarter of the returnees had been dissatisfied with their work conditions (Commonwealth Immigrant Advisory Council 1967).

Hugo (1994) estimated an overall settler loss in Australia of 21 percent over the period from 1947 to 1991. He also noted a general trend towards an increasing number of transients in the Australian immigration intake, as well as a recent trend in brain drain of an increasing number of local- and Asian-born Australians to Asia.

Kee and Skeldon (1994) have estimated that as many as 30 percent of immigrants from Hong Kong who arrived during 1990–91 were not living in Australia and were presumed to have returned home. Many of these people were skilled or business migrants and their mobility might be considered in the contexts of a global market for highly-skilled labour, the internationalisation of capital, and the success of the Asian economies during the 1980s and early 1990s (Hugo 1994; Mak 1997; Skeldon 1994). There were concerns that a settler loss of this scale represents an enormous loss of both human and financial capital to Australia. A study by Mak (1996) on the cross-cultural adjustments of professional and managerial Hong Kong immigrants found that while most were able to obtain employment soon after arrival, many were working in a different occupation than they had before. They also had difficulty adjusting to a different workplace culture.

Mak (1997) further analysed the factors in skilled immigrants' intention for either repatriation to Hong Kong or permanent settlement in Australia. A stronger intention to return to work in Hong Kong was found among young immigrants, those who had settled for a shorter period of time, and those who had lower levels of satisfaction with their career development, their latest job, or personal life. Those who did not intend to return were those with school-age children or whose reasons for migration included desiring a better future for their family. A subsequent multivariate loglinear analysis identified that career satisfaction and having school-age children constituted a parsimonious set of predictors of Hong Kong immigrants' intention for permanent settlement. The results further showed that a number of immigrants experienced a career-family dilemma, in that while they were not satisfied with their work situation, they were determined to remain permanently in Australia for the sake of their children's education. Mak's study identified work and family factors as important determinants of immigrants' intention for permanent settlement and key aspects of their adjustment as new settlers.

The importance of their children's education as a factor in Hong Kong immigrants' permanent settlement intention was not surprising. In a survey of recent immigrants, 40 percent of those from Asian countries considered educational opportunities in Australia to be 'excellent' and 52 percent said they were 'good' (findings obtained by the authors from the Longitudinal Survey of Immigrants conducted by the Department of Immigration and Multicultural Affairs during 1995–99). Presumably, many Asian immigrants would want to stay permanently so that their children could have access to these opportunities. Australia is also a favoured destination for many Asian parents considering sending their children overseas for tertiary education, because of the reputation of its universities and its geographic proximity and associated lower costs. Asian students form the vast majority of overseas students in Australia. In 1999, more than 80 percent of the 120 thousand overseas students resident in Australia were from Asian countries (Department of Immigration and Multicultural Affairs 1999b).

The Present Study

The present study is a partial replication of Mak's (1997) study in applying a multi-factorial framework consisting of background, work, and family variables to examine the intention for permanent settlement among a larger number of skilled and business immigrants from various Asian countries to Australia. The data came from the Longitudinal Survey of Immigrants to Australia, a major survey of immigrant settlement experiences funded by the Department of Immigration and Multicultural Affairs. The key indicator of immigrant adjustment used in this study was the intention to stay permanently in Australia or to return home.

The aim of the study was to examine the possible roles of various background variables (namely, country of origin, visa category, age group, and English language proficiency), work-related factors (such as labour force status, job satisfaction, and the use of educational qualifications), and family factors (having school-age children and whether immigrating for the future of the family) in whether a migrant intended to stay permanently or return (or had returned) home.

Specifically, it was hypothesised that those who were able to find employment soon after arrival, were satisfied with their jobs, and/or were able to use their qualifications, would be more likely to indicate an intention for permanent settlement. It also examined the hypothesis that those who had school-age children or those who indicated 'a better future for the family' as a reason for immigration, would be more likely to intend to settle permanently.

Methodology

Data

The data for the study came from the Department of Immigration and Multicultural Affairs' Longitudinal Survey of Immigrants to Australia (LSIA). A sample of 5,192 immigrants who arrived in Australia during the period from September 1993 to August 1995 and who resided in the major urban areas were interviewed within three to six months after arrival. A second interview was conducted one year later, and a third interview was conducted two years after the second interview. Data from the first and second interviews were used in this study.

The sample was selected at random from a total population of 75 thousand immigrants who were the principal applicants for permanent resident visas, stratified by visa category, state of residence, and country of origin. Interviews were conducted face-to-face by trained interviewers, with about one-third of the interviews involving bilingual interpreters. Further details of the survey are available from the Department of Immigration and Multicultural Affairs (1997).

Included in the survey sample were 530 immigrants from eight Asian countries — China, Hong Kong, Korea, Taiwan, Malaysia, Singapore, India, and Sri Lanka — who had come under the Concessional Family, Independent Skill, or Business Migration visa categories. Of these, the largest number was from Hong Kong (162), followed by India (90), China (88), Sri Lanka (56), Malaysia (42), Taiwan (38), Korea (29), and Singapore (25). Preliminary analyses showed that the smaller birthplace groups could be combined into regional groups because of their similar background characteristics and adjustment patterns: Korea and Taiwan; Malaysia and Singapore (Southeast Asia); and India and Sri Lanka (South Asia). However, migrants from China and Hong Kong came from very different political, economic, and English-speaking environments and had different adjustment patterns. They were retained as separate groups for analysis.

The five country groups in this study were major sources of Asian immigration to Australia in the last 15 years. Together they accounted for more than half (54 percent) of all non-humanitarian migration from Asia to Australia for the years 1986–99. They were also the main sources of skill and business migration from Asia to Australia during those years. Among immigrants from these countries who arrived during the survey sampling period of 1993–95, the percentage who were skilled or business migrants ranged from 26 percent (from China) to 72 percent (from Hong Kong). The average was 40 to 50 percent.

Measures

Intention for Permanent Settlement

The outcome measure of immigrant adjustment in this study was the migrant's permanent settlement intention reported at about 18 months after arrival in Australia. Immigrants who were adjusting well to their new place of residence would be more likely to want to stay permanently, while those who were not adjusting would be more likely to think about returning home. The LSIA asked all migrants whether they intended to return permanently to their country of origin. The skilled and business migrants in this study were divided into two groups according to their answer to this question at the second interview (about 15 to 18 months after arrival). Those who answered 'no' were the permanent settlers. Those who answered 'yes' or 'not sure' were possible returnees. Included in this group were 46 people who had participated in the first interview of the survey but not the second because they had returned overseas between the first and second interviews. Of the 530 skilled and business migrants in the study, 70 percent were in the permanent settler group and 30 percent were in the possible returnee group.

Background Variables

Migrants' background characteristics that were examined in this study were visa categories of migration, age, and English proficiency, as these had been identified in other studies as important to immigrant adjustment, especially in relation to labour market participation (e.g. Wooden 1994; Williams et al. 1997).

There were two main categories of skill migration: the Independent Skill category and the Concessional Family category (now known as Skilled–Australia-linked). Immigrants in the Independent Skill category were selected based on their qualifications, occupational skills, age, and English proficiency. Those in the Concessional Family category were also assessed for these characteristics but were sponsored by an Australian resident relative. Since the Concessional Family group had relatives in Australia, this could help in their adjustment and they might be more likely to stay permanently than Independent Skill migrants.

The points system used in the selection of skilled migrants awarded the most points for those less than thirty years of age. Younger people presumably have less difficulty adjusting to a new life. They also have more years to contribute to society in terms of their skills.

English language proficiency is important to immigrant adjustment, particularly for skilled migrants, because it is crucial for skilled employment in Australia. In this study, the measure of English language proficiency used is the immigrant's self-assessment at the first interview of his/her ability to speak English. The LSIA also collected information on reading and writing abilities. Since there was high correlation between reading, writing, and speaking ability, it was decided to use the measure based on speaking ability.

Work and Family Variables

The work and career variables included in this study were labour force status, job satisfaction, and use of qualifications in current employment, all measured at the time of the first interview (about six months after arrival).

Migrants who were employed at the time of the first interview were asked how they felt about their job. Those who replied that they "love it — (best job I ever had)" or "like it — it is a really good job" were classified as 'Very satisfied' with their job. Those who said that "The job is OK" were classified as 'Satisfied' while those who indicated that they "don't really care" or disliked or hated their jobs were classified as 'Not satisfied'. It was hypothesised that those who were very satisfied with their job would be more likely to settle permanently than those who were not as satisfied.

Employed migrants were also asked whether they used their highest qualification 'very often', 'often', 'only sometimes', 'rarely', or 'never'. It was hypothesized that those who used their qualifications often or very often would be more likely to settle permanently than those who used their qualifications only sometimes, rarely, or not at all.

Two dichotomous family measures were examined — presence of school-age children and whether 'a better future for the family' was one of the reasons for immigration. The first was a more specific measure than the second of the role of family factors.

Results

Descriptive Results

Among the study sample, 36 percent were Concessional Family migrants, 53 percent were Independent Skill migrants, and the rest were Business migrants. Because of the small size of the Business category, it was combined with the Independent Skill category in the data analysis because, like the Independent Skill category, it was not a family-sponsored category.

In the study sample, only 27 percent were under age 30, but nearly half (48 percent) were between the ages of 30 and 40. Close to 80 percent of the migrants in the study spoke English well or very well.

Just over half (52 percent) of the study sample were employed at the time of the first interview; 22 percent were unemployed and 26 percent were not in the labour force.

Of those employed, 52 percent were very satisfied with their job and 40 percent were satisfied. Eight percent were not satisfied. About 70 percent of those employed used their qualifications often or very often.

60 percent of the migrants in the study sample indicated that they had migrated to have a better future for their family and 46 percent had a school-age child in the household.

Migrant Characteristics by Country of Origin

Although all the migrants in the study were either skilled or business migrants, there were important differences in their background characteristics and work outcomes by country of origin, based on the chi-square test at probability levels of less than 0.05 (Table 10.1).

First, differences were observed by visa category. There was a higher proportion of Concessional Family migrants in the groups from China and South Asia. Business migrants made up nearly half of the group from Korea and Taiwan and one-fifth of the group from Southeast Asia but less than three percent of the groups from China and South Asia.

The Korea and Taiwan group also had an older age distribution with 46 percent aged 40 or older, followed by the Southeast Asian group with 37 percent. This was related to their larger proportion of business migrants who tended to be older than migrants in the skill categories.

The five groups also differed in their level of English proficiency. Migrants from Malaysia and Singapore had the largest proportion (91 percent) speaking English very well, while those from Korea and Taiwan had the lowest (two percent). Those from India and Sri Lanka also had a relatively high level of English proficiency.

Table 10.1: Background Characteristics of Sample of Skilled or Business Asian Migrants, by Country of Origin

	China	H.K.*	Korea/ Taiwan	Malaysia/ Singapore	India/ Sri Lanka	All Groups
	Country of Origin					
	%	%	%	%	%	%
Background Variables						
Visa Category						
Family Linked	53.4	32.7	19.4	28.4	41.8	36.4
Independent	44.3	58.0	35.8	53.7	58.2	52.5
Business	2.3	9.3	44.8	17.9	0	11.1
Age						
<30 years	27.3	32.7	13.4	35.8	24.0	27.4
30–39 years	58.0	45.8	40.3	26.9	56.8	47.7
40+ years	14.8	21.6	46.3	37.3	19.2	24.9
English-speaking Proficiency						
Very well	22.7	24.7	1.5	91.0	74.7	43.6
Well	39.8	53.1	44.8	6.0	17.1	34.0
Not well/not at all	37.5	22.2	53.7	3.0	8.2	22.4
Work Variables						
Labour Force Status						
Employed	62.5	50.6	29.9	62.7	52.1	51.9
Unemployed	10.2	16.1	16.4	14.9	41.1	21.9
Not in labour force	27.3	33.3	53.7	22.4	6.9	26.2
Job Satisfaction						
Very satisfied	34.1	19.1	22.4	43.3	25.3	26.8
Satisfied	19.3	26.5	7.5	23.3	17.9	20.9
Not satisfied	9.1	4.9	0	3.4	**	4.2
Not employed	37.5	49.4	70.1	37.3	48.0	48.1
Use Qualifications in Job						
Often	38.6	36.4	56.7	41.8	50.7	45.8
Sometimes/rarely	23.9	14.2	4.5	10.5	21.2	16.0
Not employed	37.5	49.4	70.1	37.3	48.0	48.1
Family Variables						
Have School-age Child						
Yes	50.0	36.4	56.7	41.8	50.7	45.8
No	50.0	63.6	43.3	58.2	49.3	54.2
Reason for Migration						
Better future for Family	50.0	55.6	61.2	56.7	70.6	59.6
Total	100.0	100.0	100.0	100.0	100.0	100.0
No. of Migrants	88	162	67	67	146	530

Notes: *Hong Kong
　　　**less than 5 people

In terms of work outcomes, the proportion employed within six months of arrival was highest for migrants from Malaysia, Singapore, and China and lowest for those from Korea and Taiwan. The highest unemployment rate was found for migrants from India and Sri Lanka. More than half the migrants from Korea and Taiwan and one-third of those from Hong Kong were not in the labour force at six months after arrival.

Job satisfaction also varied among the five countries of origin groups. Of those with more than half in employment, the proportion stating that they were very satisfied ranged from 69 percent of employed migrants from Malaysia and Singapore to 38 percent of those employed from Hong Kong. Only eight percent of those employed from all groups expressed dissatisfaction with their jobs.

There were also differences in the proportion using their qualifications. Of those groups with more than half in employment, those from Malaysia, Singapore, and Hong Kong were more likely to use their qualifications than those from China, India, and Sri Lanka.

The groups were also different in their proportion with at least one school-age child in the family. Half or more of skilled and business migrants from China, Korea, Taiwan, India, and Sri Lanka had a school-age child compared with just over one-third of those from Hong Kong and just over 40 percent of those from Malaysia and Singapore. The proportion who had migrated for a better future for the family was also higher among migrants from Korea, Taiwan, India, and Sri Lanka.

Covariates of Permanent Settlement Intention: All Asian Migrants

At 18 months after arrival in Australia, only 70 percent of the skilled Asian migrants in the survey indicated that they intended to settle permanently in Australia. Most of the other 30 percent were not sure and a few had returned overseas.

The migrants differed in their permanent settlement intention by a number of characteristics. In examining the individual predictors of permanent settlement intention in Table 10.2, the chi-square test with a probability level of 0.05–0.10 was used to establish a significant relation. According to this criterion, country of origin, visa category, and the family variable 'migration for a better future for the family' were significantly

Table 10.2: Skilled or Business Asian Migrants who Intended to Stay Permanently, According to Background Characteristics and Work and Family-related Factors

	China	H.K.*	Korea/ Taiwan	Malaysia/ Singapore	India/ Sri Lanka	All Groups
	%	%	%	%	%	%
Background Variables						
Origin						
China	–	–	–	–	–	76.1
Hong Kong	–	–	–	–	–	75.3
Korea & Taiwan	–	–	–	–	–	62.7
Southeast Asia	–	–	–	–	–	71.6
South Asia	–	–	–	–	–	63.0
						(p=0.063)
Visa Category						
Family Linked	78.7	81.1	38.5	89.5	73.8	76.2
Independent or Business	73.2	72.5	68.5	64.6	55.3	66.5
	(p=0.542)	(p=0.231)	(p=0.044)	(p=0.042)	(p=0.023)	(p=0.019)
Age						
<30 years	70.8	67.9	77.8	70.8	68.6	69.7
30–39 years	74.5	79.7	59.3	77.8	62.7	70.8
40+ years	92.3	77.1	61.3	68.0	57.1	68.9
	(p=0.314)	(p=0.302)	(p=0.595)	(p=0.777)	(p=0.643)	(p=0.929)
English-speaking Proficiency						
Very well	75.0	90.0	–	72.1	60.6	70.1
Well	82.9	70.5	66.7	66.7	70.3	69.4
Not well/not at all	69.7	–	58.3	–	–	70.6
	(p=0.441)	(p=0.013)	(p=0.580)	(p=0.777)	(p=0.290)	(p=0.976)
Work Variables						
Labour Force Status at Wave 1						
Employed	76.4	80.5	60.0	71.4	60.5	71.3
Unemployed	88.9	80.8	45.4	80.0	65.0	69.8
Not in labour force	70.8	64.8	69.4	66.7	70.0	67.6
	(p=0.555)	(p=0.091)	(p=0.339)	(p=0.768)	(p=0.774)	(p=0.746)

Table 10.2: (Continued) Skilled or Business Asian Migrants who Intended to Stay Permanently, According to Background Characteristics and Work and Family-related Factors

	China	H.K.*	Korea/ Taiwan	Malaysia/ Singapore	India/ Sri Lanka	All Groups
	Country of Origin					
	%	%	%	%	%	%
Job Satisfaction						
Very satisfied	70.0	83.9	60.0	65.5	67.6	70.4
Satisfied	84.0	78.4	60.0	84.6	53.9	73.0
Not satisfied/ Not employed	85.8	70.0	63.0	72.0	65.7	68.6
	(p=0.478)	(p=0.259)	(p=0.957)	(p=0.446)	(p=0.376)	(p=0.690)
Use Qualifications in Job						
Often	70.6	83.1	–	68.6	60.0	71.1
Sometimes/rarely	85.7	73.9	–	85.7	61.3	71.8
Not employed	75.8	70.0	–	72	65.7	68.6
	(p=0.441)	(p=0.208)		(p=0.655)	(p=0.805)	(p=0.796)
Family Variables						
Have School-age Child						
Yes	77.3	83.1	65.8	75.0	58.1	70.8
No	75.0	70.9	58.6	69.2	68.1	69.3
	(p=0.803)	(p=0.084)	(p=0.548)	(p=0.605)	(p=0.213)	(p=0.718)
Reason for Migration						
Better future for family						
Yes	79.6	80.0	70.7	81.6	62.1	73.1
No	72.7	69.4	50.0	58.6	65.1	65.4
	(p=0.453)	(p=0.122)	(p=0.087)	(p=0.039)	(p=0.734)	(p=0.058)

Notes: * Hong Kong
      **less than 5 people

related to permanent settlement intention for the study sample as a whole (last column in Table 10.2).

Migrants from China and Hong Kong were the most likely to want to settle permanently (75 percent) while those from Korea, Taiwan, India, and Sri Lanka were the least likely (63 percent). As expected, migrants in the Concessional Family category, who had relatives in Australia, were also significantly more likely to settle permanently than those in the Independent Skill or Business categories. Finally those whose reasons for migration included "a better future for family" were more likely to settle permanently than those who did not indicate this reason for migration.

There was very little difference by age or English proficiency. The work variables also did not show any significant relation to permanent settlement intention for the group as whole. Neither did the family variable of having a school-age child.

Covariates of Permanent Settlement for Different Country Groupings

Because the five country groupings differed in their background characteristics, it was not surprising that there were a number of differences in the factors related to their permanent settlement intention. None of the variables shown in Table 10.2 were significantly related to the permanent settlement intention of migrants from China. For skilled migrants from India and Sri Lanka, none of the variables except visa category was significantly related to permanent settlement intention. For the migrants from Korea, Taiwan, Malaysia, and Singapore, two variables — visa category and migration for a better future for the family — were significant. For migrants from Hong Kong, the significant variables included English proficiency, labour force status, and both family variables.

China

Although Chinese migrants who were in the Concessional Family visa category or had migrated to have a better future for the family were more likely to settle permanently compared with those who were in the Independent Skill category or had migrated for other reasons, the difference was not significant. It was possible that for many immigrants from China, return migration was not a viable option regardless of their work or family situation due to the costs of moving again or conditions in the country. This group had the highest proportion intending to settle permanently.

Hong Kong

In contrast, the results for skilled Hong Kong migrants showed that their permanent settlement intention was related to level of English proficiency as well as some of the work and family variables. Being in the labour force and having a school-age child were significantly related to permanent settlement intention. Those who had migrated for a better future for the family were also more likely to settle permanently than those who had not migrated for this reason although the relation was weaker than that shown for the presence of school-age children. Those who were more satisfied with their job or able to use their qualifications were also more likely to settle permanently than those who did not have these characteristics.

Korea and Taiwan

Although visa category was related to permanent settlement intention for this group, the relation was the opposite of that expected. The lower percentage intending to stay permanently among Concessional Family migrants compared with Independent/Business migrants is difficult to explain. Having relatives in Australia apparently had not helped in their settlement. For this group, migration to provide a better future for the family was strongly related to permanent settlement intention.

Malaysia and Singapore

Family factors had a very strong relation to the permanent settlement intention of this group. Those who had relatives in Australia or who had migrated for a better future for the family were much more likely to intend to stay permanently than those who had not. However, none of the work variables showed any relation to permanent settlement intention.

India and Sri Lanka

None of the variables except visa category was related to permanent settlement intention for this group. There was no relation between any of the work or family variables with permanent settlement intention. Other factors not examined in this study must be affecting their permanent settlement intention since the proportion in this group intending to settle permanently was relatively low — less than two-thirds.

A Summary Analysis

While the above analyses had identified the background variables and work and family measures that have a strong relation to skilled migrants' permanent settlement intention, it was also useful to examine how effective these factors considered together were as predictors of permanent settlement intention. Table 10.3 shows the results of loglinear models to examine country of origin, visa category, and migration for a better future for the family as predictors of permanent settlement intention.

Table 10.3: Goodness-of-fit Statistics for Loglinear Models of Permanent Settlement Intention of Asian Skilled Migrants

	Model 1	Model 2	Model 3	Model 4
Independent variables	1. A	1. B	1. A	1. A
	2. B	2. C	2. C	2. B
				3. C
Likelihood ratio chi-square	10.60	4.73	0.80	18.28
d.f	4	4	1	13
Probability	0.0315	0.3157	0.3706	0.1473
Number of cases	530	530	530	530

Notes: Independent variables — (A) Visa category; (B) Country of origin; (C) "Better Future for family"

The model that best fit the data was Model 3, which had only visa category and migration for a better future for the family as predictors of permanent settlement intention. Model 2, which has country of origin and family reason for migration, as predictors and Model 4, which has all three variables, also showed a satisfactory fit but not as good as Model 3. When the reason for migration variable was excluded (Model 1), the fit became unsatisfactory, confirming the importance of this variable in predicting permanent settlement intention among Asian skilled migrants. In all the models, all the independent variables were significantly related to permanent settlement intention.

The results confirmed the importance of family factors in immigrant adjustment as measured by permanent settlement intention. Skilled migrants whose migration was family-related — as measured by visa category or reason for migration — were more likely to be permanent settlers than those whose migration was not family-related.

Discussion

Asian skilled immigration to Australia, including a large proportion of ethnic Chinese, represents an important new wave of immigration of skills and capital to Australia since the 1980s. However, there has not been a systematic study of the various Asian groups' intentions for permanent settlement. The longitudinal analyses of two waves of data collected in Australia in the mid-1990s reported in this chapter aim to address this important gap in our understanding of the adjustment of recent skilled immigrants from Asia.

Asian Immigrants as a Whole

It was significant that when asked at 18 months after arrival in Australia whether they intended to settle permanently in Australia, only 70 percent of skilled Asian immigrants said "yes". Further analysis of the data indicates that family factors are important in determining the intention for permanent settlement among these migrants. Those who have relatives in Australia — who have migrated in the Concessional Family visa category — are much more likely to settle permanently than the

Independent skilled or Business migrants. Those who have migrated because they want a better future for their family are also more likely to settle permanently than those who have migrated for other reasons. The latter finding is consistent with Inglis and Wu's (1994) observation that immigrant families, such as Hong Kong Chinese families, with school-age children often value the educational opportunities available in Australia, and the freer and less competitive nature of Australian schooling. Moreover, immigrant children can often quite quickly adjust to the Australian school system, and over time may not have maintained a level of literacy in their first language (e.g. Chinese) necessary to switch back smoothly into the local school system in their country of origin.

Although skilled and business migrants are selected for migration on their occupational and business skills, the results show that employment status, job satisfaction, or use of qualification are not as important in influencing the permanent settlement intention of most skilled migrants from Asia, with the possible exception of those from Hong Kong.

Skilled Immigrants from Hong Kong

The study shows that for immigrants from Hong Kong, whether occupational skills can be transferred successfully is important in influencing permanent settlement intention. For these migrants, children's education was also important as demonstrated by the greater likelihood of permanent settlement among those with school-age children, confirming the results of Mak's (1997) study. This may be related to the school curriculum in Hong Kong or Hong Kong parents' greater reluctance to disrupt their children's education. It may also be that these migrants consider it particularly important that they settle permanently so that their children can have access later to the tertiary education opportunities in Australia.

Mak (1997) has indicated that skilled immigrants from Hong Kong considering returning to work in Hong Kong could be caught in a career versus family dilemma that can be further complicated by different levels of career satisfaction of husband and wife in dual-career families. Mak (in press) has further suggested that parents with school-age children intending to repatriate to Hong Kong face the difficult decision of choosing one of three solutions. First, they would have to enrol their children in one of the highly expensive and exclusive English-speaking international schools in Hong Kong. Second, only the father would return to work in Hong Kong, frequently flying back to Australia for family reunions, becoming the so-called 'astronaut'. Third, both parents would return to Hong Kong, leaving their teenaged children — the so-called 'parachute children' — to continue with their schooling in Australia.

Skilled Immigrants from China

It is interesting to note that the study's findings relating to skilled immigrants from China are different from those for similar immigrants from Hong Kong, even though both groups are ethnic Chinese. This suggests the different orientation of the two groups to permanent settlement that may be related to conditions back in the home country and whether return migration is a realistic option. It is possible that return migration is a less realistic option for immigrants from China than for immigrants from Hong Kong. This would explain the lack of impact that their employment situation and other factors examined in this study have on their permanent settlement intention.

Skilled Immigrants from Singapore and Malaysia

The important factors affecting the permanent settlement intention of this third group of mainly ethnic Chinese immigrants also differ from those for the other two groups above. The permanent settlement intention of this group is most strongly influenced by family factors, with the findings that those who had been sponsored to migrate by family members and/or had migrated for a better future for the family are much more likely to want to settle permanently. Career factors have not been important factors in their permanent settlement intention. However, compared to the previous two groups, this group has adjusted better in terms of their employment, with the highest proportion using their qualifications and being satisfied with their jobs. It is also noteworthy in this regard that they are all highly proficient in English.

Putting Families First

Overall, present findings have highlighted the importance of family factors in the permanent settlement of skilled Asian immigrants. Those with existing family ties and who had migrated for a better future for their family were more likely to indicate an intention for permanent settlement. Contrary to the original hypotheses, immigrant employment outcomes did not appear to constitute discerning factors for such an intention, with the exception of the Hong Kong-born.

Immigrant community observations have shown that many new immigrants could have decided to settle permanently primarily because of their spouse's or extended family's preferences, and/or for the sake of their children's schooling and future. Mak (1991) has referred to some of these immigrants as Contented Settlers. They are resigned to the career disadvantages associated with their non-English-speaking immigrant background and have shifted their focus on career development to raising children with outstanding academic performance. After settling down in a job with a steady income, Contented Settlers would devote a lot of time and energy to their familial roles and invest in their children's education. They hope that their children will eventually succeed in prestigious professional careers or lucrative businesses in Australia; such expectations could ease the disappointments caused by the curtailment in their own career development (Mak & Chan 1995). Data from the 1996 Census have already shown that a higher proportion of the second generation whose parents are born in China, Hong Kong, or Malaysia have tertiary qualifications compared to all second generation persons. While 17 percent of Australian-born residents over the age of 15 with one or both parents born overseas had tertiary qualifications in 1996, the equivalent percentages for those with one or both parents born in China, Hong Kong, or Malaysia were 31, 25, and 22 percent respectively (Department of Immigration and Multicultural Affairs 2000a; 2000b; 2000c).

Implications for Immigration Programmes

There has been increased emphasis on skilled migration in Australia's immigration policies and programmes in recent years. Migrants in the skilled visa categories made up nearly 40 percent of all visa-bearing immigrants in 1999/2000 compared to just 25 percent in 1995/96. The increase has been due to the government's efforts to 'balance' the immigration programme, which was dominated by family reunion migration in the first half of the 1990s. Temporary entry arrangements were also introduced in 1997 that allowed employers to sponsor the migration of skilled labour for up to four years' stay. These arrangements have resulted in an increase in the temporary entry of skilled migrants.

Australia is not the only country that is keen to attract skilled migrants. The European and North American countries are also looking to import skilled foreign labour, particularly in information technology, and can be considered to be in competition with Australia in the global market for skilled migrants. At the same time, skilled labour is becoming increasingly internationally mobile in response to this global market and can afford to consider the options available in different countries. In the context of this global competition for skilled migrants, the results of this study can be useful in suggesting how countries can attract and retain skilled migrants from Asia and that is to highlight the resources and opportunities — including educational opportunities — available to their families and their children's future.

Educational opportunities for shaping a better future for the family are attractive to various groups of Asian immigrants. Community observations have also suggested that among ethnic Chinese Australian families, despite the diversity of their countries of origin, socioeconomic backgrounds, and religious affiliations, they often share a core family value of achieving security and prosperity (Mak & Chan 1995). Accruing human capital in the form of qualifications and skills is highly regarded as these achievements are associated with improved prospects for financial security.

Immigration programmes that emphasise educational opportunities and offer academic support for children from non-English-speaking backgrounds, such as the Australian programme, are likely to be attractive to prospective Asian immigrants looking for an adopted country to raise their children, as well as to lure them to settle permanently. On the other hand, a better understanding of the sizeable loss of settlers can be gained in light of a global trend towards increasing mobility of highly-skilled labour, especially among those without existing family ties in the new country. The career-family dilemma faced by Hong Kong and Taiwanese Chinese immigrants has contributed to the increase in the numbers of 'astronaut fathers' and 'parachute children', posing a threat to the cohesiveness of the family. At a time when the phenomenon of the Chinese diaspora has continued to develop, the traditional Chinese value in rendering their children good educational opportunities apparently remains unabated, even though for some highly-skilled immigrants, this may mean putting the children's future ahead of their own career considerations.

CHAPTER 11

No Longer Migrants: Southern New Zealand Chinese in the 20th Century

Niti Pawakapan

Most previous studies of the New Zealand Chinese have been concerned with immigration restrictions and the racial discrimination that the Chinese have encountered in New Zealand (see Buckingham 1974; Forgie 1969; Fyfe 1948; Kay 1973; O'Connor 1968; Willis 1974). A major conclusion is that the prejudice against the Chinese, socially and politically, by the Europeans,[1] especially in the 19th century, was the main factor that created social distance between the two peoples. It is said that injustice and, on several occasions, violence against the Chinese were the results of this prejudice. Previous studies often show little hesitation in agreeing that the Chinese were nothing but the victims of the White mistreatment, putting the blame on the Europeans for unfavourable and bitter racial relations in New Zealand. There seems to be a common view of the Europeans as racists.

I do not deny that discrimination exists. New Zealand's immigration restrictions and other laws imposed in the past provide clearly proof of racial discrimination. Yet, the issue of racism, in my view, has been over-emphasised. For instance, to the New Zealand Chinese (and some of those who conducted research on the Chinese), perhaps the least popular person — with the exception of Lionel Terry who shot dead a Chinese man in Wellington — has been Richard John Seddon, a former Prime Minister. Although a hero of the European working class, to the

Chinese he was a troublemaker and an enemy, and was even described as a "quite savage racist" (O'Connor 1968, p. 42). This judgment was not, however, entirely fair. It is apparent that:

> "While strongly set against Chinese immigration he (Seddon) did not relish discrimination against those already admitted for settlement. Even when working hard in 1880 for virtual prohibition of Chinese immigration, he fought against moves to remove Chinese names from voting lists and asked for an inquiry into reports that police had used unnecessary brutality in breaking up a Chinese card-game: Chinese in New Zealand, he insisted, 'ought to have the same personal freedom as people of other nations'. It was not till some years later that he swung over full-scale discrimination" (Price 1974, 208).

Seddon, in a role of politician, was neither more nor less racist than were others of his time.

This paper focuses on the Chinese who migrated to Dunedin, in New Zealand's South Island, between the 1920s and the 1940s. Unlike previous studies, I argue that social distance between the Chinese and the Europeans in the past occurred as the result of Chinese migrants' attempts to settle and establish their "self-employed" businesses in the new country. Social distance between the two groups was often due to economic circumstances rather than racial prejudice.

The early Chinese migrants in New Zealand were miners, whose main goals were to make a fortune from gold mining and then to return to China a wealthy man. None of these early migrants planned to settle in New Zealand. By contrast, Chinese migrants who arrived in Dunedin in the 1920s, and the following decades,[2] were intent on settling permanently in their new home. This was due, on the one hand, to war, bandits, drought, and famine in China, and, on the other hand, to new opportunities in New Zealand and a feeling of security. They also differed from the older Chinese gold miners in that after a number of years working in the new country, most of them had earned adequate experience and money to become self-employed.

Because of the nature of their jobs and the location of their places of work, which they also used as places of residence, the Chinese were isolated socially as well as physically. Since most of their time was occupied by work, these Chinese had little chance to associate with either their fellow Chinese or with Europeans. In addition, the lack of public transportation infrastructure reduced mobility. Most contacts with outsiders were, therefore, restricted to working relationships. This sort of way of life separated the Chinese from the host society and limited the time they could spend cultivating social relationships. Thus, interaction between the Chinese and the Europeans was at a minimum. It took several decades for both groups to narrow social distance between them, and for the Chinese themselves to develop their enterprises, and to change and establish a new lifestyle.

Some jobs, such as laundry, required special skills that can be acquired only by working. Although apprenticeship has long been practised by the Chinese, outside of China apprenticeship systems vary from place to place. For instance, the systems that were established among the Chinese in the Philippines are said to be rather complex and widespread (Omohundro 1978, pp. 97–98). In the United States, on the other hand, such apprentice systems are rare among second-generation Chinese, and are restricted to those with specific, close relationships such as father and son and those in laundries (Barnett 1960, p. 43). In Dunedin, Chinese newcomers who worked in the laundries had to learn new skills, such as ironing and starching, by taking up apprenticeship. Apprenticeship was also important among young men who worked in fruit and vegetable shops. One must learn to buy and sell products at the prices that were profitable, to auction at the auction markets, to keep the products in good condition, to select a 'good business' location for a new shop, and so on. Such knowledge was transferred from an older shop owner or shopkeeper to a younger apprentice — in most cases, between father and son, uncle and nephew or close relatives — only by working.[3]

The Arrival of the Chinese

The Chinese had been arriving in New Zealand since the 1860s, working in the goldfields of Central Otago, a rough and dry inland area in the South Island. Almost all of them were Cantonese, whose hometowns were located in Guangdong Province in southeastern China. Generally, these people worked under contracts with Chinese merchants and most of the latter lived in New Zealand. Under such a contract, the miner's travelling expenses, food, and all necessary supplies were taken care of by the merchants. In return, the miners would pay back their debts, with a high interest added, to the merchants. While working in the goldfields of South Island, Chinese miners hardly made a living, let alone a fortune, out of gold mining. Thus, it took several years to pay off their debts. Life was hard, they were poor, and there was not much hope for success. Some died and many became old, unable to start a new life or return to China.

By the turn of the century, gold became difficult to find. Consequently, the region's prosperity slowly declined. Most of the population, including the Chinese, moved to the big cities in North Island, searching for a new fortune. Many Chinese, however, remained in Central Otago, turning to other jobs such as picking fruit, thinning turnips, shearing, or fencing. Some were cooks or worked in local hotels (Don, *A.I.T.*, 1901, p. 24). Several of my informants agreed with the above statement, insisting on the presence of Chinese cooks in hotels during the first two decades of the 20th century, especially in North Island. Yet, until the late 1920s a few elderly Chinese were still seen around the West Coast of South Island, working as market gardeners/hawkers, and one or two lived on charity (Adshead & Johnson 1988, pp. 28–36).

Dunedin and the Chinese

A number of Chinese moved from the goldfields to Dunedin, trying to find jobs. A few of them, who had some savings and were lucky enough to find some Europeans who agreed to lease a small piece of land to them, grew vegetables and hawked their produce on the city's streets. Some Chinese were also seen selling pork, fish, and bought old rags, bottles, bones, sacks and scrap metals (Lee 1977, pp. 65–66 & 129). Others found work as cooks or kitchen-hands.

Dunedin, located almost at the bottom of South Island, was the most flourishing city in New Zealand during the days of the gold rush. It was the port where the earliest Chinese gold miners landed before travelling inland to Central Otago. It was here that they rested, met their relatives, friends, or sponsors, took their supplies, learnt how to live in a new country, and so on. Here the history of the New Zealand Chinese began. Nonetheless, around the beginning of the 20th century, Dunedin's population began to shrink gradually because of migration to North Island. The city became less significant, but still had its peculiar characteristics. There were libraries, museums, public baths, parks, and recreation grounds (Olssen 1981, p. 253). Electricity was used both for public enterprises, such as tramways, and, as early as the 1920s, for domestic purposes, for ranges, water heaters and several other appliances (see good collections of photographs during this period in Knight 1983–85). In the early 20th century, the city's residents also witnessed the coming of new vehicles, that is, motorcars and lorries, mostly owned by wealthier families.

In the late 19th and early 20th centuries, most Chinese lived in boarding houses, the so-called "Chinese clubs", in downtown Dunedin. This was one of the city's most crowded areas, known as the "Devil's Half-Acre" or the "Dunedin Slums", where most of the residents were Chinese and Lebanese. It was an area of unpleasantness, minimal facilities, dirt, gambling dens, and brothels. Its residents were ignored and left to live on their own for many years until the turn of the 20th century, when the danger of epidemics and unsanitary buildings raised public awareness. In 1900, the area was inspected by the city council. Many buildings were reported to be unfit for living and were ordered to be demolished. Thus, Rev. Alexander Don, a missionary who worked among the Chinese, and representatives of the Chinese community discussed the problem of homelessness if the buildings were to be demolished. It was clear that a large number of the Chinese could not find or afford to have new residences. Many of them were old and poor. Possible solutions were either to send them to the Old Men's Home or for the city council to provide them with houses, if the demolition was carried out. Finally, it was agreed that the action would be postponed until the Chinese residing in these buildings found new accommodation. They were ordered, however, to keep the places scrupulously clean to protect against disease (O.D.T., 19/6/1900, p. 7). It is also worth noting that some Chinese at the time lived in the Old Men's Home,[4] or Benevolent Institution, and a few in the asylum.

Former Chinese gold miners who turned market gardeners/hawkers earned adequate money and lived reasonably well. These people and their fellow Chinese migrants were among the pioneers who established themselves in some self-employed occupations, such as market gardening, fruit and vegetable retailing, and laundering. Their expectation, nevertheless, was not to achieve business success, nor to become permanent residents of the new country. Their dream was to return to China as rich men. Although many of them lived frugally, trying to save as much money as they could, their savings were not used towards increasing capital for re-investment in the business, but was instead sent to their families in China. This obviously limited the development of their businesses. In addition, since the Chinese at this time did not intend to settle in New Zealand, social activity, particularly with Europeans, was also limited.

The Newcomers

Despite government restrictions on immigration and the poll tax, the Chinese were still coming to New Zealand in the 1900s and the following decades. The 1920s saw a new era for the New Zealand Chinese. Young men, mostly in their teens or early twenties, travelled by sea from China via Sydney and would have landed at Wellington or perhaps Auckland. Unlike previous immigrants who worked under contracts, these newcomers were financially supported by their fathers or close relatives who had worked in New Zealand for some time and saved an adequate amount of money to pay for the new immigrants' travelling and other expenses. Thus, these young men were not bound by any legal contracts. Living with relatives — or, in some cases, senior fellow villagers or close friends — in the cities, they learnt where to find jobs and how to survive in a new country. Some stayed, but many shifted to Christchurch and other county towns. Several young Chinese came to Dunedin. These newcomers proved to be quite different from their predecessors.

In Dunedin, Chinese newcomers, in their early twenties, worked as market gardeners, fruit and vegetable retailers, grocery sellers, and launderers, more or less the same kinds of jobs they had held in China before emigration. These businesses were either handed down from their fathers or other older male relatives to the newcomers or bought from the previous owners. Although these were largely family enterprises, outsiders would sometimes be taken in as partners or as employees. A notable remark, however, is that while the Chinese who migrated to New Zealand before 1920 had one inspiration for starting their self-employed enterprises, that is, to return to their homeland with wealth to ameliorate their former poverty, the new immigrants of the 1920s did more than just become wealthy. They were the first Chinese to settle permanently in New Zealand. For any Chinese, China remained home, but as famine and war continued to prevail in the homeland, the new immigrants had no choice but to stay in a foreign country. After years of hard work, their businesses became successful and the Chinese discovered new prosperity and a new home.

However, because their jobs were extremely time-consuming, the Chinese were often deprived of social life, both with their own community as well as with others. This was one of the main factors that affected relations both among the Chinese and with the Europeans. All of these will be described further below.

It must be noted that the Chinese female population at this time was very small. This was due to New Zealand immigration legislation, the poll tax, and Chinese custom (Ip 1990, Chapter 2). Chinese women and their children only began to arrive in larger numbers just before and during World War II, as war refugees.

Market Gardening

Market gardening became one of the most characteristically Chinese occupations in New Zealand. It can be traced back to the days of the gold rush (Don, O.C.M.). There is some evidence to show that the Chinese initially grew vegetables only for their own consumption, but later became the source of supply for their neighbours and Europeans. With the growth of urbanisation, especially at the turn of the century, Chinese market gardeners had become major suppliers for the people in the cities and rural towns of South Island.

Chinese had become conspicuous as market gardeners in Dunedin during the second half of the 19th century.[5] According to one newspaper, five Chinese men, possibly disenchanted with mining, leased land in Great King Street and established a garden (O.W., 7/10/1867). Between

June and July 1889, there were 290 Chinese men in Dunedin, including the suburbs and Sawyers Bay, of whom 110 were gardeners (approximately 80 gardeners at Andersons Bay, Forbury and Caversham), 70 shopkeepers, 66 hawkers (possibly including vegetable hawkers) and seven hotel cooks (Don, O.C.M., 1/6/1889: 222 and 1/7/1889: 3). At the same time, Chinese market gardeners were seen in other places throughout the country, for example in Christchurch (Leach 1984, p. 120).

During the 1890s and the 1900s, land was taken up for market gardens at Sawyers Bay, around North-East Valley, in Kaikorai Valley, and on the Flat at Tainui, Forbury, and South Dunedin (between Burns and Barker Street). Owing to legislation forbidding Asians to hold freehold land, the gardening areas were not owned by the Chinese, but were instead leased from year to year. According to Stedman, rentals varied from £5 per acre per annum (in 1900) for two acres on the Ings' property at Bay View Road to £14 per acre for 16 acres on the McIndoe land at Macandrew Road, although it has been estimated that, on average, the amount paid was £12 per acre per annum in 1908 (which was quite high — see further). The yearly rates levied by the Borough Councils of Caversham and South Dunedin averaged about £1 per acre at this time. Approximately 50 acres at Forbury and South Dunedin, and a further 60 acres on the Tainui Flat were leased to Chinese gardeners. Individual holdings ranged in size from two to ten acres but most were between three and eight acres (Stedman 1966, p. 133).

Chinese methods of cultivation in New Zealand were based on the traditional Chinese peasant pattern, and were not influenced very much by the new physical environment. Cropping was necessarily intensive and followed a strict rotation system. Field stubble and horse manure, the latter obtained from the stables at Macandrew Road, were regularly dug in so as to maintain fertility, since leaching rapidly drained the soil of nutrients. Irrigation was unnecessary and the main concern of the tenant farmer was to drain off surface water. For this purpose, a complicated system of ditches was developed, leading — at Forbury — to the large open channel in Macandrew Road. During winter, treadmills (typically Chinese) were operated to hasten run-off of floodwater. As in China, there was an intensive application of labour to the soil, six or seven men working the average farm — about five acres (Stedman 1966, p. 134).

Seven main crops were grown: potatoes, cabbages, cauliflower, lettuce, spinach, carrots and parsnips (*ibid*).[6] There was little specialisation and the majority of farmers grew most, if not all, of these vegetables, conditions in China having taught them the dangers of monoculture (Stedman 1966, p. 134). In addition, Chinese market gardeners preferred fertilised and flat land, whether irrigated or not (Helen Leach, per. comm.).

A distinctive characteristic of market gardening in New Zealand appears to be a preference for areas of basalt — dark coloured soil of volcanic origin, rich in fertiliser and therefore excellent for vegetable growing. Dunedin, especially around Sawyers Bay, is a basalt area. Interestingly, basalt areas in Auckland have been cultivated by Chinese market gardeners as well (Lee 1974; Hunt 1956).

Before the 1920s, the crop was usually sold door-to-door by hawkers around South Dunedin and St. Kilda, and also in the city, the vegetables being carried, as in the homeland, in baskets attached to a (bamboo) pole across the vendor's shoulders. While people occasionally called at the gardens to buy produce, stalls were not set up until 1965. In 1908, it was said that a man working on a garden and hawking his crops from there could expect a clear profit of £130–140 per annum, whereas the same person operating a shop on the Flat or in town, and buying in most of his produce, could expect only £60–70 (Stedman 1966, p. 135).

One of the oldest Chinese market gardeners in Dunedin said that when he arrived here in 1920, his father had a small garden at Forbury, then moved to Kaikorai Valley. A few years later, he handled the job for his father, who returned to China, and moved to North Taieri, Outram, and, finally, to Momona. In his case, the reason for shifting was typical in that market gardeners gradually moved to increase the size of their holdings. Normally, a market gardener would start to lease a small piece of land, often near the residential areas, owing to the convenience of transportation and the number of consumers. Years later, when he could save enough money to lease more land, he would probably find another area if the former garden could not be expanded, especially those located next to residential areas, such as around North-East Valley, and the Flat at Forbury and South Dunedin. Thus, a new garden had to be established in the outskirts, further and further from the community. In other words,

Chinese market gardens, that from the early 1920s had been developed from small parcels of land around the suburbs of Dunedin, became in the next three decades, along with the expansion of suburban residential areas, large commercial gardens surrounded by sheep farms.

Owing to limited capital, labour, and other inputs, one gardener usually could lease and work only about four to five acres of land. In other places in the country, "acreage leased, ... depended largely on the number of men who were willing to work together. Hand-cultivation, planting, weeding and picking limited the amount cultivatible by any one person to two to three acres" (Sedgwick 1982, p. 322). However, Chinese market gardens in Dunedin in the 1920s were rarely larger than ten acres and the average acreage per man varied. Outside of Dunedin, again, "the land in many cases was uncleared and non-productive ... so European owners found the arrangement attractive ... leases, after all, were word-to-mouth agreements and could be terminated at any time by the owners" (Sedgwick 1982, p. 321). It is confirmed that conditions in Dunedin were similar.

According to my informants, cleared land (ready for cultivating) was leased for between £7 and £8 an acre per year. In comparison, a small plot of land in Christchurch at the turn of the century would be leased at a rate of £5 to £10 an acre per year, but the sources do not mention whether the land was cleared or not (Sue *et al.* 1982, p. 13). Another document states that "Land ... could be leased for seven shillings an acre for uncleared land in the first year, increasing to £1 to £2 in the second year and perhaps £4 to £5 in the third year" (Sedgwick 1982, p. 322). Unfortunately, the locations of these gardens are not indicated, but possibly they were in the big cities of North Island. In Dunedin, when a Chinese wanted to lease a piece of cleared (and possibly productive) land, averaging about five acres, he often had to pay £200 to £300 to "buy lease" from his predecessor. This so-called "buy lease", often based on individual agreements, was used by the Chinese to indicate the commercial value of land which the gardener had been working for a number of years and had developed from uncleared and non-productive to cultivated land.

Usually, if a market gardener wanted to leave the land for some reason, usually because he had to return to China, he would ask another Chinese, who was interested in the land, to take his garden and pay the "buy lease" to him. If the agreement were made, the former proprietor would receive a lump sum of a few hundred pounds. It is worth noting that fruit and vegetable retailers and launderers also had to pay the "buy lease" if they wanted to lease a shop. In this case, it represented the value of a shop, and its business — which depended on several factors, such as its location and size — that had been established for some time.

Leasing the land, moreover, was in the interest of both Chinese and Europeans " ... not only because of the rent gained especially during the Depression, but also because ... the Chinese developed the land, making it particularly suitable for pasture once they vacated the gardens" (Sedgwick 1982, p. 378). The Europeans, however, became interested in market gardening and selling vegetables much later (Mr George Goddard, per. comm.). Thus, contacts, rather business-like ones, between these two groups grew into a social intimacy of sorts.

Owing to the small size of gardens and efforts to save money, many gardeners did not employ any workers, but preferred to work alone or accompanied by sons or relatives rather than outsiders. If someone needed help, however, especially after the Depression when market gardening had been expanding, he probably hired a fellow countryman for £4 a week plus board and lodging. By contrast, the Chinese in Christchurch were hired to work " ... on the gardens [for wages which] were quite meagre, probably £1 to £2 per week" (Sue et al. 1982, p. 13). Several informants insisted that the higher wages of a market gardener, in comparison with the wages of a worker in a fruit and vegetable shop, were due to the harder work demanded by gardening.

On the other hand, it is not clear how much a gardener did earn per year from his garden, although it can be believed that his income was reasonably good. An old ex-market gardener indicated his preference for a higher income, involving harder work, to the lower income to be earned in other jobs. This gave him one reason to maintain the job for more than half of his life. In any case, income attracted the workers as well. It was said that a hardworking and frugal labourer could probably save enough money to lease a small garden after three or four years of work.

Life in the garden, nevertheless, was never easy. The long working hours gave both gardener and worker little time for outside activities. Work started early in the morning and often continued until dark. A son of an ex-market gardener who had a garden at Sawyers Bay and died many years ago, said that he often saw his father working in the garden after dark for one or two hours, depending upon seasonal demands, by the light of paraffin lamps or candles covered by tall cylinder-shaped glasses. Average working hours, therefore, could be between nine to nine and a half hours a day in winter and more than twelve hours in summer, seven days a week (Shum 1956, p. 10; Yee 1968, p. 35; Hunt 1956, p. 21). Paraffin lamps and candles were still in use in the 1950s in Christchurch market gardens where there was no electricity (Shum 1956, p. 12). In other words, a Chinese market gardener's life was isolated because of the long hours of hard work. To this was added the desire to save money, which made life simple and frugal, but not uncomfortable, and the distance of the gardens from the community.

A market gardener seldom went to the city, owing to the lack of public transportation. The only reasons for such a trip would be to take the crop to auction or to sell to retailers. Some of the market gardeners even had little contact with the Chinese community. One informant, for example, said that he spent most of the time in his garden and did not visit the Chinese clubs either at Stafford or MacLaggan Streets. Another case involved an ex-gardener of Sawyers Bay who lived with his family near the garden. He often had to get up at three o'clock in the morning to carry his vegetables on a horse-cart to markets.

Being isolated, however, did not mean living poorly. Living conditions were adequate and often comfortable, but far from luxurious. Provided with a large amount of vegetables and poultry that were usually kept in the gardens, the Chinese could have a highly varied diet, to which they often added from the city supplies, such as meat and fruit; consequently, they easily maintained their own good health (Shum 1956, pp. 10–11; Chin 1954, pp. 11–12).

In many places, Chinese market gardening in the pre-1950s has been described as unmechanised and labour-intensive. This was probably true, but the reasons were complex. Before World War II, particularly during the 1930s when market gardening was mainly the work of younger men who had just arrived in the country, the Chinese formed " ... an extremely busy community in which an intense work ethic developed" (Sedgwick 1982, p. 326). Cultivated land, averaging five to ten acres, was small in area and was leased. With a small amount of capital, none of the Chinese, at least in the first four or five years, could afford to buy any machinery for his garden. One of the old ex-market gardeners bought his first small lorry — the single wheel — to replace a horse and cart in 1925, but it was not until 1933 that he used a small (early model) tractor in his garden at Outram and dispensed with his Clydesdales, because of the larger land area and the efficiency of the new machine.

This case is perhaps typical. Starting from a small piece of land and hard work, a market gardener worked and saved for years. Then, unless he left for China or turned to other jobs, he re-invested in this business. As happened with overseas Chinese in other countries, most of the capital in the business, before modern sources of investment, came from the owner's savings, which implied a slow development and expansion of the business. In any case, using unmechanised and labour-intensive production was not merely a simple conservative activity, but an early step in comparison with the development of the occupation itself. However, the pattern of smallholdings in the early 20th century in Dunedin was slightly different from other places, such as Nelson, Otaki, Wanganui, Fielding, Palmerston North, Foxton, Napier, Gisborne, and Auckland, where the scale of market gardening ranged from one man on a single acre to an enterprise of 14 or more working as many as 41 acres (Sedgwick 1982, p. 318). Thus, Dunedin's market gardening was in this respect unique.

Fruit and Vegetable Retailing

It is unclear when the fruit and vegetable retailing business was first established in Dunedin. Nonetheless, since market gardening had begun in the last century, this business may well have appeared a short while later. One Chinese, for example, left the goldfields at the turn of the century, then turned to odd jobs before arriving to Sawyers Bay and becoming a market gardener who leased a small piece of land. Several years later, he leased a shop with his savings and changed it into a fruit and vegetable retailing business. At the same time, he was still a gardener. All the vegetables sold in the shop were from his garden. He, however, was an exception.[7] Although many gardeners had become shop owners, most of them did not continue gardening, nor did many shop owners acquire gardens.

According to informants, the early retailers were itinerant hawkers. As mentioned above, hawkers had been active since the days of the goldfields and, later, the practice spread into many towns throughout the country. By 1910, nevertheless, in Dunedin the Chinese retailers carried their vegetables on horses and carts selling door-to-door,[8] especially around the suburbs, to housewives who usually lacked their own vehicles and found the prices reasonable and the service convenient. This delivery service still operated in the 1930s and the early 1940s, when lorries replaced horses and carts. A retailer would usually buy and sell cheap vegetables, make a small profit, and give his customers attractive service without any charge. Thus, he could maintain his business in the long run.

In Dunedin during the 1920s and the 1930s, unfurnished shops were leased for between £3 to £5 per week depending upon the location. For instance, at the time when the Exchange, the centre of cable-cars and electric trams, was the busiest area, one Chinese fruit and vegetable shop on Rattray Street was operated by three partners and two or three part-time workers. Its lease was higher than in other areas. Shop leases in the areas around South Dunedin and Caversham were cheaper. It was said that in the city, along George Street, from Knox Church to the Octagon, there were eight fruit and vegetable shops. A European ran only one of them and the rest were run by Chinese.

Most of the fruit and vegetable shop owners started as workers or shop assistants. After a few years' of work and some saving of capital, they would become the partners or even the owners if the capital was adequate and the opportunity arose, such as when someone left the business. A Chinese person who wanted to have his own shop needed an average capital investment of between £150 to £200. This amount of money would be separated into £150 for the "buy lease" and the rest for running the business. Since the capital was small, most of the shops were never decorated. In other words, they were empty shops adorned by fruit and vegetables. According to some informants, however, the "buy lease" was sometimes abandoned, particularly during the great Depression when a lot of shops were left empty and many businesses collapsed. A new investor, who wanted to re-open the shop and could assure the owner of paying the lease regularly, could easily start his business without any requirement because no one occupied the shop. If he had any guarantors, usually relatives or friends, he could ask for the "credit-account" at the auction markets to buy fruit and vegetables. A new retailer who had a "credit-account" could operate his business with a small amount of cash and, possibly, if working hard and keen on saving, could become a successful business owner.

When lorries became more common, the retailers could also conveniently buy vegetables either from the auction markets or some gardeners. On the major auction days, which were Tuesday and Thursday, the gardeners of the Taieri carried their crops to the auction markets where they would sell most of them, and then delivered the rest to the retailers directly by lorry. In this case, the gardeners would contact the retailers beforehand, asking their requirements, then calculating how much they could sell without any waste. On the one hand, the gardeners were satisfied with the small profit that had been made outside the system of the auction market, which charged a ten percent commission for the service. On the other hand, retailers could buy vegetables, distributed directly to the shops, more cheaply than at the markets.

Normally, a shop assistant was employed for two pounds and ten shillings to three pounds per week plus board and lodging, which often consisted of a storeroom behind the shop. The owners themselves lived upstairs. In China, a shop and the living quarters were usually the same place. Therefore, living in the shops was not only due to financial difficulties, but also to the Chinese way of life. It took years before the Chinese could afford to buy a house and alter this lifestyle. In the 1930s, a young teenager was sometimes paid less than £2 per week. Jobs were difficult to find, and this was considered a juvenile wage. This compares with the wages of £2 a week for a young European girl working in a factory at the same time (Mrs Howell, per. comm.). By contrast, a shop owner could earn on average £300 to £400 per annum. It was said that some shops in busy areas, for instance the Exchange, might have earned up to £500 a year. According to one informant, in the latter half of the 1930s some shop owners hired high school students to serve in the shops or to deliver goods to housewives who lived near by, on foot or by bicycle, if there were any. These students mostly worked after school and/or during school holidays. In addition, some were hired to work in the market gardens on the Taieri during summer holidays as well. They travelled daily between their homes and the gardens on the gardener's lorries.

The shops opened early, at seven or seven-thirty o'clock in the morning. The shops closed at ten-thirty or eleven o'clock in the evening, but on Friday and Saturday evenings they stayed open even later. Most of the shops were cleaned on Saturday night (after closing) or on Sunday morning. This meant that the Chinese rested on only one day or even half a day of the week. Life in the shop during weekdays was rather busy, and was, if not physically hard work, time consuming. Early in the mornings, especially on market-days, a shop owner would go to the auction markets to buy fruit and vegetables. If he was the only person in the shop, he probably asked his relatives or friends or hired someone to deliver the goods. Then the goods had to be sorted for either storage or sale and, after washing, arranged for display. Regular customers could expect home deliveries by lorry. These activities did not allow the shop owners and/or assistants to have lunch before two o'clock or dinner before seven o'clock, but they always stopped to serve customers who came into the shops during meals.

The location of the shops and the long workday were important to the success of any business. A shop at Sawyers Bay, which supplied vegetables for local people, hotels, and ships[9] anchored at Port Chalmers, was described as a good business before the Depression. At the other end of the city, in South Dunedin, considered a working-class area during the 1930s and the 1940s, business was also profitable owing to the large population and the cheap leases. Although, during the Depression, life was uncomfortable and many families could not afford to buy as much as usual, the shops were still run with an adequate profit. An ex-shop owner, who had operated his own shop in Hillside Road, South Dunedin, since the late 1930s, described the area in his days as full of activity. Housewives, after taking their children to school, came to buy food for dinner, and men often came to buy fruit during lunchtime. He had his own lorry and sometimes hired three or four Chinese to serve and deliver. During the Depression, however, a large number of people grew their own vegetables — if land was available, since not many people at the time could afford to own a house with a piece of land — or they bought them in summer, owing to the cheaper prices and greater number of varieties, to preserve for winter. Therefore, the quantity of vegetables sold in winter was less than in summer and there were fewer varieties available in winter.

"Credit-account"

There were six auction markets in Dunedin, where both growers and retailers sold or bought their products. Crucial to this market system was the purchasing process. With credit given by the markets, any sellers and buyers were allowed to pay their debts at the end of every month. The monthly payment was very convenient for the growers and retailers who had small amounts of capital for their businesses.

Growers could sell their products without restrictive regulations. The only dealing with the market owners was the obligatory commission for service of ten percent of the total goods sold, paid by each grower. Nonetheless, the growers undoubtedly could make enough profit, and were satisfied to maintain their business relations. The market owners did make a small profit through the buying and selling of produce on their own behalf, but their main source of income was the ten percent commission.

Retailers who owned small shops, but had never had a contract before and were limited by the amount of capital at their disposal, had to pay cash immediately for any goods bought at auction. This prevented them from buying more goods and expanding their businesses. Thus, most retailers entering the market for the first time preferred to seek a guarantor from a permanent customer of the market, which would allow him to become a "credit-account" customer. Any retailer who had a "credit-account" could buy an unlimited amount of goods without paying cash until the end of the month. In this case, the "credit-account", which allowed a small shop owner to accumulate a little capital before having to pay his monthly account, would give him an opportunity to maintain, or even expand, his business.

The retailer who had a "credit-account" was required to pay his debt regularly. If any retailer did not pay the account when it was due, he was probably suspended in one of two ways. Either his "credit-account" was cancelled and he was ordered to pay cash immediately — until his balance was in credit again, or, if he was considered to be insolvent, he would be suspended and banned by all markets as all had close connections with one another. This sanction could force the retailer out of business altogether and he could lose everything. According to informants, some retailers were suspended by the markets and, after losing their businesses, they turned to other occupations. One common reason for business failure was gambling debt.

Laundering

Chinese laundries, as well as fruit and vegetable retailing, were very early Chinese enterprises in urban areas. With the increasing number of white-collar workers in cities, the laundries were a valuable service because of the dress requirement of city business life.

It is reported that "the laundry business [in the early 20th century] was usually passed on by each successive tenant or group of tenants. The newcomer and his partners, if he needed them for capital, would purchase the business for £300–£400, which would give them the basic necessities — large coppers for boiling water heated with coke, a gas-heated roller, a wringer and some large, heavy irons" (Sedgwick 1982, p. 323). In comparison with Dunedin in the 1930s, the investment capital could sometimes be up to £500, so the newcomer, who usually had limited capital and was not able to borrow money from the bank, often needed one or two partners not only for investment purposes but also for labour, especially if the shop was a good business. For example, an informant, who came from Toy San and had worked for three years in a laundry shop whose owner was a relative, invested in a shop with two partners for £180 per person in 1925. Like fruit and vegetable shops during the late 1920s and the 1930s, the "buy lease" was unnecessary if the shop was left empty for some time.

In the 1930s, furthermore, there were about ten to twelve laundry shops in Dunedin where coal gas or coal was used for boiling the water, and coke, which produced less smoke than coal, for the drying rooms — the so-called "heating room" — because of the cold and wet climate. Three such businesses used electricity for power, and two had electric washing machines. In Chinese laundries in Christchurch, on the other hand, " ... All the work was done by hand as there were no electric washing

machines in those days [presumably at the turn of the century]"
(Sue *et al.* 1982, p. 15). Three decades later, laundry shops in Dunedin
were more modern. The same informant insisted that although work in
the laundries was harder than in the fruit and vegetable shops,
electrification made work easier during the 1930s and 1940s than in earlier
times. In short, the amount of investment capital in a laundry was usually
higher than in a fruit and vegetable shop owing to the need for equipment
and the cost of heating.

Average earnings for one laundry shop were from £300 to £600 a year.
This is similar to Sedgwick's information which insists that income
was between £6 and £10 a week, or £300 to £500 gross a year before
rent, rates, overheads, and remittances were subtracted (Sedgwick 1982,
p. 323). Meanwhile, an ex-laundry owner in Dunedin informed me
that his shop was shared with three other partners; each of them earning
about £200 per annum. The wages of a labourer in a laundry were about
£3 a week, similar to the rate in a fruit and vegetable shop. Working in a
laundry, however, was often physically harder work, and the most
unpleasant task, particularly in winter, was hand washing, which took
hours every day. For many informants who had been laundrymen, it was
one of the reasons for changing jobs.

Unlike fruit and vegetable shops that were located throughout the
city, even in the suburbs and working-class residential areas, the laundries
were always in the downtown area where the customers could drop off
and take out their washing easily. In Dunedin, the customers of laundries
included both well-to-do families and factory workers. A woman, for
instance, who had been working in a factory in the 1930s, said that part
of her day-to-day work was to bring the factory's garments to a Chinese
laundry near Moray Place every week at the expense of the factory's
owner. Normally, men's shirts and evening apparel were the major work
in Chinese laundries. However, women's dresses, tablecloths and other
linens were sometimes laundered as well (Mrs Wilson and Mrs Rae
Vernon, per. comm.). The costs of the service were quite high, and only
white-collar workers could easily afford them. The charges (probably in
the 20th century) were four pence for a starched collar and five or six
pence for a shirt (Sedgwick 1982, p. 323). In the 1930s, the charges were
not much different unless the laundry needed special attention; for

example, an evening shirt requiring starching of the chest would cost one shilling.

Chinese laundering was always uncomfortable work. The day usually started at five to half past five in the morning, with the boiling of the water, and finished around nine to ten o'clock at night, seven days a week. Again, as in fruit and vegetable shops, times for meals were flexible. It must be understood that although the laundry was a labour-intensive kind of work, skill or experience in some tasks, particularly ironing, was required for the best service. This skill was one distinctive feature among those that characterised Chinese laundries for over half a century.

Other Jobs

Between the 1920s and the 1940s, according to informants, there were only a few Chinese grocery shops in Dunedin. Sew Hoy and Sons Limited at the time was probably the biggest Chinese enterprise involved mostly in importing and exporting. At the time, it had not yet invested in the textile industry. All the Chinese imported goods, either food or other goods such as Chinese medicines, were sold in the shop on Stafford Street. Most of the customers were Chinese, since Europeans were not interested in Chinese food or products.[10] A fruit and vegetable shop on George Street, which was very busy and at times employed several Chinese workers, sold some imported products as well. I was informed that the Sew Hoy family was one of the most notable merchant families who sponsored the Chinese to come to New Zealand until, at least, the early 1920s.

During the gold rush, groceries had supplied services as well as goods. Some served cooked meals as well as alcohol and operated as meeting places and informal news exchanges (Don, O.C.M., 1/9/1882: 45).[11] It is also confirmed that during the first two decades of the 20th century some Chinese in New Zealand, as well as in New South Wales and in Queensland, Australia, deposited their savings in Chinese stores and, on the other hand, could borrow bank loans to start new businesses (Yong 1977, p. 46). After the 1920s the shops in Dunedin provided consumer goods rather than services. Fruit and vegetable shops stocked few groceries, owing to the smaller demand for them at such outlets.

During the late 1930s and the 1940s, some young Chinese were seen working in factories, such as the woollen mills. These men would either live with friends or in the fruit and vegetable shops of relatives, helping in various ways in the shops after work and/or on the weekend for free board and lodging.

Conclusion

While previous Chinese immigrants intended to return to China, young men who migrated to Dunedin since the 1920s were inclined to settle permanently in New Zealand. It was also a starting point when most Chinese newcomers were supported by their fathers or close relatives to come to New Zealand and, if they wanted, could start their own businesses independently after a few years of their arrival or after paying their debts if they had borrowed from relatives. After migrating to New Zealand, they were employed in the businesses of market gardening, fruit and vegetable retailing, and laundries. These were family businesses where fathers and sons or uncles and nephews or elder and younger male relatives worked side by side. The businesses grew slowly and when the former gardeners or shopkeepers retired or returned to China, the new immigrants replaced them in these jobs. Work was hard, but profitable. Most of them went home a few times either to visit their families or to marry, but found that hardships and difficulties in China were unbearable. Returning to New Zealand, the Chinese began to establish their second home.

Chinese newcomers in Dunedin started their businesses with small savings and developed their own. Since the Dunedin Chinese came from a farming background, rather than a commercial one, their business successes are due to frugality, hard work, and a general understanding of how to work with their business counterparts and how to satisfy their customers. Usually, the capital for business was accumulated by either savings or through partnership. Many informants insisted that they did not borrow from the banks because they did not want to be in debt nor have to deal with a faster-growing business. They felt more comfortable with long-term but secure investment. It took several decades to build up the business and became credit-worthy. For most of the Chinese who started with little capital, the financial problem was always the first obstacle. Hunt (1956) and Tweedie (1950), for instance, described Chinese market gardeners as conservatives who relied upon manual labour and ignored machines. To my knowledge, the reasons for not using machinery were mostly economic.

Many Chinese probably had some experience in business in the market towns of their country before they came to New Zealand (Mawson 1927, pp. 1–2; Sedgwick 1982, p. 66; for the functions of markets in China, see Skinner 1964–65). Those who were itinerant hawkers, either in China or New Zealand, probably found no difficulty in selling goods. For shop owners, nonetheless, the businesses were more complicated. A successful shop owner had to know how to handle the business, the prices of goods, when to buy and sell, how to deal with the customers, and so on. Such knowledge had to be gained individually in New Zealand, and was transferred from one generation to the next in the work situation. Younger workers and newcomers in shops and gardens, therefore, not only earned a wage on which to live and to save, they also gained experience and specialised knowledge about their jobs. A job like laundering required special skills, such as starching and ironing; these experiences were seldom found in the market towns of China. This apprentice/worker system developed independently over several generations in New Zealand.

Most importantly, unlike previous studies which emphasize that racial prejudice against the Chinese in New Zealand was the main factor that barred any relationship between the Europeans and the Chinese for many decades, my research has discovered that in Dunedin, and perhaps in many places, economic circumstances played a major role in these misunderstandings. It is quite clear to me that the nature of Chinese occupations was one of the main factors that kept social distance between them and the others in place. Firstly, because most Chinese were self-employed, contacts with outsiders, particularly those of market gardeners, were often not necessary. Only when the Chinese did go to the auction markets or hire some school students did they come face-to-face with the Europeans. Secondly, their jobs were extremely time consuming. Both gardeners or shop owners/shopkeepers worked about twelve to sixteen hours a day, six or perhaps seven days a week. A little leisure time was spent for rest or with families or, every now and then, with other relatives and friends. Life was little more than work.

Thirdly, the location of their workplace was isolated, therefore, travelling was always limited by the distance between the main community and their living places. The market gardens of Dunedin, especially when many residents took to the suburban areas, were usually set in the outskirts far away from the main communities. At the time, it was a great difficulty for a market gardener to travel between his garden and the city. Transport was rare and although a few Chinese did own lorries, driving to the city was not very pleasant, owing to the bad condition of the roads and the distance involved. The road to Sawyers Bay, for example, which was over ten kilometers from downtown Dunedin, was quite winding, or, worse, hills and steep roads isolated market gardens in the Kaikorai Valley. Lack of adequate time to travel was also a serious problem.

Finally, but not least, isolation from the host society was due to the language barrier. Many Chinese at the time could scarcely speak English, let alone fluently. When a Chinese communicated with a European, conversations were always brief and business-like, consequently, language skill improved very slowly. In other words, it means that the fewer contacts the Chinese had with the outsiders, the slower they could become fluent in English. Obviously, the limitation of language fluency barred and socially isolated the Chinese from the English speakers for many years.

All of these aspects separated the Dunedin Chinese from others for a long time and, therefore, reduced social contact to a minimum. However, employment could sometimes create an intimacy. For instance, either market gardeners on the Taieri who hired high school boys or those in North Island who hired the Maori (for the latter see Sedgwick 1982, pp. 355–362; Ip 1990, pp. 133–135) certainly had more contact with others. In short, social distance between the Chinese and the others in Dunedin was a matter of economic rather than social or racial prejudice.

Notes

[1]The term "Europeans", instead of "White people" or "White New Zealanders", will be used in this paper.

[2]Hereafter, these groups of Chinese will be referred to as the "newcomers". It must be noted, however, that most of these younger migrants travelled between

New Zealand and China more than once, either to marry a Chinese woman, visit their families, or for other personal reasons. Therefore, they were not in fact "new" to New Zealand. The use of such a term is to distinguish them from the previous generations of Chinese migrants who were gold miners, many of whom, despite living in the new country for several years, were still in poverty and could not afford to return home. I would also like to note that this paper focuses upon Chinese males. The population of Chinese females in New Zealand before the 1940s was very small and information regarding them is limited.

[3]Apprenticeship also provided a source of capital accumulation. In New York's Chinatown in the late 19th century the newcomers who worked in the laundries "are subjected to a six-month apprenticeship, first at the steaming washtubs, then wielding the eight-pound irons, then on to finish work". If a newcomer worked hard and was frugal, he could become a laundry owner "after a year or two" (Hall 1998, p. 78).

[4]There were at least 13 old Chinese in 1909, and 12 in 1910, in the Home (Don, *A.I.T.* 1909–1911, pp. 5 & 26, respectively). None of them, however, lived in the "Ross Home", Dunedin's well-known nursing home, although many of the residents were retired Europeans miners, who were single and came from Australia and Britain (*Ross Home Admission Register*, from 1918–1985).

[5]By comparison, Chinese vegetable growing in Auckland was seen in the late 1870s, however, it was a long time before market gardening became a commercial activity (Coleman 1967, pp. 105–106 & Lee 1974, p. 8).

[6]My informants also mentioned the existence of these seven crops, plus silver beet in winter, and beans and green peas in summer.

[7]The reasons were due to the lack of capital and/or the nature of the work, which was extremely time consuming (for comparison, see Ip 1990, p. 132).

[8]In the 1930s and 1940s, the Chinese still sold vegetables door-to-door in Auckland (Ip 1990, p. 130).

[9]One informant, who had lived in Auckland for many years during the 1920s before coming to Dunedin, said that there were two big Chinese shops in Auckland at the time supplying fruit and vegetables for the hotels and ships as well. One of them sometimes employed up to 20 workers, including part-time workers, for service and delivery.

[10]It may be interesting to note that Chinese food in Dunedin was not widely consumed until much later. The first Chinese restaurant in Dunedin was open in the early 1950s.

[11]By comparison, the Chinese stores in Hawaii had similar functions, such as meeting places, news exchange, and the like. Also, one could find job information, or even present one's political opinion freely. In the stores, especially in the area of *Chinatown*, the Chinese felt themselves respectable and, more or less, important, as they were at home (Glick 1980, pp. 139–143).

CHAPTER 12

Singapore Chinese Society in Transition: Reflections on the Cultural Implications of Modern Education

Lee Guan Kin

Introduction

Spanning a period of 183 years, the modern history of Singapore includes 146 years of colonial rule and 37 years of independence. Within the past 37 years, Singapore has undergone major transformations in the various spheres of politics, economics, society, culture, and education. The character of the Singaporean Chinese community, especially, has also transformed rapidly. In the first part of this paper, I shall examine briefly the social, educational, and cultural background of this community to facilitate further discussion.

Singapore is essentially an immigrant society. After its founding in 1819, people from China, India, Malaya, Indonesia, and other places arrived in Singapore, forming a multiracial and multicultural society. The cultures transported here by immigrants of the three major races were basically agrarian cultures. They were definitely not representative of the Chinese, Indian, and Muslim civilisations. Thus, a Chinese majority made up mostly of labourers characterised Singapore. After the Second World War ended, immigration from China ceased but the unique structure of an immigrant society was already formed in Singapore. At the beginning of the 1990s, an influx of immigrants to Singapore occurred again with the government's encouragement to import foreign talent. The largest group of immigrants consists of ethnic Chinese from China, Malaysia, and other places, reviving the immigration phenomenon within the Chinese Singaporean community. However, unlike immigration patterns before the War, immigration in the recent decade is predominantly of a knowledge-based nature. Thus, immigration, especially within the Chinese community in post-independent Singapore, declined for some years before gradually increasing again.

The education system of Singapore experienced substantial changes with the convergence in 1987 of four language streams of education into one stream that places English as the dominant language. In the colonial era, the colonial rulers were only interested in developing the English schools so as to produce clerical staff and a small group of loyal professionals. The other streams of education were left to their own means. With a strong sense of nationalism and ethnic identity, the Chinese community worked hard to sustain the provision of education in their mother tongues. During the days of nation-building, education in Singapore was caught in a paradoxical situation. Due to several factors, including that of the English language's superior status as an international language, the general anti-Communist stance, and discrimination against ethnic Chinese in Southeast Asia, the multiracial makeup of Singapore, and the local political leaders themselves being mostly English-educated, an English-medium education was chosen to be the national form of education for Singapore. Ironically, this decision, made when Asians themselves were in power, led to the repression of education in their mother tongues.

The third historical aspect of Chinese Singapore society to be introduced here is culture. Singapore has become increasingly westernised due to the changes in language and educational policies. During the colonial period, the colonial rulers made English the language of administration, business, education, and so on, leaving the mother tongues and cultures of the various races to their own fates. To the ethnic Chinese, the vibrancy of the Chinese schools ensured the continuity and development of their culture. After independence, the usage domain of the English language was widened even more with the incoming of a pragmatic government. As a result, the status of the English language was elevated even higher in independent Singapore than during the colonial period, while the mother tongues of the three main races were rendered second languages. As a consequence, the problem of inheritance was created for the cultures transmitted via these languages. Thus, although independent Singapore had politically moved away from the colonial period and was free from colonial rule, culturally, it had entered a neo-colonial phase (Teng 2000, pp. 69–71). This neo-colonial phenomenon was especially poignant within the Singaporean Chinese community.

From the above narrative, one can see that the courses that society, education, and culture took in Singapore are all interwoven with its political path. Employing a historical perspective, this paper serves to reflect on the impact of some of Singapore's major modern language policies in the realm of education on the Chinese community. Emphasis will be given to the challenges these policies pose to Chinese culture and their effects in the wider cultural sphere of Singapore. The Chinese community discussed here includes both the Chinese-speaking and English-speaking groups. As for the term, 'culture' employed here, it refers not to 'Culture' in the broadest sense of the word. In the context of this article, 'Chinese culture' (*zhonghua wenhua*) is the culture the forebears (in China) of the Chinese in Singapore have created and 'Singapore Chinese culture' (*xinhua wenhua*) is the Chinese culture inherited but modified by Singaporean Chinese as they adapted their forebears' culture to the local context. Finally, the 'modern education' considered here refers to those educational policies implemented after independence and which had a strong influence on Chinese culture.

This topic is worth exploring as, despite the plethora of material successes that Singapore can display today, it is found desperately wanting in the area of cultural cultivation. Since its independence, Singapore has managed to establish international fame, significantly improved the living standards of its people, and has groomed many professionals. However, to the intellectual observer, it is not difficult to discover that there exists in Singapore a contradictory mentality of regarding western culture with suspicion and prejudice, on the one hand, while allowing the various ethnic cultures to weaken, on the other. Taking into consideration that the Chinese make up three quarters of the population, the cultural depth of the ethnic Chinese naturally determines to a great extent the average cultural calibre of the nation.

The following questions will be explored in the event of the discussion: What path of development did the education and culture of the Singaporean Chinese take during the colonial period? What foundation did Chinese culture in Singapore have and what restrictions to development did it face? What setbacks did Chinese culture suffer in the independence era under the new educational policies? What were the consequences? Was there a twist of fate? Now, with rapid economic advancement in China, the rise of Chinese education and Chinese culture in Southeast Asia, and the reception of more and more immigrants from China, how will Chinese culture in Singapore be affected? Will it rise up to the challenges in the new century brought about by external and internal changes?

Chinese Cultural Developments and Limitations
in the Colonial Period

Singapore was a sparsely populated island until British colonization, which ushered in the mass immigration of ethnic Chinese. The early Chinese immigrants in the colonial period came to Singapore from Malaya, mostly from Malacca and Penang. They formed the Straits Chinese community. A number of prominent businessmen and intellectuals emerged from this group. Later, with mass immigration from China, a sizeable Chinese immigrant community appeared in Singapore comprising mainly of labourers. Chinese society, formed by the two above-mentioned groups, was thus distinctly of a working class nature. A small number of capitalists and several traders made up the merchant class, while a minority of officials and intellectuals from China created a class of literati (shi) (Yen 1986, pp. 141–143). This last group later only expanded with the springing up of local English and Chinese schools.

The level of cultural cultivation within the early Chinese community in Singapore was thus very low. Most of the immigrants who came to Singapore to make a living were barely educated, except for the handful of Confucian scholars cum merchants (*rushang*) and a small group of literati. Thus the task of developing Chinese culture fell on the officials who made business and political trips to Singapore from China, and intellectuals who came on social visits, to seek refuge, or to make a living. As these people had no wish to see the de-culturalisation of the Chinese immigrants either due to political reasons or ethnic pride, they gathered the merchants to establish literary societies, publish newspapers, and set up schools. The end of the 19th century witnessed a flourishing Chinese cultural scene in Singapore created with the efforts of the Chinese Consulate as well as the intellectuals. Induced by political developments in China, a local Confucian movement was launched. Subsequently, modern schools, news press, and dramas with underlying patriotic messages filled the local Chinese cultural scene for a few decades. With Singapore becoming a focal centre for education, Confucian studies, and press and literary activities in Southeast Asia, Chinese culture was thriving.

However, the very same political influence of China that contributed to the vibrancy of Singapore's Chinese cultural scene, arrested the development of the Singapore Chinese culture before the Second World War. Leaders' enthusiasm for the Confucian movement waxed and waned with the transformations of political circumstances (Lee 2001). The fate of newspapers, cultural organisations and activities was also dictated by politics. The unfortunate linkage between cultural activities and politics made it difficult for the enthusiastic literati to further contribute to the nurturing and transmittance of Chinese culture. In short, its connection to politics before the war placed Chinese culture in a paradoxical situation: it both flourished and stagnated at the beck and call of politics.

In theory and in reality, Chinese schools were the most important locale of cultural transmittance. The history of Chinese schools in Singapore spans almost a period of 140 years. With the avid support of Chinese merchants, Chinese education was able to extend its sphere from the pre-primary level to the tertiary level by the 1950s. In fact, the Chinese schools, from primary to pre-university levels, consistently had the leading number of enrolment amongst all the educational language streams before 1954. Efforts exerted by Chinese schools over a century stimulated the growth of Chinese culture and established a foundation upon which Singapore Chinese culture could develop.

Unfortunately, neglect by the colonial authorities contributed to the difficulties that Chinese education encountered and to its eventual ill fate. With meagre public financial aid, Chinese schools were constantly confronted with problems in the areas of finance, administration, facilities, staff recruitment, curriculum and so on. The Great Depression of the 1930s, the oppressive times under the Japanese Occupation in the 1940s, and the political interference of the 1950s and 1960s arrested the progress of Chinese education. This in turn impeded the systematic development of Chinese culture and retarded the maturing of Singapore Chinese culture.

The Setbacks and Waning of Chinese Culture after Independence

Both the transmittance of the Chinese culture and the growth of Singapore Chinese culture required time. Time was also needed for revision and improvement. Regrettably, towards the end of the colonial era, the internal and external circumstances Singapore found itself in were disadvantageous to the continuous development of Chinese culture. Internally, although Chinese education recovered its momentum after the war, English education progressed at such an fast pace that it threatened the progress of the Chinese schools. Externally, the international status of the English language, the Communism advocated in the region, racism, and the widespread discriminatory politics against ethnic Chinese provided a harsh environment for Chinese education and culture in Southeast Asia. Such a situation persisted without easing even at the eve of Singapore's independence. The future path of Chinese education was paved with greater obstacles after the internal struggles of the People's Action Party (PAP, the party that took to the political centre-stage) ended with its English-educated members led by Lee Kuan Yew defeating their Chinese-educated counterparts.

Against such historical circumstances, the government implemented two important language-related policies after a decade of independence. The policies had a tremendous effect on the Chinese community and to a great extent, shaped not only Singapore's educational system, but also its social structure and cultural path. Together, they made the development of Chinese culture an insurmountable task.

The First English-dominant Education Policy

Under the new education system in which priority was given to English, the Chinese schools and Nanyang University merged with the English schools and University of Singapore respectively. This signified a major reform in the history of education in Singapore. From then on, Singapore only had English-medium schools and universities.

Due to the colonial government's education policy after the Second World War, the development of English schools progressed more rapidly than the other three streams of education. In fact, it contributed greatly to the decline of the non-English language schools. Between 1946 and 1954, enrolment for Chinese schools (from pre-primary level to post-secondary level) that originally surpassed that of the English schools by 30 percent, fell drastically to 1.5 percent lower than the English schools (Lee 1994, p. 95). Before obtaining self-government, the enrolment of primary school students in Chinese schools outnumbered the enrolment for English schools. But after 1959, Chinese education went into decline and the disparity in school enrolment between the two education medium institutions widened. The difference in enrolment increased from 4.7 percent in 1959 to 39.7 percent in 1974, and eventually rose to 77.1 percent in 1982 (*ibid*, p. 96, Table 4). The plummeting numbers of Chinese primary school students brought an end to Chinese-medium education.

The crisis of Chinese schools became increasingly evident after independence. However, it must be said that both the government and the Chinese community did attempt to salvage the situation, but their efforts were futile. In their struggle to survive, Chinese schools shed their Chinese language-orientation, drawing closer to the English schools. This facilitated the gradual merger between Chinese and English schools, and eventual formation of a single stream of education. In December 1983, the government finally announced the plan for the Chinese, Malay, Indian, and English streams to merge into a single stream of education from 1984. This merger was to be completed by 1987.

Nanyang University (Nantah), the highest level Chinese educational institution faced a similar fate as the Chinese schools. The development of Nantah was full of obstacles. The problems encountered by the university included student strikes in the 1950s and 1960s; the delayed recognition of its degrees by the government; the difficulties job-seeking graduates faced, and so on. These issues adversely affected the university's recruitment of students. Between 1959 and 1966, the ratio of graduates from Nantah and the University of Singapore was 1:1. From 1967 to 1976, the ratio was 1:2, and it fell to a further 1:3 between 1977 and 1980 (*ibid*, 97, Table 6). In order to ensure its survival, reforms were constantly introduced to Nantah, and teaching in English was reinforced. In 1978, students sat for the English-medium examinations held jointly by Nantah and the University of Singapore. In the same year, a combined campus was created for both universities and, in 1980, as suggested by the government, the two universities merged to form the National University of Singapore.

Thus, Chinese culture was moving towards the door of crisis with the difficulties faced by the Chinese schools surfacing in the 1960s and the plunge in recruitment numbers of students in the 1970s, resulting in the irreversible and helpless situation of Chinese education in 1980s. When the enrolment numbers for Nantah also fell drastically, forcing it to merge with the University of Singapore in 1980, Chinese culture suffered yet another major blow. With the dismantling of the Chinese educational system after the colonial period, Chinese culture in Singapore not only lost the opportunity to refine itself and develop steadily, it also faced the threat of losing whatever it had already accumulated and established.

During this time, the Singaporean Chinese were split in their views with regards to the preservation of Chinese culture. One group was of the opinion to stress Chinese schools as the guardian of Chinese culture while the other group thought that the preservation of the Chinese language was adequate in preserving Chinese culture. Wolfgang Franke, a Sinologist, who was the Head of the Chinese department at the University of Malaya, pointed out that the tragic loss of culture was produced by an English-medium education. Franke articulated the fears of many Chinese-educated in Singapore who were deeply anxious about what they perceived as the gradual demolishing of culture by the Chinese themselves allowing the disappearance of the Chinese schools (*Sin Chew Jit Poh* 6 September 1965, 12 May 1967). The second view, which regarded the bilingual policy implemented by the national leaders as a way of safeguarding the continuity of Chinese teaching given the crisis of Chinese education, brought a glimpse of hope to some Chinese-educated amidst the pessimism (*Lianhe Zaobao* 22, 23, 31 December 1983, 3 & 19 January 1984, 20 February 1984). However, many more Chinese-educated expressed grave doubts towards the cultural function of a Chinese language that would be taught at a lowered standard and reduced to the operative medium of only one teaching subject (*Nanyang Siang Pau* 15 July 1982, 6 August 1982; *Lianhe Zaobao* 19 April 1983, 15 June 1983).

To the Chinese-educated, the drastic impact of the closing of schools on Chinese culture was well understood and they had constantly worked towards contributing to the welfare of Chinese schools. Within a short period of 28 years of self-government, the Chinese-educated had witnessed the decline and eventual closing down of the Chinese schools and Nantah. This was certainly a severe blow to them. For the academics, teachers, intellectuals, literati, artists, and others. involved in Chinese education, this period and the time after were filled with a sense of pessimism and futility (Lee 1994, pp. 74–85). The aspirations and the conditions for the refinement of Chinese culture and the re-creation of a Singapore Chinese cultural legacy were dissipated.

The Second English-dominant Education Policy

Another important educational policy of the state, was the promotion of an English-dominant, bilingual education. This policy reduced the mother tongues of the three main races to secondary languages.

After obtaining self-government, Singapore authorities emphasized the importance of studying a second language in a multiracial society. Primary and secondary school students had to learn a second language from the years 1960 and 1966, respectively, and sit for second language exams from the years 1966 and 1969, respectively. In the 1960s and 1970s, English stream students could opt for the mother tongue of another race as a second language of study. Beginning from 1980, it was compulsory for the ethnic Chinese students of English schools to study Chinese as a second language and take the exams set for the subject. With the converging of the four streams into one in 1987, all ethnic Chinese students (except those studying Chinese as a first language) were required to study and be examined in Chinese as a second language.

To ensure the successful implementation of bilingual education among the ethnic Chinese, besides assigning Chinese as a second language the status of a compulsory subject, the weight given to it in primary school departure examinations was greatly increased. Students also have to attain a minimum grade in order to qualify for secondary schools, junior colleges and university entry. The usage of simplified Chinese characters and the hanyu pinyin system were introduced by the Ministry of Education, and a state-sponsored Speak Mandarin Campaign was held annually to aid students in mastering their command of Chinese as a second language.

The rationale behind this bilingual education system was that the mother tongue can impart cultural values while English language is to be learnt for its practical functions. The transmission of traditional Chinese culture was perceived to lie within the parameters of the teaching of Chinese as a second language. Through his frequent contact with Chinese-educated students during political encounters, then prime minister, Lee Kuan Yew, had observed what he perceived as their superior character that he felt was lacking among the English-educated students. This, in Lee's view, in turn attested to the importance of Chinese education and culture to the establishment of character and values. Unfortunately, preservation of traditional culture became problematic with the demise of the Chinese schools. To counteract this problem, the government actively promoted bilingual education with the intention of employing Chinese as a second language to function as a cultural tool.

Could the bilingual education policies really perpetuate the growth and development of Chinese culture? This is actually debatable. Let us first examine the actual implementation, the problems faced in the process, and the consequences brought about by these problems.

Firstly, bilingual education policies before 1990 were not consistent. The policies regarding Chinese language in the educational system were constantly revised. For instance, the time allocated to Chinese second language teaching was supposed to increase gradually through the years. It was to increase from 18 percent to 25 percent in 1973, and then to 33.33 percent in 1974, and 40 percent in 1975. However, this was never realised due to certain difficulties. Another instance is the weight given to the language. Beginning in 1973, the Chinese and English languages were accorded the same double weight in comparison to Mathematics and

Science in the primary school leaving examinations. Yet, in 1980, the Ministry of Education revised the policy so that the two languages came to share the same weight as Mathematics and Science. The volatility of the policies further dampened the confidence and enthusiasm of Chinese educators.

Secondly, there were discrepancies in the policies made for Chinese and English language teaching. First, the mother tongue was relegated to a 'second language'. This not only affected the morale of the educators and the mindset of the students, but also influenced people's value judgements on the language. Despite breaking away from the label of 'second language' by 1992, it was nevertheless still perceived as a language of secondary importance. Second, the mother tongue only formed a subject in school, and thus the time allocated to teaching it, the number of words learnt, and usage of the language were restricted. Therefore, even though Chinese language is commonly used amongst ethnic Chinese students, the standard of the language used has significantly declined. Third, despite the mother tongue being perceived to function as a cultural language (the language in which culture is transmitted), it functioned in reality more as a cultural vehicle for the passing down of traditional values. In terms of application, the usage domain of the mother tongue was too constricted. From a cultural perspective, the responsibilities the mother tongue had to bear was too great a load and the content taught, too shallow. The conflicting expectations afforded to language teaching affected the motivations of the students to learn the language and limited the content of the teaching.

Thirdly, dialects were sacrificed under the bilingual education policies. In 1979, Singapore's long-running campaign, the Speak Mandarin Campaign, was launched for the first time. This campaign aimed to alter the Chinese habitual use of dialects and promote the use of Mandarin as a common language amongst the ethnic Chinese. The campaign fit into the bilingual educational policies schema from the educational point of view. Lee Kuan Yew had thought that the average child would encounter difficulties learning two languages and a dialect and thus, the use of dialects had to be discouraged for the student to better concentrate on the two languages taught in school. Mandarin gradually and eventually substituted the Chinese dialects after years of effort put into the campaign.

A survey carried out by the Ministry of Education showed that the use of Mandarin as a household language had increased from 26 percent to 64.7 percent from 1980 to 1992, while the use of the dialects had decreased from 64.4 percent to 3.6 percent (Ong 1992). The campaign was aimed at complementing the bilingual system, while the bilingual policies were intended to contribute towards preserving traditional values. The question to raise here then is: Has the declining use of dialects and the promotion of widespread usage of Mandarin benefited the development of Chinese culture?

It is worth scrutinising the third point above. Undeniably, the family acts as the cradle for traditional culture and ethics. In the past, when Chinese schools and English schools co-existed, the English-educated kept their links with traditional culture and values through speaking dialects at home. Many among them were eastern-oriented. However, when the dialects suffered a fall in status, the role family education could play diminished. The dialect-speaking elderly monolingual grandparents who spoke neither English nor Mandarin could not transmit culture and values to the younger generations. Perhaps Mandarin could replace dialects in the long run, but a crisis has already quietly crept in. According to the same survey mentioned above, the number of students of Chinese ethnicity who use English at home is increasing at an accelerating rate. This number has risen from nine percent in 1980 to 31 percent in 1992, indicating the gradual substitution of Mandarin by English as a home language. Anxious over the phenomenon, the political leaders are worried that traditional culture and values would be lost as a result of the common usage of English (Goh 1991).

Is the widespread usage of spoken and written Mandarin a positive phenomenon even if Mandarin is not replaced by English? The answer does not seem to offer any optimism. This is due to the different emphasis given to the languages under the state's linguistic policies and the bilingual educational system that adversely affected learners' enthusiasm and standard of the Chinese language. What makes things worse is the separation of Chinese language into the spoken and written realms. This in turn resulted in students learning the spoken form with superficial knowledge of the Chinese language and thus they are incapable of absorbing the rich cultural values that could be transmitted through written Chinese. Together with a general disinterest in reading, the lack of a good foundation of written Chinese caused Chinese students to grow up unappreciative of the language. Chinese language, hence, is reduced to a mere colourless communicative tool that possesses no cultural depth in Singapore.

Where Is Singapore Chinese Culture Heading in the 21st Century?

The Crisis of Chinese Culture

Educational changes have greatly shaped the development of Chinese culture in Singapore and contribute to the crisis it is facing now. Except for those who studied Chinese at a higher level in secondary schools and junior colleges, and the minority who majored in Chinese at local and overseas universities, the young Chinese Singaporeans of today have a poor command of the language. Their verbal, written, and reading abilities in Chinese are less than satisfactory. Often, they have to resort to using a dialect or English when holding a conversation in Mandarin due to their limited knowledge of Chinese words.

Many of these young people possess interest in singing popular Chinese songs and watching Chinese drama serials, but reading the Chinese newspapers is too demanding a task, one that they would rather not attempt since there are just too many characters foreign to them. They are strangers to Chinese culture, they cannot differentiate the 'Qin' dynasty from the 'Qing' dynasty in Chinese history, and they know very little about Confucius and Lao Tzu. When it comes to literary appreciation, remembering one or two lines from Li Bai's poem is considered no mean feat.

Perhaps a comparison would illuminate the problem better. The average young Chinese Singaporean's identification with and knowledge of his or her mother tongue not only paled in comparison to that of the young Chinese in Malaysia, but also could not match that of his or her Malay peers. Indeed Chinese culture is fading away in Singapore at a speedy rate and this in turn brought about certain effects.

The effects can be highlighted through the examination of the differences between the Chinese communities in Singapore and Malaysia.

Singapore was formerly part of Malaysia and both countries shared the same historical experiences. Chinese schools were established at both places at the same time. Nantah was built with the efforts of both sides. When Singapore was separated from Malaysia, the path Chinese education took at both places diverged. The Malaysian Chinese continued to develop Chinese education partly due to the fact that although a minority, the Malaysian Chinese made up nearly a third of the total population, and also partly because despite being under Malay political leadership, they believed firmly in the superiority of Chinese culture and refused to be assimilated into Malay culture. The spring up of Chinese High Schools in the 1970s and the establishment of the Southern College, New Era College and Han Chiang College in the 1990s are concrete evidence of the Malaysian Chinese effort toward developing Chinese education. The Malaysians' efforts enabled the progressive growth of the Chinese schools that in turn perpetuated the evolution of Chinese language and culture.

Chinese-educated youth have achieved a substantial command of the Chinese language. When the Chinese Malaysian debating team were champion and runner-up in separate years recently for the International Varsity Chinese Debate Competition, the world turned its attention towards these ethnic Chinese bred in a Malay-dominant country. For many years, Malaysian students and Chinese-language writers have constantly gained honours in various Taiwanese literary competitions (Tu 2000, Chong 2001). In the Nanyang Technological University (the predecessor of the Nanyang University) the author teaches among other courses, General Chinese History, a course attended by both Malaysian and Singaporean students. Not surprisingly, the Malaysian students exhibit a comparatively higher level of literary and historical knowledge. Also, in an important student organisation within the university, the Chinese society, Malaysian students dominate the leading positions. During the month of August 2000, the drama group of the society performed in public a Chinese play entitled, "The Nantah Story". The key people involved in the production of the play, such as the scriptwriter and director, were Malaysians. With the history of Nanyang University as its narrative, the play expressed the students' sentiments for Chinese education (How 2000, p. 67).

Whereas Malaysian Chinese academics and intellectuals are actively critiquing and making suggestions to the development of Chinese culture in Malaysia, Chinese educators and intellectuals in Singapore can only preoccupy themselves with the declining standard of Chinese language.[1] The anxiety in the latter case is deep and depressing. Both the disappearance of the Chinese schools and the unbalanced bilingual policy that weakens the Chinese language abilities of the younger generations have already caused a serious problem in terms of a lack of qualified Chinese-language workers and a cultural rupture.

Firstly, there is a serious shortage of new blood with adequate language ability and strong cultural knowledge to fill the positions of teachers, journalists, presenters, editors, secretaries, administrators, and others in the spheres of education, print and television media, publication, and commercial advertising. This has affected the quality of work and production. The Ministry of Education thus has to resort to employing foreign Chinese-language teachers to fill teaching positions. The number of foreign Chinese teachers has increased from 33 in 1998 to 62 in 1999 and 81 in 2000 (*Lianhe Zaobao* 14 January 2001). A more embarrassing phenomenon of incoherent sentences and misuse of characters in Chinese commercial advertisements, documents, publicity pamphlets, and so on is created by the lack of qualified translators. A Chinese handbook to introduce Singapore to foreigners entitled "Contact Singapore", published by the Ministry of Manpower in Hong Kong and Shanghai, had to be withdrawn in December 2000 due to several linguistic errors. Nevertheless, the publication had been circulated overseas for over a year and this has adversely affected the image of Singapore (*Lianhe Zaobao* 8, 9, 13, 18 January 2001).

Secondly, there is a cultural rupture. When Chinese schools were functioning, Chinese-language based social and cultural organisations had developed vibrantly resulting in a wonderful array of publications and literary activities that employed Chinese as the medium. But after the decline and eventual demise of Chinese schools, many organisations such as Chinese clan associations found difficulty in getting successors to carry on the work that has been done.[2] The Chinese press and publishers had to watch anxiously the number of readers dwindling rapidly while the Chinese drama circle witnessed an extensive period of poor box office sales.[3] This really makes Chinese intellectuals wonder: what could be used to construct a Singaporean's ideal multicultural Singapore and what could be done to achieve the state's ideal of the Renaissance vibrancy for the local arts scene (e.g. Chua 2001, pp. 61–63; Chong 2001)?

As mentioned earlier, the fast waning of Chinese culture in Singapore could be illustrated from the stark contrast between the Chinese lack of identification with their mother tongue and the Malay enthusiasm for their mother tongue. Both the Chinese and Malays share similar historical experiences. After independence, both Chinese and Malay schools have declined and Singaporeans who are presently below 35 years of age, are the product of modern bilingual education. Yet the developmental paths of Chinese and Malay cultures has diverged significantly. With Islam as its anchor, Malay culture is imparted through the Malay language, with the school, family, and the mosque sharing educational responsibilities. The impact of the closure of Malay schools as well as of westernisation upon the Malay culture is thus comparatively less. Moreover, the preservation of some Islamic schools aid in the maintenance of Malay culture.

Unfortunately, unlike the Malay community, the Chinese did not have a common religion that is intimately connected to their ethnic identity. The absence of a strong religious hold on the ethnic group means that there are no religious institutions or religious scriptures to count on for cultural transmission. It appears that the main forts of Chinese culture are the Chinese schools, followed by the family. So when vernacular schools disappeared, the young Singaporean Chinese lost touch with their culture at a faster rate than their Malay peers although both were growing up under the bilingual education system. The situation was made worse with English replacing dialects and Mandarin as the home language of more and more Chinese families.

Here, I shall draw upon two survey reports to demonstrate the faster rate of decline of the Singaporean Chinese mother tongue and culture compared to those of the Malays. According to the Singapore Census of Population 2000 published by the Singapore Department of Statistics, a general phenomenon of cultural loss across all ethnic groups amongst the young Singaporeans is observed (see Advance Data Release No. 3, Table 4). However, the Chinese has the most rapid rate of loss. The percentage of 5–14 year old children using Mandarin and Chinese dialects at home had fallen from 76.5 percent in 1990 to 63.9 percent in 2000. The rate of decline is 12.6 percent while the percentage of children speaking just Mandarin only increased by two percent. English speakers however, increased by 12.5 percent from 23.5 percent in 1990 to 35.8 percent in 2000. Conversely, the percentage of Malay children of the same age group using Malay at home decreased only by 1.5 percent from 91.6 percent in 1990 to 90.1 percent in 2000, and those speaking English increased by a mere 1.1 percent from 8.3 percent to 9.4 percent. Through this contrast of home language used between Chinese and Malay children, one can imagine how the shift in language used amongst the Chinese has weakened the family's ability to impart Chinese culture. Thus, the declining educational role of the family in culture caused further distress to Singapore Chinese culture.

The other survey is one done on ethnic identification. At the end of 1999, a Sociology lecturer of the National University of Singapore, Dr. Chang Han Yin, made known to the public a survey report regarding the identification of young Singaporeans (*Lianhe Zaobao* 4 December 1999, *Straits Times* 14 December 1999). The report revealed that only 78.4 percent of the young Singaporean Chinese would choose to be born ethnic Chinese if there is the possibility of rebirth after death. The report stirred up a great commotion within the Chinese community. Despite several scholars' criticisms of the methodology and analysis of the report (*Straits Times* 19 December 1999, *Lianhe Zaobao* 22 December 1999), what is of interest here is that the analysis in the same report shows that 91.9 percent of the young Singaporean Malays have chosen to be born into the same ethnicity if there is a next life. The response of youths from the two ethnic communities diverged distinctly. Obviously, the decline of education in the mother tongue and English-dominant bilingual education seemed to have a greater impact on the Chinese community and culture. The alienation from the mother tongue has decreased cultural knowledge and identification, which in turn has influenced adversely the ethnic identification of some Chinese. Some of these youths hoped that they could either be born white or Japanese, some did not care whether they are Chinese, and others merely regarded themselves as a citizen of the world. This display of weariness in ethnic identification naturally weakened cultural identification. With almost a quarter of the Chinese youths giving up the choice of being Chinese, the anxieties and worries of the Chinese communities over cultural issues are sparked off again.[4]

Arising Opportunities

Despite the obstacles faced, hope is not lost for Chinese culture in Singapore. In fact, its darkest moments since Singapore's independence are over. Spoken and written Chinese are increasingly recognised for their cultural, ethical, and economic values due to internal and external factors. This, in turn, spells development opportunities for long-suffering Chinese language and culture.

Externally, the waves of anti-communism and anti-Chinese sentiments have since calmed down in Southeast Asia and the relationship between the PRC and the region has improved from the late 1970s. Internally, after more than a decade of nation-building, the Singaporean leaders in confronting supposed "western decadence" started to feel confident enough to turn to Chinese culture for moral support. Thus, recognition of the cultural and moral value of Chinese language has allowed the mother tongue of the ethnic Chinese some breathing and breeding space. This recognition subsequently led to the establishment of the SAP schools in the 1970s and Confucian Studies in the 1980s in the education sector, and also the appearance of the Speak Chinese Campaign and Confucianist revival movement in the social sector.

The PRC began opening its doors to the world in the late 1970s. After the mid-1980s, the interest of Southeast Asian countries in the PRC's market increased and the Singaporean state started to discuss the economic value of spoken and written Chinese. In 1985, the government for the first time in the history of the Speak Chinese Campaign began to talk about the economic benefits of Chinese knowledge (Ong 1985). In the 1990s, its economic value increased enabling Chinese language and culture to secure more breathing space. The government gradually developed Higher Chinese and Language Elective Programs (LEP) in schools. At the beginning of 1999, BG Lee Hsien Loong announced that in the new Chinese language education policy, the top 30 percent scorers at the primary school departure examination would be eligible to study Higher Chinese when they enter secondary schools. This was 20 percent more than the quota in the year before. There was also an increase in the number of SAP schools from nine to ten, while the number of junior colleges teaching LEP increased from two to three (*Straits Times* 21 January 1999).

With the cultural values and economic values of Chinese language in mind, the Singapore government proposed in the late 1990s to groom a Chinese cultural elite. At the opening ceremony of the Speak Mandarin Campaign in 1998, Minister for Information and the Arts, George Yeo mentioned that "To transmit Chinese culture and the Chinese language effectively to successive generations of Chinese Singaporeans, we need a Chinese intellectual and cultural elite. We need political and cultural leaders, intellectuals and scientists, writers and poets, principals and teachers, editors and journalists, and many others who [will have] master[ed] Chinese at a high level" (Yeo 1998). One of the main aims of the new Chinese language teaching policy announced by B. G. Lee in 1999 is to foster a Chinese elite who "should be able to play the role that they should through the development of Chinese culture to promote and shape Singapore into a metropolitan city and economy in the twenty-first century" (*Straits Times* 21 January 1999).

The rapid rise of the PRC's economy and its friendly foreign relations policy, on the other hand, have also catalysed the revival of interest in Chinese education in the Southeast Asian region which in turn is a positive influence on Chinese culture in Singapore. After its decline in Southeast Asia between 1950s and mid-1980s, Chinese education was revived as the governments in the region relaxed their educational policies. Three colleges built in the 1990s have extended the realm of Chinese education in Malaysia to include higher education. The three varsities, together with over a thousand Chinese primary schools and over 60 independent Chinese secondary schools, form a complete Chinese education system. In Indonesia, restrictions on the learning and usage of Chinese language have gradually relaxed and with this, Chinese education of different forms appeared, including the setting up of a Taiwanese school for the children of Taiwanese businessmen. Upon entering the threshold of a new century, the fever of Chinese school establishment saw Indonesia turning to China and Malaysia for assistance (*Lianhe Zaobao* 31 December 2000, 2 February 2001). There is also the setting up of new schools or revitalisation of old institutions and in Thailand, Vietnam, and Cambodia. Thus motivated by neighbouring countries, as well as pragmatic needs, Chinese education in Singapore did not regress with the constant re-adjustment of Chinese language teaching under the bilingual policy.

This recognition of Chinese language and culture by the state has altered the distant attitude of some parents towards Chinese and encouraged some students of the SAP and LEP programme to continue studying Chinese at local or overseas universities and even pursuing a Master's or Ph.D degree in it. These young people who have a good command of two languages and are well informed of western theories and technology, inject new life into Chinese culture. Some of them are also involved in Chinese literary, drama, and academic activities.

Finally, immigration and the mobility of talents are major factors acting as stimulants for Chinese culture. Immigrants from China and Malaysia have increased since the early 1990s. This immigration consists predominantly of knowledge workers of whom some have joined culture-related professions in the academic, education, media, and publishing sectors. Besides assisting the resolution of cultural rupture, these immigrants can also transform the linguistic and cultural environment of the Chinese community in Singapore. Moreover, more and more Singaporeans are arriving in China to work or study. The individual may benefit and perhaps even labour for Chinese culture after an immersion of three or more years in the culturally rich Chinese atmosphere.

Restrictions and Challenges

Despite the opportunities arising from a dawning age, the development of Chinese culture still faces many restrictions. While restrictions are posed by complicated situational circumstances and old modes of thinking, challenges present themselves in the form of new experiences and new difficulties.

The first of the restrictions is the geopolitical location and demographic make-up of Singapore. As Singapore is situated in a Malay region, it has to be cautious of sensitive racial issues frequently raised by its neighbours. The ethnic composition of Singapore also contributes to the problem. The country is made up of four races, and the Chinese, after independence, was again divided along linguistic educational mediums. National leaders often cite stability and national unity as reasons for not allowing the majority of Chinese to emphasize their mother tongues and culture. This position is still held by the state. During the launch of *The Encyclopedia of the Chinese Overseas* published by the Chinese Heritage Centre in Singapore on 26 October 1998, Prime Minister Goh Chok Tong remarked, "The Singaporean Chinese recognize and accept [that] ... Chinese culture and Mandarin must be advanced within the multiracial context of Singapore and the political and social milieu of Southeast Asia" (*Straits Times* 27 October 1998). In fact, besides keeping in consideration the minority when handling Chinese language and cultural matters, the issue is also a sensitive subject with the English-speaking Chinese community. The development of Chinese culture thus faces many restrictions internally.

The second restriction stems from the linguistic environment. Although spoken and written Chinese was not a language of power in the colonial days, it had important educational, cultural, and commercial functions for the Chinese community. However, after independence, spoken and written English prevailed in almost every sector and became the working language in the academic, educational, economic, technological, and other spheres. Singaporeans could function in English in every aspect of their daily lives. Chinese became a mere examination subject in school that could be left behind when one leaves school. Even the graduates of the SAP and LEP programmes lose touch with their mother tongue as they have few occasions to use Chinese if they do not engage with Chinese-related occupations after leaving schools. Under the rhetoric of convenience and efficiency in Singapore's English-dominant society, it becomes common for Chinese bilinguals to lose their competence in the Chinese language through the lack of usage. In short, the linguistic environment in Singapore has wasted linguistic resources, ultimately retarding the growth of Chinese culture.

Among the challenges Chinese language and culture face, westernisation and globalisation, the development of Chinese culture in neighbouring countries, and the construction of Singapore culture are the most prominent. Singapore is a westernised country to a certain extent. Its colonial past and the predominance of English in the post-independence era led it inevitably onto the path of westernisation. This is evident from the increased usage of English in households, the much higher sales figures of English newspapers, and the prevalence of western popular culture. As Singapore tries to catch up with the pace of information circulation and globalisation, the rate of westernisation will accelerate. Given that the average young Singaporean does not like to read Chinese books and newspapers and does not write in the Chinese language, Chinese culture will have to be prepared to rise up to tougher challenges if enduring development in Singapore is desired.

In facing the challenge from the Chinese cultures in its neighbouring countries, Singapore has already lagged far behind its closest neighbour, Malaysia. The alarm had already sounded for Chinese culture in Singapore when collections of Chinese books could find no home on the island but were kept like treasure by the Malaysian Chinese who housed them with care. The warning signal was on when Chinese students from Singapore broke out in sweat before their Malaysian peers during interaction due to their inadequate knowledge of the Chinese language and culture.

Singaporeans often debate over the issues of Singaporean culture. Some believe that Chinese culture should not be emphasized as what Singapore needs instead is a Singaporean culture. Others think that multiculturalism should not be built on the basis of an empty ideology of culture. Since Chinese culture is an integral part of Singaporean multiculturalism, its content should not be neglected. If the second view offers a more realistic conceptualisation of Singaporean culture, the role Chinese culture plays in Singaporean cultural formation is not a minor one. Moreover, Singapore is currently trying to attract foreign talent. Much of the present foreign talent consists of Chinese from Malaysia, China, Hong Kong, and Taiwan who come perceiving a relative ease in adaptation partly due to Singapore's own ethnic composition. A rich Singaporean cultural atmosphere would pose an added attraction for such foreign talent to choose to come here rather than elsewhere.

Conclusion

The developmental path of Chinese culture in Singapore, whether Chinese culture (*zhonghua wenhua*) or Singapore Chinese culture (*xinhua wenhua*), has been a rocky one. After facing various constraints in the colonial period and experiencing several setbacks after independence, it still has to confront numerous difficulties today. However, despite its long history of struggle, the end of Chinese culture may not be imminent. For continued development, it would depend on how Chinese culture manoeuvres around the sets of opportunities and crisis for its survival.

Notes

[1]Huang Jin Shu's *Mahua Wenxue Yu Zhongguo Xing* [The Spirit of China in Chinese Malaysian Chinese Literature] published in 1997 and Ho Khai Leong's *Wenhua Mahua: Jicheng Yu Pipan* [Malaysian Chinese Culture: Succession and Criticism] published in 1999 are two critical works on Malaysian Chinese Culture. As for critical articles on the standard of the Chinese language in Singapore, numerous examples include Huawen 2000a, 2000b, 2000c, 2000d.

[2]Articles expressing such anxieties are abundant, Han Shanyuan's article, (1999) is one typical example. The writer remarks, "We have nurtured large numbers of the younger generation who know nothing or little about Chinese traditional culture and who are unable to write and speak Chinese. They have almost severed all ties with their cultural roots. As a result, our society has paid a high price for it and the lack of new blood for clan associations is one instance that exemplifies the cost."

[3]According to statistics provided by the National Arts Council, between 1995 to 1999, the average visits to the English language theatre each year was over 80 thousand while the average visits to the Chinese language theatre each year was only 16 thousand. See Han 2001.

[4]Within six weeks (4 December 1999 to 18 January 2000) there were in total 33 articles published in *Lianhe Zaobao* discussing the survey. In an interview with *Lianhe Zaobao*, Professor Eddie Kuo, Dean of the School of Communication Studies at the Nanyang Technological University pointed out that the survey results reinvigorated the worries over culture that have been haunting Chinese society.

Bibliography

Adorno, Theodor W. 1991. *The Culture Industry: Selected Essays on Mass Culture*. Edited with an introduction by J.M. Bernstein. London: Routledge.

Adshead, Rona & Johnson, Jillian. 1988. *Valley of Little Towns: The 120 Years of Marsden Valley's History, 1866–1986, Grey County, Central Westland*. Invercargill: Craig Printing.

Ahern, Emily M. 1975. "Sacred and Secular Medicine in a Taiwan Village: A Study of Cosmological Disorders". In Kleinmen 1975: 91–114.

Ais. 1915. "Acting Inspector of Schools to Government Secretary". 26 March 1915. Secretariat File. No. 267.

Albert Associates of Canada. 1987. *Project Report: Access to Trades and Professions in Ontario, Toronto, May 6*.

Albert Task Force On The Recognition of Foreign Qualifications 1992. *Bridging the Gap: A Report on the Task Force on the Recognition of Foreign Qualifications*. Edmonton: Government of Alberta.

Anglican Church, Diocese of Sabah. 1987. *Diocese of Sabah Silver jubilee, 1962–1987*. Kota Kinabalu.

Appleyard, R. 1962a. "The Return Migration of United Kingdom Migrants from Australia". *Population Studies* 15:214–25.

─────────── 1962b. "Determinants of Return Migration". *Economic Record* 38.83:352–68.

Ayers, William. 1971. *Chang Chih-tung and Education Reform in China*. Cambridge, Massachusetts: Harvard University Press.

Bachelard, Gaston. 1964. *The Poetics of Space*. Translated by Maria Jolas. Boston: Beacon Press.

Badets, J. 1999. *Report of the Expert Panel on Skills: Background Papers — Immigrations and Educational Levels in Canada*. Statistics Canada, 1–4.

Baker, M., Sloan, J. and Robertson, F. 1994. *The Rationale for Australia's Skilled Immigration Program.* Canberra: Australian Government Publishing Service.

Barnett, Milton L. 1960. "Kinship as a Factor Affecting Cantonese Economic Adaptation in the United States". *Human Organisation* 19: 40–46.

Basavarajappa, K.G. and Verma, R.B.P. 1985. "Asian Immigrants in Canada: Some Findings from 1981 Census". *International Migration* 23.1: 97–121.

Basel Christian Church of Malaysia. 1963. *Basel Christian Church of Malaysia, 1963 Report and Membership Record.* Jesselton. [In Chinese]

Basel Christian Church of Malaysia. 1983. *BCCM Centenary Magazine, 1882–1982.* Kota Kinabalu: BCCM. [In Chinese and part English and Malay]

Basran, G.S. 1983. "Racial and Ethnic Policies in Canada". In S. L. Peter and B. S. Bolaria (eds.), *Racial Minorities in Multicultural Canada.* Toronto: Garamond Press, pp. 3–14.

Basran, G.S. and Bolaria, B.S. 1985. *A Statistical Profile of Saskatoon Sikh Community.* Department of Sociology, University of Saskatchewan.

Basran, G.S. and Zong L. 1998. "Devaluation of Foreign Credentials as Perceived by Visible Minority Professional Immigrants". *Canadian Ethnic Studies* 30.3: 6–23.

Battershill, C. 1993. "Migrant Doctors in a Multicultural Society: Policies, Barriers and Equity". In V. Satzewich (ed.), *Deconstructing A Nation: Immigration, Multiculturalism & Racism in 90's Canada.* Halifax: Fernwood Publishing, pp. 243–261.

Beach, C. and Worswick, C. 1989. "Is There A Double-Negative Effect on the Earnings of Immigrant Women?" *Canadian Public Policy* 16.2: 36–54.

Benjamin, Walter. 1979. *One Way Street and Other Writings.* London: New Left Books.

Biers, D. & Vatikiotis, M. 1999. "Back to School". *Far Eastern Economic Review* 8 April: 10–14.

Birrell, B. and Hawtorne, L. 1997. *Immigrants and the Professions in Australia.* Melbourne: Centre for Population & Urban Research, Monash University.

Blanchot, Maurice. 1987. "Everyday Speech". *Yale French Studies* 73.

Boyd, L.A. 1977. *The Immigration Restriction Amendment Act, 1920.* Unpublished Postgraduate Diploma dissertation. Department of History, University of Otago.

Boyd, Monica. 1985. "Immigration and Occupation Attainment in Canada". In Monica Boyd, John Goyder, Frank E. Jones, Hugh A. McRoberts, Peter C. Pineo, and John Porter (eds.), *Ascription and Achievement: Studies in Mobility and Status Attainment in Canada*. Ottawa: Carleton University Press, pp. 393–445.

Brook, T. (ed.). 1997. *Culture and Economy in Eastern Asia*. Ann Arbor: University of Michigan, pp. 155–86.

Brown, R.A. (ed.). 1995. *Chinese Business Enterprise in Asia*. London: Routledge.

Buckingham, P. 1974. *The Report of the Chinese Immigration Committee, 1871: With Respect to Some Aspects of Public Opinion in Otago Province*. Unpublished Postgraduate Diploma dissertation. Department of History, University of Otago.

Bureau of Immigration, Multicultural and Population Studies Research. 1996. *English Proficiency and Immigrant Groups: Statistical Report No. 21*. Canberra: Australia Government Publishing Service.

Butler, J. 1989. *Gender Trouble: Feminism and the Subversion of Identity*. London: Routledge.

Casson, M. (ed.). 1990. *Entrepreneurship*. Aldershot: Edward Elgar.

Chan K.B. (ed.). 2000. *Chinese Business Networks. State, Economy and Culture*. Singapore: Prentice Hall.

Chan K.B. & Chiang, C. 1994. *Stepping Out — The Making of Chinese Entrepreneurs*. Singapore: Prentice Hall.

Chang, Peng-yuan and Shen, Huai-yu (eds.). 1987. *Minguo zhengfu zhiguan nianbiao, 1925–1949 (Lists of the Officials of the Government of the Republic of China, 1925–1949), Vol. 1*. Taipei: Institute of Modern History, Academic Sinica.

Char Yong (Dabu) Association. 1998.

Chelliah, David D. 1948. *A History of the Educational Policy of the Straits Settlements with Recommendations for a New System Based on Vernaculars*. Kuala Lumpur: Government Press.

Chen, Bisheng and Chen, Yimin. 1986. *Chen Jiageng nianpu (The Chronology of Tan Kah Kee)*. Fuzhou: Fujian renmin chubanshe.

Chen, Liren. "The Development of Chinese Education in Singapore in the early 20th century", 1987/1988. BA. Hons Academic Exercise, Department of Chinese Studies, National University of Singapore.

Cheng, C. 1996. *Masculinities in Organizations*. Thousand Oaks: Sage.

_____ 1999. "Marginalized Masculinities and Hegemonic Masculinity: An Introduction". *The Journal of Men's Studies* 7: 295–315.

Chihwa Primary School. 1989. *Majalah Kenangan SRJK Chi Hwa, Sandakan Sabah*. Sandakan: Chi Hwa Primary Schoool. [In Chinese]

Chin, J.C. 1954. *Chinese Families*. An unpublished M.B.Ch.B. dissertation. Medical School, University of Otago.

Chirot, Daniel & Reid, Anthony. 1997. *Essential Outsiders: Chinese and Jews in the Modern Transformation of Southeast Asia and Central Europe*. Seattle: University of Washington Press.

Chong, Wing Hong. 2000. "Duoshao Wenyi? Xian Kan Duoshao Yangfen." [How Much of Arts and Culture? It All Depends on the Amount of Nutrients] in *Lianhe Zaobao*, 3 December 2000.

_____ 2001. "Bujing Shi Yuyuan Shuiping Wenti." [Not Just an Issue of Language Standard] in *Lianhe Zabao*, 19 February 2001.

Chua, Chin Kang. 2001. "Zai Muyu Chengdu Diluo De Huanjing Li Wenyi Fuxing: Tan Women Qianque Le Shenme?" [Renaissance and the Low Standard of Mother Tongue: What are we Lacking?] in *The Tangent*, Singapore, No. 2, 61–63.

Chua, Peter and Fujino, Diane. 1999. "Negotiating New Asian-American Masculinities: Attitudes and Gender Expectations". *The Journal of Men's Studies* 7: 391–413.

Citizenship and Immigration Canada. 1992. *Immigration Statistic*. Ottawa.

Clough, Patricia T. 1992. "Poststructuralism and Postmodernism: The Desire for Criticism". *Theory and Society* 21.4.

Coleman, B.P. 1967. "The Effect of Urbanisation on Agriculture". In Whitelaw 1967: 102–111.

Committee to Advise on Australia's Immigration Policies. 1988. *Immigration: A Commitment to Australia*. Canberra: Australia Government Publishing Servcie.

Commonwealth Immigrant Advisory Council. 1967. *The Departure of Settlers from Australia: Final Report of the Committee on Social Patterns*. Canberra.

Compte Reude. 1992.

Connell, R.W. 1987. *Gender and Power: Society, the Person and Sexual Politics*. Oxford: Polity Press.

_____ 1995. *Masculinities*. St. Leonards: Allen and Unwin.

_____ 1996. "Politics of Changing Men". *Arena Journal* 6:53–72.

_____ 1997. "Men in the World: Masculinities and Globalization". A paper delivered at the *Masculinities: Renegotiating Genders* Conference. University of Wollongong.

_____ 2000. *The Men and the Boys*. St. Leonards: Allen and Unwin.

Coronil, Fernando. 1997. *The Magical State: Nature, Money, and Modernity in Venezuela*. Chicago: University of Chicago Press.

Da, Wei Wei. 1997. "The Changing Public Construction of Masculinity in Modern China". A paper delivered at *TASA* Conference. University of Wollongong.

De Eredia, *Emanuel Godinho*, translated by J. V. Mills. 1930. "Eredia's Description of Malacca, Meridional India and Cathy". *Journal of Malayan Branch of RoyalAsiatic Society* 8.1.

Denzin, Norman K. and Lincoln Yvonna, S. (eds.). 1994. *Handbook of Qualitative Research*. Thousand Oaks: Sage.

Department of Immigration and Multicultural Affairs. 1997a. *Immigration Update June Quarter 1997*. Canberra.

_____ 1997b. *The Migrant Experience: Wave One, Longitudinal Survey of Immigrants to Australia*. Canberra.

_____ 1999a. *Key Facts in Immigration, Fact Sheet No. 2*. Canberra.

_____ 1999b. *Temporary Entrants 1997–98*. Canberra.

_____ 2000a. *Community Profiles 1996 Census: China-born*. Canberra.

_____ 2000b. *Community Profiles 1996: Hong Kong-born*. Canberra.

_____ 2000c. *Community Profiles 1996: Malaysia-born*. Canberra.

_____ 2000d. *Immigration Update June Quarter 2000*. Canberra.

Derrida, Jacques. 1986. *Glas*. Translation by John P. Leavey, Jr. and Richard Rand. Lincoln: University of Nebraska Press.

Don, Alexander. 1879–89. *Our Chinese Mission (hereafter, O.C.M.)*. Dunedin: The New Zealand Presbyterian.

─────── 1886–1911. *Annual Inland Tours (hereafter, A.I.T.)*. Dunedin: Otago Daily Times.

Donaldson, M. 1993. "What is Hegemonic Masculinity?" *Theory and Society* 22: 643–57.

Doraisamy, T.R. 1969. *150 Years of Education in Singapore*. Singapore: TTC Publications Board, Teachers Training College.

Eagleton, Terry. 1990. *The Ideology of the Aesthetic*. Oxford: Basil Blackwell.

Edgar, Don. 1997. *Men, Mateship, Marriage: Exploring Macho Myths and the Way Forward*. Sydney: Harper Collins Publishers.

Employment and Immigration Canada. 1993. *Occupational Standards and Certification: Recognition of Foreign Qualifications, Report 4*. Ottawa: Minister of Supply and Services.

Ers. 1911. "Educational Report on Sandakan 1910". *British North Borneo Official Gazette*. 1 June 1911. CO874/287.

Fernando, T. and Prasad, K.K. 1986. *Multiculturalism and Employment Equity: Problems Facing Foreign-Trained Professionals and Tradespeople in British Columbia*. Vancouver: Affiliation of Multicultural Societies and Service Agencies of B. C.

Financial Mail. 1981. "Chinese Community: No Politics Please". 10.7.1981.

Fleming, Scott. 1989. "Asian Lifestyles and Sports Participation". In Alan TOMLINSON (ed.), *Leisure, Labour and Lifestyles: International Comparisons*. Sussex university, Brighton: Leisure Studies Association, pp. 82–98.

Forgie, A. 1969. *Anti-Chinese Agitation in New Zealand, 1887–89: Its Results and Causes*. An unpublished M.A. dissertation. Department of History, University of Otago.

Friedland, J. 1991. "Kuok the Kingpin". *Far Eastern Economic Review* 7 Feb.

Fyfe, F. 1948. *Chinese Immigration to New Zealand in the Nineteenth Century*. An unpublished M.A. dissertation. Department of History, University of New Zealand (Victoria).

Geertz, Clifford. 1973. "Deep Play: Notes on the Balinese Cockfight". In Clifford Geertz (ed.). *The Interpretation of Culture*, Selected Essays. New York: Basic Books.

George, K.M. 1987. "The Contributions of Mission Schools to the Development of the Church and the State of Sabah". In *Anglican Church* 1987.

Gilroy, Paul. 1997. "Diaspora and the Detours of Identity". In Woodward 1997: 299–346.

Glick, Clarence E. 1980. *Sojourners and Settlers: Chinese Migrants in Hawaii.* Honolulu: The University Press of Hawaii.

Godley, Michael R. 1981. *The Mandarin-capitalist from Nanyang: Overseas Chinese Enterprise in the Modernization of China, 1893–1911.* Cambridge: Cambridge University Press.

Goh, Chok Tong 1991. Speech at the Speak Mandarin Campaign Launching Ceremony, 30 September 1991.

Gomez, T.E. 2000. *Chinese Business in Malaysia: Accumulation, Accomodation and Ascendence.* Honolulu: University of Hawaii Press.

Gpc. 1918. "Governor Pearson to Chairman". 4 April 1918, CO874/477.

Grindstaff, C.F. 1986. *A Socio-Demographic Profile of Immigrant Women in Canada, 1981, by Age at Immigration, for Women Age 30–44.* London: University of Western Ontario.

Gwee, Yee Hian. "Chinese Education in Singapore". In Doraisamy 1969.

Guo, Fang. 1999. *Zai-Nichi kakyô no aidenthithi no henyô* (The Changing Identity of Overseas Chinese in Japan). Tokyo: Tôshindô .

Guo, Zhuzhen (ed.). 1986. *Xuelane Fujian huiguan bainian jinian tekan, 1885–1985 (The Souvenir Magazine of Centenary Celebration of the Selangor Hokkien Association, Kuala Lumpur).* Kuala Lumpur: Selangor Hokkien Association.

Gungwu, W. 1991. "Among Non-Chinese". *Daedalus* 120.2.

Hall, Bruce Edward 1998. *Tea That Burns: A Family Memoir of Chinatown.* New York: The Free Press.

Hamashita, Takeshi. 1997. "The Intra-Regional System in East Asia in Modern Times". In Kaatzenstein & Shiraishi 1997: 113–35.

Han, Shanyuan. 1999. "Huiguan Jiebanren Hechu Xun" [Where are the New blood to Lead the Clan Associations?]. *Lianhe Zaobao* (24 April).

Han, Sin Fong. 1975. *The Chinese in Sabah East Malaysia*. Taipei: The Oriental Cultural Service.

Han, Yong Hong. 2001. "Bianyuanhua: Huayu Juchang Buke Taobi De Mingyun?" [Marginalization: The Inescapable Fate of Chinese Language Theatre?]. *Lianhe Zaobao* (23 February).

Handley, P. 1996. "Growing Fast: the CP Way". *Institutional Investor* October 1996.

Hartley, Robyn (ed.). 1995. *Families and Cultural Diversity in Australia*. Sydney: Allen and Unwin.

Haw, S.G. 1990. *China: A Cultural History*. London.

Hawthorne, L. 1994. *Labour Market Barriers for Immigrant Engineers in Australia*. Canberra: Australia Government Publishing Service.

Hefner, R.W. (ed.). 1998. *Market Cultures: Society and Morality in the New Asian Capitalism*. Boulder: Westview.

Heng, P.K. 1997. "Robert Kuok and the Chinese Business Network in Eastern Asia: A Study in Sino-Capitalism". In Brook 1997: 155–86.

Hiscock, G. 1997. *Asia's Wealth Club*. Sydney: Allen & Unwin.

Ho, Khai Leong 1999. *Wenhua Mahua: Jicheng Yu Pipan* [Malaysian Chinese Culture: Succession and Criticism], Kuala Lumpur: Omnipresence Publisher.

How, Woen Liang. 2000. "Nanda: Sousuo He Gandong." [Nantah: to Search and to Move] in *Yuan*, Singapore: No. 50, 1.

Hsu, Francis L.K. & Serrie, Hendrick (eds.). 1998. *The Overseas Chinese: Ethnicity in National Context*. Lanham: University Press of America.

Hondagneu-Soleto, Pierrette. 1992. "Overcoming patriarchal constraints: The reconstruction of gender relations among Mexican immigrant men". *Gender and Society* 6: 393–415.

Hondagneu-Soleto, Pierrette and Messner, Michael A. 1994. "Gender Displays and Men's Power: The 'New Man' and Mexican-American Man". In Brod and Kaufman (eds.), *Theorizing Masculinities*. Thousand Oaks: Sage, pp. 200–218.

Huang, Jin Shu. 1997. *Mahua Wenxue Yu Zhongguo Xing* [The Spirit of China in Chinese Malaysian Chinese Literature], Taipei: Meta Media International Company.

Huawen. 2000a. "Huawen Qianjing Ling Ren Danxin" [The Anxiety over the Prospect of Chinese Language]. *Lianhe Zaobao* (4 June).

Huawen. 2000b. "Huawen Mingyun Konglong Hua?" [Chinese Language Shares the Fate of Dinosaurs]. *Lianhe Zaobao* (13 August).

Huawen 2000c. "Huawen Hui Miejue Ma?" [Will Chinese Language Die Off?]. *Lianhe Zaobao* (18 August).

Huawen 2000d. "Huawen Shi Weilai De Chufang Yuyuan" [Will Chinese Language become a Language Confined to the Kitchen?"]. *Lianhe Zaobao* (6 September).

Hugo, G. 1994. *The Economic Implications of Emigration from Australia.* Canberra: Australia Government Publishing Service.

Hunt, Donald T. 1956. *Market Gardening in Metropolitan Auckland.* An unpublished M.A. dissertation. Department of Geography, University of Auckland.

Ichikawa, Nobuchika (ed.). 1987. *Kakyô shakai keizairon josetsu* (An Introduction to Overseas Chinese Society and Economy). Fukuoka City: Kyûshû daigaku shuppankai.

_____ 1988. Kakyô gakkô kyôiku no kokusai teki hikaku kenkyû (A Comparative Study of Chinese Education for Overseas Chinese). Report for the Toyota Foundation.

Inglis, C. and Wu C.T. 1992. "The 'New' Migration of Asian Skills and Capital to Australia". In C. Inglis, S. Gunasekaran, G. Sullivan and C. T. Wu (eds.), *Asians in Australia: The Dynamics of Migration and Settlement.* St. Leonards, NSW: Allen and Unwin, pp. 193–230.

_____ 1994. "The Hong Kong Chinese in Sydney". In R. Skeldon (ed.), *Reluctant Exiles: Migration from Hong Kong and the New Overseas Chinese.* Hong Kong: Hong Kong University Press, pp. 197–214.

Ip, Manying 1990. *Home away from Home: Life Stories of Chinese Women in New Zealand.* Auckland: New Women's Press.

Ip, D.F. 1993. "Reluctant Entrepreneurs: Professionally Qualified Asian Migrants in Small Business". *Asian and Pacific Migration Journal* 2: 57–74.

Ip, D.F., Kawakami, I. Duivenvoorden, K. and Tye, L.C. 1994. *Images of Asians in Multicultural Australia.* Sydney: Multicultural Centre, University of Sydney.

Iredale, R. and Newell, P. 1991. *Taking Few Chances: The Employment of Overseas Trained Professionals and Technicians in Australia.* Wollongong: Centre for Multicultural Studies, University of Wollongong.

Jameson, Federic. 1983. "Pleasure: A Political Issue". In *Formations of Pleasure*. London and Boston: Routledge.

Jones, L.W. 1962. *Sabah Report on the Census of Population*. Kuching: Government Printing Office.

Kaatzenstein, Peter & Shirarishi, Takeshi (eds.). 1997. *Network Power: Japan and Asia*. Ithaca: Cornell University Press.

Kay, G. 1973. *Seddon and Asian Immigration Legislation, 1896–99*. An unpublished Postgraduate Diploma dissertation. Department of History, University of Otago.

Kee, P.K. and Skeldon, R. 1994. "The Migration and Settlement of Hong Kong Chinese in Australia". In R. Skekdon (ed.), *Reluctant Exiles: Migration from Hong Kong and the New Overseas Chinese*. Hong Kong: Hong Kong University Press, pp. 183–96.

Kee, P.K., Shu, J., Dang, T., and Khoo, S.E. 1994. "People Movements between Australia and Asia-Pacific Nations: Trends, Issues and Prospects". *Asian and Pacific Migration Journal* 3.2–3: 311–37.

Khoo, S.E., Kee, P., Dang, T., and Shu, J. 1994. "Asian Immigrant Settlement and Adjustment in Australia". *Asian and Pacific Migration Journal* 3.2–3: 339–71.

Khor, Eng-hee. 1958. *The Public Life of Dr. Lim Boon Keng*. An unpublished B. A. Honours Thesis, University of Singapore.

Kiong, Beng Huat. 1953. *Educational Progress in Singapore, 1870–1902*. An academic exercise — Department of Malaya, University of Malaya.

Kleinmen, Arthur, *et al.* 1975. *Medicine in Chinese Cultures*. Washington, D.C.: U.S. National Institute of Health.

Knight, Hardwicke 1974. *Dunedin Then*. Dunedin: John McIndoe.

_____ 1983–85. *Otago Cavalcade. Vol. 1–7 (1901–1935)*, Dunedin: Allied Press.

Kôbe Shinbunsha (ed.). 1987. *Sugao no kakyô* (Real Faces of Overseas Chinese). Kyoto: Jibun shoin.

Koh, Soh Goh (Xu, Shuwu). 1950. *Xinjiapo Huaqiao Jiaoyu Quanmao* (Chinese Education in Singapore). Singapore: Nanyang Shuju.

Kok, Loy Fatt. 1978. *Colonial Office Policy Towards Education in Malaya 1920–1940*. Thesis (M. Ed.) — Fakulti Pendidikan, Universiti Malaya.

Kô yama Toshio. 1979. *Kôbe Ôsaka no kakyô* (Overseas Chinese in Kobe and Osaka). Kobe: Kakyô mondai kenkyûjo.

Kreta Ayer Citizens' Consultative Committee. 1993. *Kreta Ayer, Faces and Voices*. Singapore: Landmark Books Pte Ltd.

Kun Zheng Girls School. 1968. *Kun Zheng (Kuen Cheng) nuxiao liushi zhounian jiniankan (Souvenir Magazine of 60th Anniversary Celebration of the Kuen Cheng Girls' School)*. Kuala Lumpur: Kuen Cheng Girls School.

Leach, Helen 1984. *1000 Years of Gardening in New Zealand*. Wellington: A.H. & A.W. Reed.

Lee, Guan Kin. 1990. *Lin Weiqing de suxiang: zhongxi wenhua de huiliu yu maodun (The Thoughts of Dr. Lim Boon Keng: Convergence and Contradictions between Eastern and Western Cultures)*. Singapore: Singapore Society of Asian Studies.

Lee, Guan Kin. 1994. "Xinjiapo Huawen Jiaoyu Bianqian Xia Zhishi Fenzi De Baogen Xintai (1959–1987)." [Changes in Chinese Education in Singapore and the Attitude of Intellectuals towards the Preservation of Roots (1959–1987)'] in Yeo Song Nien. (ed.) *Chuantong Wenhua Yu Shehui Bianqian*, Singapore: Tung Ann District, 47–97.

_____ 2001. "Xinma Rujiao Yundong De Xiandai Yiyi (1894–1911): Yi 1980 Niandai Xinjiapo Ruxue Yundong Yanzheng Zhi". [The Modern Significance of the Confucian Movement in Singapore and Malaya, 1894–1911: Light Shed by the Confucian Movement in Singapore in the 1980s] in Lee Guan Kin. (ed.) *The Nantah Scholar*, Singapore: Nanyang Technological University.

Lee, John A. 1977. *Early Days in New Zealand*. Martinborough: Alister Taylor.

Lee, Kam Hing and Chow, Mun Siong (eds.). 1996. *Biographical Dictionary of the Chinese in Malaysia*. Petaling Jaya: Pelanduk Publications.

Lee, Lai To (ed.). 1987. *The 1911 Revolution — The Chinese in British and Dutch Southeast Asia*. Singapore: Heinemann Asia.

Lee, Siong Kong. *History of the Li Family as told by Li Zhenggao* (unpublished).

Lee, Ting Hui. 1957. *Policies and Politics in Chinese Schools in the Straits Settlements and the Federated Malay States, 1786–1941*. Singapore: University of Malaya.

Lee, Thong Ling. 1974. *Chinese Market Gardening in the Auckland Region*. Unpublished M.A. dissertation. Department of Geography, University of Auckland.

Lemmer, E.M. 1995. "The Education system of the People's Republic of China" In E. Dekker & O.J. van Schalkwyk, *Modern Education Systems*. Durban.

Li, Guilin (ed.). 1989. *Zhongguo jiaoyushi (A History of Chinese Education)*. Shanghai: Shanghai jiaoyu chubanshe.

Li, Gushen and Lin, Guazhang (eds.). 1936. *Xinjiapo Duan Meng xuexiao sanshi zhounian jiniance (Souvenir Magazine for the Commemoration of 30th Anniversary of the Founding of the Tuan Mong School*. Singapore: Duan Mong School.

Li, P.S. 1992. "The Economics of Brain Drain: Recruitment of Skilled Labour to Canada, 1954–86". In V. Satzewich (ed.), *Deconstructing A Nation: Immigration, Multiculturalism and Racism in '90s Canada*. Halifax, Nova Scotia: Fernwood Publishing, pp. 145–62.

_____ 1996. *The Making of Post-War Canada*. Toronto: Oxford University Press.

Li, Wanzhi. 1997. "Wo he Shenhu zhonghua tongwen xuexiao" [Kôbe *Tongwen* Chinese School and I]. In Yasui 1997.

Lim, Haw Seng. 1995. "Li Guangqian de qiye wangguo" (The Business Empire of Lee Kong Chian). In Lim Haw Seng, *Xinjiapo huashe yu huashang (Singapore Chinese Society and Ethnic Chinese Business*. Singapore: Singapore Society of Asian Studies.

Lin, Tongchun. 1997. *Hashi wataru hito: Kakyô haran banjô shishi* (Bridge-Crossing Man: My Own Turbulent History as a Chinese Resident in Japan). Kobe: Epikku.

Lin, Yun (ed.). 1966. *Daonan xuexiao chuangxiao liushi zhounian jinian tekan (Tao Nan School 60th Anniversary Souvenir, 1906–1966*, Singapore: Dao Nan School.

Liu, Hong. 1998. "Old Linkages, New Networks: The Globalization of Overseas Chinese Voluntary Associations and Its Implications". *China Quarterly* 155: 582–609.

_____ 2000. "Sino-Southeast Asian Studies: Toward a New Analytical Paradigm". Paper presented at the "Approaching Asia from Asia Workshop", Sariska, India, 20–22 February.

Lutz, Jessie G. and Lutz, Rolland Ray. 1998. *Hakka Chinese Confront Protestant Christianity, 1850–1900, with the Autobiographies of Eight Hakka Christians and Commentary*. London: M.E. Sharpe, East Gate Books.

Mac An Ghaill, Mairtin. 1994. *The Making of Men: Masculinities, Sexualities and Schooling.* Buckingham: Open University Press.

—————— (ed.). 1996. *Understanding Masculinities: Social Relations in Cultural Arenas.* Buckingham: Open University Press.

Mackie, J.A.C. 1992. "Overseas Chinese Entrepreneurship". *Asia-Pacific Economic Literature* 6.1: 41–64.

—————— 1996. "Introduction". In Reid 1996: xii–xxx.

—————— 1998. "Business Success among Southeast Asian Chinese: the Role of Culture, Values and Social Structures". In Hefner 1998: 129–46.

Mahathir bin Mohamad. 1970. *The Malay Dilemma.* Singapore: Donald Moore for Asia Pacific Press.

Mak A. 1996. *Careers in Cross-Cultural Transition: Experiences of Skilled Hong Kong Immigrants.* Canberra: Australia Government publishing Serivce.

—————— 1997. "Skilled Hong Kong Immigrants' Intention to Repatriate". *Asian and Pacific Migration Journal* 6.2: 169–84.

—————— (in press). *Hong Kong Professionals and Managers in Australia.* Hong Kong: Centre of Asian Studies, University of Hong Kong.

Mak A.S. 1991. "From Elites to Strangers: Employment Coping Styles of New Hong Kong Immigrants". *Journal of Employment Counselling* 28: 144–56.

Mak A.S. and Chan H. 1995. "Chinese Family Values in Australia". In Hartley 1995: 70–95.

Mak A.S. and Nesdale, D. (in press). "Migrant Distress: The Role of Perceived Racial Discrimination and Coping Resources". *Journal of Applied Social Psychology.*

Mak Lau Fong. 1995. *The Dynamics of Chinese Dialect Groups in Early Malaya.* Singapore: Singapore Society of Asian Studies.

Malaixiya Huaxiao Jiaoshi Lianhehui Zonghui. 1987. *Dongzhong sanshi nian (Thirty Years of the Federation of the Chinese School Presidents of Malaysia) Vol. 1.* Kuala Lumpur.

Manitoba Culture, Heritage and Citizenship. 1997. *Working Towards Accreditation and Recognition in Manitoba: An Analysis of the Credentials Recognition Program.* Citizenship and Multiculturalism Division, Immigrant Credentials and Labour Market Branch. November.

Manitoba Working Group on Immigrant Credentials. 1992. *Issues, Trends and Options: Mechanisms for the Accreditation of Foreign Credentials in Manitoba.* Manitoba.

Mansour, M. 1996. *Qualifications Alone Will Not Get You the Job You Want: Integrating into the Quebec Labour Market with Foreign Credentials.* Unpublished Master thesis, Department of Geography, Concordia University, Montreal, Quebec, Canada.

Mao, Lijui and Shen, Guanqun (eds.). 1988. *Zhongguo jiaoyu tongshi (General History of Chinese Education Vol. 5).* Jinan: Shandong jiaoyu chubanshe.

Marx, Karl. 1972. *The Economic and Philosophic Manuscript of 1844.* Edited by D. J. Struik. New York: International Publishers.

Mata, F. 1994. "The Non-Accredentation of Immigrant Professionals in Canada: Societal Impacts, Barriers and Present Policy Initiatives". An unpublished paper presented at the *Sociology and Anthropology Meetings of the 1994 Learned Societies* Conference, University of Calgary, June 3–18, Calgary, Alberta.

Mawson, William 1927. *The Chinese Immigrants in New Zealand.* Institute of Pacific Relation.

Mcbsec. N.d. "Marriage Certificates of the Basel Self-Established Church, 1921–1930", North Borneo Secretariat File, No. 1063.

Mcdade, K. 1988. *Barriers to Recognition of the Credentials of Immigrants in Canada.* Ottawa: Institute for Research on Public Policy.

Mckeown, Adam. 1999. "Conceptualizing Chinese Diasporas, 1842–1949". *Journal of Asian Studies* 58.2: 306–337.

Millar, R. 1972. *Early Reactions and Attitudes to Chinese Immigrants in Otago, 1866–1870.* Unpublished B.A. (Hons) dissertation. Department of History, University of Otago.

Min, Zi. 1997. *Lin Tongchun chuan* (Biography of Lin Tongchun). Beijing: Zhongguo huaqiao chubanshe.

Mitchell, C., Tait, C. and Castles, S. 1990. *The Recognition of Overseas Professional Qualifications.* Canberra: Australia Government Publishing Service.

Mosley, J. 1973. *The Chinese Immigrants Act, 1881.* An unpublished B.A. (Honours) dissertation. Department of History, University of Otago.

Murphy, Brian. 1993. *The Other Australia: Explorations of Migrations.* Melbourne: Cambridge University Press.

Nanyang Hua Qiao Zhongxue. 1969. *Nanyang Hua Qiao zhongxue jinxi jinian tekan (Souvenir Magazine of the Golden Jubilee Celebration of the Singapore Chinese High School).* Singapore: Singapore Chinese High School.

National Heritage Board. 1997. *Collecting Memories — The Asian Civilisations Museum at the Old Tao Nan School.* Singapore: National Heritage Board.

Ng, Benjamin W.M. 1988. "A Critical Review of Japanese Scholarship on Overseas Chinese in Modern Japan". *Sino-Japanese Studies* 11: 1 (October): 61–67.

Ng, D. 1962. *Ninety Years of Chinese Settlement in New Zealand, 1866–1956.* Unpublished M.A. dissertation. Department of Geography, University of Canterbury.

Ng, E. 1972. *The 'Yellow Peril' — Myth or Reality (1878–1881).* Unpublished B.A. (Hons) dissertation. Department of History, University of Otago.

Niew Shong Tong. 1993. "A Brief History of the Hakka Immigrants in East Malaysia". *Asian Culture* 17: 187–95 (June). [In Chinese]

Oades, Rizalino. 1961. *Chinese Emigration Through Hong Kong to North Borneo Since 1880.* M.A. Dissertation, Hong Kong University.

O'Connor, P.S. 1968. "Keeping New Zealand White, 1908–1920". *The New Zealand Journal of History* 21: 41–65.

O'Connor, P. 1972. *Asian Immigration to New Zealand, 1896 to 1899.* Unpublished M.A. dissertation. Department of History, University of Otago.

Olssen, Erik 1981. "Towards a New Society". In Oliver & Williams 1981: 250–78.

_____ 1984. *A History of Otago.* Dunedin: John McIndoe.

Oliver, W.H. & Williams, B.R. (eds.). *The Oxford History of New Zealand.* Wellington: Oxford University Press, pp. 250–78.

Omohundro, John T. 1978. "Merchant Culture and Chinese Ethnicity in the Philippines". *Southeast Asian Journal of Social Science* 6.1–2: 90–102.

Ong Teng Cheong 1985. Speech at the Speak Mandarin Campaign Launching Ceremony, 28 September 1985.

Ong Teng Cheong 1992. Speech at the Speak Mandarin Campaign Launching Ceremony, 1 September 1992.

Ong, Yen Her. 1975. *The Politics of Chinese Education in Singapore During the Colonial Period, 1911–1959*. Thesis (M. Soc. Sci.) — Department of Political Science, University of Singapore.

Ontario, Ministry of The Attorney General. 1980. *The Report of the Professional Organizations*. Committee, Toronto.

Ontario, Office of The Deputy Premier. 1984. *The Proceeding of the Visible Minority Women: A Conference on Racism, Sexism and Work*, September 30–October 2, 1983, Toronto.

Ornstein, M.D. and Sharma, R.D. 1983. "Adjustment and Economic Experience of Immigrants in Canada: An Analysis of the 1976 Longitudinal Survey of Immigrants". A Report to Employment and Immigration Canada. Toronto: York University Institute for Behavioural Research.

The Otago Daily Times (hereafter, *O.D.T.*). Hocken Library, University of Otago.

The Otago Witness (hereafter, *O.W.*). Hocken Library, University of Otago.

Palanca, E. 1995. "Chinese Business Families in the Philippines since the 1980s". In Brown 1995: 197–213.

Pan, L. (ed.) 1998. *The Encyclopedia of the Chinese Overseas*. Singapore: The Chinese

Pretoria Chinese School. 1984. *50 Anniversary*. Pretoria.

Parcell, W., Sparkes, L. and William, L. 1994. *A Brief Historical Outline of Skill Migration in Australia, 1980–83*. Canberra: Australia Government Publishing Service.

Parry, R.E. 1946. "Colony of North Borneo, Five Year Plan of Education Development for the years, 1947–1952". 28 August 1946. CO 531/43/1.

Peake, Cyrus H. 1970. *Nationalism and Education in Modern China*. New York: Howard Fertig.

Peirol, P. 1996. "Skilled Immigrants Meet Job Barriers". *Globe and Mail*. November 19, A1 & A8.

Pendakur, K. and Pendakur, R. 1996. "The Colour of Money: Earnings Differentials among Ethnic Groups in Canada". Research on Immigration and Integration in the Metropolis, Working Paper Series, *http://www.sfu.ca/riim*. 96.3: 1–27.

Pretoria News. 1978. "City Chinese Study Language Heritage". 6.2.1978.

Price, Charles 1974. *The Great White Walls are Built: Restrictive Immigration to North America and Australia 1836–1888*. Canberra: Australian National University Press.

Purcell, Victor. 1980. *The Chinese in Southeast Asia*. London: Oxford University Press (Reprint).

Rajagopal, I. 1990. "The Glass Ceiling in the Veritcal Mosaic: Indian Immigrants to Canada". *Canadian Ethnic Studies* 22: 96–105.

Ralston, H. 1988. "Ethnicity, Class and Gender among South Asian Women in Metro Halifax: An Exploratory Study". *Canadian Ethnic Studies* 20.3: 63–83.

Rbmab. 1946. "Report of BMA in Borneo, 10 June 1945–15 July 1946". WO 203/2400.

Reid, Anthony (ed.). 1996. *Sojourners and Settlers: Histories of Southeast Asia and the Chinese*. St. Leonard's, Australia: Allen and Unwin.

Ren, Gueixiang. 1989. *Huaqiao dierci aiguo gaochao (The Second High Tide of Overseas Chinese Patriotism*. Beijing: Zhonggong dangshi ziliao chubanshe.

"Report of the Proceedings at an Educational Conference Held in Singapore (Conference)". 1925.

Richmond, A.H. 1984. "Immigration and Unemployment in Canada and Australia". *International Journal of Comparative Sociology* 25.3–4: 243–55.

——————— 1996. "Skilled Immigrants". *Globe and Mail*. November 20, A22.

Rivera, T. and Kenji K. 1995. *The Chinese-Filipino Business Families and the Ramos Government*. Tokyo: Institute for Developing Economies.

Ross Home Admission Register. 1918–85. Dunedin.

Rutherford, J. (ed). 1990. *Identity: Community, Culture, Difference*. London: Lawrence and Wishart.

Sato, Y. 1993. "The Salim Group in Indonesia: the Development and Behavior of the Largest Conglomerate in Southeast Asia". *The Developing Economies* 31.4 (December): 408–441.

SCCC. 1991. *Sandakan Chinese Chamber of Commerce Centenary, 1891–1991*. Sandakan. [In Chinese]

Schama, Simon. 1995. *Landscape and Memory*. London: HarperCollins.

SR. 1911. "School Returns 1910". *British North Borneo Official Gazette*. 1 June 1911

Schwartz, A. 1994. *Nation in Waiting. Indonesia in the 1990s.* Sydney: Allen & Unwin.

Searle, P. 1999. *The Riddle of Malaysian Capitalism. Rent-seekers or Real Capitalists?* Sydney: Allen & Unwin.

Sedgwick, Charles 1982. *The Politics of Survival: A Social History of the Chinese in New Zealand.* Unpublshed Ph.D. dissertation. Department of Sociology, University of Canterbury.

Segal, Lynne. 1997. "Sexualities". In Woodward 1997: 184–238.

Selegor Zhong Hua High School. 1946. *Xuelane Zhong Hua zhongxue fuxiao tekan, 1946 (Souvenir Magazine of the Zhong Hua High School of Selangor for 1946).* Kualal Lumpur: Selangor Zhong Hua High School.

Shahidian, Hammed. 1999. "Gender and Sexuality Among Immigrant Iranians in Canada". *Sexualities* 2: 189–222.

Shum, K.C. 1956. *Environment and Health Hazards in Market Gardening.* Unpublished M.B.Ch.B. dissertation. Medical School, University of Otago.

Sili Zun Kong Zhongxue. 1965. *Sili Zun Kong zhongxue gaochuzhong biye tekan, yijiu liuwu nian (Souvenir Magazine of Graduation of the Senior and Junior Middle Three of the Confucian High School, 1965 Batch).* Kuala Lumpur: Confucian High School.

Simpson, J. 1998. "The Economy's Saviours: Young Women and Immigrants". *Globe and Mail.* April 16, P22.

Singapore Chinese High School. 1969. *Nanyang Hua Qiao zhongxue jinxi jinian tekan (Souvenir Magazine of Golden Jubilee Celebration of the Chinese High School of Singapore).* Singapore: The Chinese High School.

"Singapore Improvement Trust Files" (SIT).

Skeldon, R. 1994. "Hong Kong in an International Migration System". In R. Skeldon (ed.), *Reluctant Exiles: Hong Kong Communities Overseas* Hong Kong: Hong Kong University Press, pp. 21–51.

Skinner, G. William. 1957. *Chinese Society in Thailand: An Analytical History.* Ithaca, New York: Cornell University Press.

——————— 1964–65. "Marketing and Social Structure in Rural China". *The Journal of Asian Studies* 24(1): 3–43; 24(2): 195–228; 24(3): 363–99.

Song, Ong Siang. 1967. *One Hundred Years' History of the Chinese in Singapore.* Singapore: University of Malaya Press.

_____ 1984. *One Hundred Years' History of the Chinese in Singapore*. Singapore: Oxford University Press.

The Star. 1980. "Chinese Lukewarm on New System". 19.6.1980.

The Star. 1986. "Chinese Role in TED Schools Unchanged: Gibson Reacts". 19.2.1986.

State of North Borneo. *North Borneo Establishment List, 1922–28*, and 1931–37.

Stedman, G. 1966. *The South Dunedin Flat: A Study in Urbanisation 1849–1965*. Unpublished M.A. dissertation, Department of Geography, University of Otago.

Stoler, Ann Laura. 1995. *Race and the Education of Desire: Foucault's History of Sexuality and the Colonial Order of Things*. Durham: Duke University Press.

Straits Settlements Government Gazette (SSGG). 1920.

Straits Settlements Annual Report (SSAR). 1925.

Strauss, Anselm and Corbin, Juliet. 1998. *Basics of Qualitative Research: Techniques and Procedures for Developing Grounded Theory*. (2nd Edition). Thousand Oaks: Sage.

Su, Xiaoxian. 1948. *Zhangzhou shishu lu Xing tongxianglu (The Directory of the Zhangzhou People in Singapore)*. Singapore.

Sue, Vanessa, *et al*. 1982. *Chinese of Christchurch*. Christchurch: no publisher.

Sugawara, Kôsuke. 1979. Nihon no kakyô (Chinese Residents in Japan). Tokyo: Asahi shinbunsha.

Suryadinata, Leo (ed.). 1997a. *Ethnic Chinese as Southeast Asians*. Singapore: Institute of Southeast Asian Studies.

_____ 1997b. "Ethnic Chinese in Southeast Asia: Overseas Chinese, Chinese Overseas or Southeast Asians?" In Suryadinata 1997a: 1–24.

Sutch, W. B. 1966. *The Quest for Security in New Zealand, 1840 to 1966*. Wellington: Oxford University Press.

Szado, D. 1987. *Access to Careers for Immigrant Women, Final Report*. Toronto: COSTI-IIAS Immigrant Services. March.

Tan, Kah Kee. 1993. *Nanqiao huiyi lu (The Memoirs of Tan Kah Kee)*. River Edge, USA: Global Publishing Co. Inc. (New Edition).

Tan, Liok Ee. 1997. *The Politics of Chinese Education in Malaya, 1945–1961*. Kuala Lumpur: Oxford University Press.

Tan, Yeok Seong. 1963. "Malai huawen jiaoyu fazhanshi (The Commencement of the History of the Chinese Education in Malaya". In Gao Xin and Zhang Xizhe (eds.), *Huaqiaoshi lunji (Essays on the History of Overseas Chinese)*. Taipei: Guofang yanjiuyuan.

Tan, Yeok Seong (Chen, Yusong). 1983. *Yeyingguan Wencun* (Collected Writings from the Ye-yin Studio), Singapore: South Seas Society.

Tan, Yeok Seong. 1984. *Yeyingguan wencun (The Literary Collections of Yeyinguan)* Volume 2. Singapore: South Seas Society.

Tar. 1925. "Tawau Annual Report of 1924". In *Supplement to the North Borneo Official Gazette*, 1925.

Task Force on Access to Professions and Trades in Ontario. 1989. *Access: Task Force on Access to Professions and Trades in Ontario*. Toronto: Ontario Ministry for Citizenship.

Tausig, Michael. 1987. "History as Commodity in Some Recent American (Anthropological) Literature". *Food and Foodways* 2: 151–69.

Tay, Lian Soon and Gwee, Yee Hean. 1975. *Malaixiya Xinjiapo Huawen zhongxue tekan tiyao, fu xiaoshi (Chinese High Souvenir Magazine of Malaysia and Singapore, with School Histories)*. Kuala Lumpur: Department of Chinese Studies, The University of Malaya.

Tay, Lian Soon (Zheng Liangshu). 1986. "Development of Chinese Education in Malaysia before the Second World War" (in Chinese) published in *Chinese Culture in Malaya and Singapore*. Vol. 2. Singapore: South Seas Society.

——————— 1997. "Xin Ma huashe zaoqi de nuzi jiaoyu" (Early Female Education in the Chinese Communities in Singapore and Malaysia). *Malayxiya huaren yanjiu xuekan (Journal of Malaysian Chinese Studies)*. Kuala Lumpur: Huazi Resource and Research Centre No. 1.

——————— 1998. *Malaixiya huawen jiaoyu fazhanshi (A History of the Chinese Education in Malaysia) Vol. 1*. Kuala Lumpur: Federation of Chinese Teachers' Association of Malaysia.

——————— 1999. *Malaixiya huawen jiaoyu fazhanshi (A History of the Chinese Education in Malaysia) Vol. 2*. Kuala Lumpur: Federation of Chinese Teachers' Association of Malaysia.

Taylor, A. 1987. Manager, Counselling Services, Women Immigrants of London, Correspondence. October 6.

Teng, Siao See. 2000. "Weihe Xuyao Hou Zhimin Yishi? Xinjiapo Duli 35 Nian De Ling Yi Zhong Fansi." [Who Needs Postcolonial Consciousness? An Alternative Contemplation on Post Independent Singapore] in *The Tangent*, Singapore, No. 1, 67–77.

Tiglao, R. 1996. "Tan Triumphant". *Far Eastern Economic Review* 26 Sept. 1996: 60–65.

Toh Lum School Graduation Souvenir Magazine. 1925

Toh Lum School 85ᵗʰ Anniversary Magazine. 1991.

Trempe, R., Davis, S. and Kunin, R. 1997. *Not Just Numbers: A Canadian Framework for Future Immigration.* Canada: Minister of Public Works and Government Services (Cat No. Ci63-21/1998E).

Trovato, F. and Grindstaff, C.F. 1986. "Economic Status: A Census Analysis of Immigrant Women at Age Thirty in Canada". *Review of Sociology and Anthropology* 23.4: 569–687.

Tuan Mong School 25th Anniversary Magazine. 1931.

Tu, Weiming. 2000. "Mother Tongue: Anchor of Our Life and Spirit." in *Lianhe Zanbao*, 4 January 2000.

Twang, P.Y. 1998. *The Chinese Business Elite in Indonesia and the Transition to Independence.* Kuala Lumpur: Oxford University Press.

Tweedie, Alan D. 1950. *Metropolitan Dunedin: A Geographic Contribution to Land-Use Planning.* An unpublished M.A. dissertation, Department of Geography, University of Otago.

Ulmer, Gregory L. 1985. *Applied Grammatology.* Baltimore: John Hopkins University Press.

Verchere, I. 1978. "The Changing World of Robert Kuok". *Insight* (August).

Wang, Gungwu. 1992. *Community and Nation: China, Southeast Asia and Australia.* St. Leonard's, Australia: Allen & Unwin.

Wang, Siow-Nam (Wang, Xiunan). 1970. *Xingma Jiaoyu Fanlun.* (A General Discussion on the Education of Malaya), Hongkong: Dongnanya Yanjiusuo.

_____ 1974. In Song, Zhemei (ed.), *Xingma Jiaoyu Yanjiu Ji* (Studies on the Education of Malaya). Hong Kong: Hongkong: Dongnanya Yanjiusuo.

Wang, Zengbing and Yu, Gang. 1981. *Chen Jiageng Xingxue ji (Tan Kah Kee's Contributions to Modern Education).* Fuzhou: Fujian jiaoyu chubanshe.

Wang, Zuo (ed.). 1963. *Pei Feng wushinian: jinxi jinian tekan (Fifty Years of Pei Feng: Souvenir Magazine of the Golden Jubilee Celebration)*. Malacca: Pei Feng High School.

Watson, I. 1995. "NESB Immigrants and Access to the Managerial Labour Market". *BIMPR Bulletin* 14: 43–44.

Weekend Argus. 1986. "Chinese, Japanese Pupils Must Apply". 6.9.1986.

White, Hayden. 1987. *The Content of the Form: Narrative Discourse and Historical Representation*. Baltimore: John Hopkins University Press.

Whitelaw, J.S. (ed.). 1967. *Auckland in Ferment*. Auckland: New Zealand Geographical Society.

Williams, L., Murphy, J. and Brooks, C. 1997. *Initial Labour Market Experiences of Immigrants: Results from the Longitudinal Survey of Immigrants to Australia*. Canberra: Department of Immigrations and Multicultural Affairs.

Willis, Katie and Brenda, Yeoh. (eds.). 2000. *Gender and Migration*. Cheltenham: Elgar Publishing Limited.

Willis, M. 1974. *The Chinese Question, 1896–99: A Study in Conflict*. Unpublished Postgraduate Diploma dissertation. Department of History, University of Otago.

Willmott, D. 1960. *The Chinese of Semarang*. Ithaca: Cornell University Press.

Wilson, Harold E. 1978. *Social Engineering in Singapore: Education Policies and Social Change, 1819–1972*. Singapore: Singapore University Press.

Wong, Lin Ken. 1978. " Singapore: Its Growth as an Entrepot Port, 1819–1941". *Journal of Southeast Asian Studies* Vol. 9.1, Singapore.

Wong, Tze-Ken, Danny. 1998. *The Transformation of an Immigrant Society: A Study of the Chinese of Sabah*. London: Asean Academic Press.

_____ 1999. "Chinese Migration to Sabah Before the Second World War". *Archipel* 58.3: 131–58.

_____ 2000. "The Chinese in Sabah: An Overview". In Lee Kam Hing and Tan Chee Beng (eds.), *The Chinese in Malaysia*. Kuala Lumpur: Oxford University Press, pp. 382–406.

Wooden, M., Holton, R., Hugo, G. and Sloan, J. (eds.). 1994. *Australian Immigration: A Survey of the Issues* (2nd edition). Canberra: Australia Government Publishing Service.

Wooden, M. 1994. "The Labour Market Experience of Immigrants". In Wooden *et al*. (eds.) 1994.

Woodward, Kathryn (ed.). 1997. *Identity and Difference*. Milton Keynes: The Open University.

Xie, Pinfeng. 1965. "Yin Sin xuexiao shilue" (A Brief History of Yin Sin School). In Lin, Zhigao (ed.), *Singzhou Ying Ho huiguan yibai sishiyi zhounian jinian tekan* (*Souvenir Magazine for the Commemoration of 141 years Anniversary of the Singapore Yin Ho Association*). Singapore: Yin Ho Association.

Xinjiapo Nanyang Wenhua Chubanshe (ed.). 1956. *Nanyang daxue chuangxiao shi* (*A History of the Founding of the Nanyang University*). Singapore: Xinjiapo Nanyang wenhua chubanshe.

Xu, Suwu. 1949. *Xinjiapo huaqiao jiaoyu quanmao* (*The Overview of the Chinese Education in Singapore*). Singapore: Lianshu yinwu yuxien gongsi.

Xuebu (Ministry of Education). 1906. *Xuebu guanbao* (*The Gazette of the Ministry of Education of the Qing Government*) Vol. 9 (December).

Xuelane Zhong Hua Zhongxue. 1946. *Xuelane Zhong Hua zhongxue fuxiao tekan* (*Souvenir Magazine of the Zhong Hua High School of Selangor for 1946*). Kuala Lumpur: Zhong Hua High School of Selangor.

Yang Zheng Xue Xiao. 1956. *Yang Zheng xuexiao jinxi jiniankan* (*Souvenir Magazine for the Commemoration of Golden Jubilee Celebration of the Yang Zheng School, Singapore*). Singapore: Yang Zheng School.

Yap, M. & Mann, D. 1996. *Colour, Confusion and Concessions*. Hong Kong.

Yasui, Sankichi (ed.). 1997. *Kinhyakunen Nicchû kankei no shi teki tenkai to Hanshin kakyô* (The History of Sino-Japanese Relations in the Last Century and Overseas Chinese in Osaka and Kobe). Research Report. Kôbe: Kôbe kakyô kajin kenkyûkai. March.

Yasui, Sankichi & Chen, Laixing (eds.). 1996. *Hanshin daishinsai to kakyô* (The Kobe-Osaka Earthquake and Overseas Chinese). Research report, May.

Yeap, Chong Leng (Ye ZhongLing). 1990. "The Founding of Nanyang Overseas Chinese Marine and Navigation School by Tan Kah Kee" (in Chinese). In Yen Ching-hwang (ed.), *Asian Culture No. 14: Special Issue on Ethnic Chinese Abroad*. Singapore: Singapore Society of Asian Studies.

Yee, Sze Onn 1968. *Some Aspects of the Contemporary Agricultural Land Use of the Taieri Plain and Adjacent Hills*. Unpublished M.A. dissertation, Department of Geography, University of Otago.

Yen, Ching-hwang. 1976. *The Overseas Chinese and the 1911 Revolution: With Special Reference to Singapore and Malaya*. Kuala Lumpur: Oxford University Press.

_____ 1982. "Overseas Chinese Nationalism in Singapore and Malaya, 1877–1912". *Modern Asian Studies* Vol. 16.3. Cambridge: Cambridge University Press.

_____ 1986. *Coolies and Mandarins: China's Protection of Overseas Chinese during the Late Ch'ing Period (1851–1911)*. Singapore: Singapore University Press.

_____ 1988. "The Response of the Chinese in Singapore and Malaya to the Tsinan Incident, 1928". *Journal of the South Seas Society* Vol. 43. Singapore: South Seas Society.

_____ 1993. "Early Fukienese Migration and Settlements in Singapore and Malaya before 1850". In Chang Pin-Tsun and Liu Shih-Chi (eds.), *Essays in Chinese Maritime History Vol. 5*. Nankang, Taipei: Sun Yat-sen Institute for Social Sciences and Philosophy, Academia Sinica.

_____ 1995a. *Community and Politics: The Chinese in Colonial Singapore and Malaysia*. Singapore: Times Academic Press.

_____ 1995b. "Ch'ing China and the Singapore Chinese Chamber of Commerce, 1906–1911". In Leo Suryadinata (ed.), *Southeast Asian Chinese and China: The Politico-Economic Dimension*. Singapore: Times Academic Press.

_____ 1998a. "The Overseas Chinese and the Second Sino-Japanese War, 1937–1945". *Journal of the South Seas Society* Vol. 52. Singapore: South Seas Society.

_____ 1998b. "Tan Kah Kee and the Overseas Chinese Entrepreneurship." *Asian Culture* 22. Singapore: Singapore Society of Asian Studies.

Yen, Ching Hwang. 1986. *A Social History of the Chinese in Singapore and Malaysia, 1800–1911*, Singapore: Oxford Press.

Yeung Ching School Magazine. 1957.

Yin Sin School Magazine. 1937.

Yock Eng School 70th Anniversary Cum Graduate Magazine. 1980.

Yong, C.F. 1977. *The New Gold Mountain: The Chinese in Australia 1901–1921*. South Australia: Raphael Arts.

_____ 1987. *Tan Kah Kee. The Making of an Overseas Chinese Legend*. Singapore: Oxford University Press.

Yong, Ching Fatt. 1980. *Zhanqian de Chen Jiageng yanlun shiliao yu fenxi (Tan Kah Kee in pre-war Singapore: Selected Documents and Analysis)*. Singapore: South Seas Society.

Yoshihara, K. 1988. *Ersatz Capitalism in South-east Asia*. Singapore: Oxford University Press.

Yuen-Fan Wong, L. 1992. *Education of Chinese Children in Britain and the USA*. Clevedon.

Zeng, Yongsheng, et. al. (eds.) 1993. *Malaixiya Fujianren xingxue banjiao shiliaoji (Historical Materials of the Promotion of Chinese Education by the Hokkiens in Malaysia)*. Kuala Lumpur: The Federation of Hokkien Association of Malaysia.

Zhang, Zidong. 1963. *Zhang Wenxiang gong quanji (The Complete Works of Zhang Zidong*. Taipei: Wenhai chubanshe.

Zheng, Bangying. 1968. "Benxiao jianshi" (A Brief History of Kuen Cheng Schoool)." In *Kun Cheng (Kuen Cheng) liushi nian: Kun Cheng nuxiao liushi zhounian jiniankan (Sixty Years of Kuen Cheng: Souvenir Magazine of the 60th Year Anniversary of the Kuen Cheng School)*. Kuala Lumpur: Kuen Cheng Girls School.

Zheng, Bingshan. 1997. *Li Guanqian Zhuan (A Biography of Lee Kong Chian)*. Beijing: Zhongguo Huaqiao chubanshe.

Zhu, Huiling. 1993. *Zai-Nichi kakyô ni okeru aidenthithi no saikôchiku* (Reconstructing Identity among Overseas Chinese in Japan). MA thesis: Rikkyô University.

——————— 1996. *Dangdai Riben huaqiao jiaoyu* [Chinese Education in Contemporary Japan]. Taiyuan: Shanxi jiaoyu chubanshe.

Zhu, Shoupeng (ed.). 1963. *Shierchao donghualu, Guangxi chao (The Donghua Records of the Twelve Reigns of the Qing Dynasty, Guangxi Reign)*. Taipei: Wenhai chubanshe.

Zizek, Slavoj. 1993. *Tarrying With the Negative*. Durham: Duke University Press.